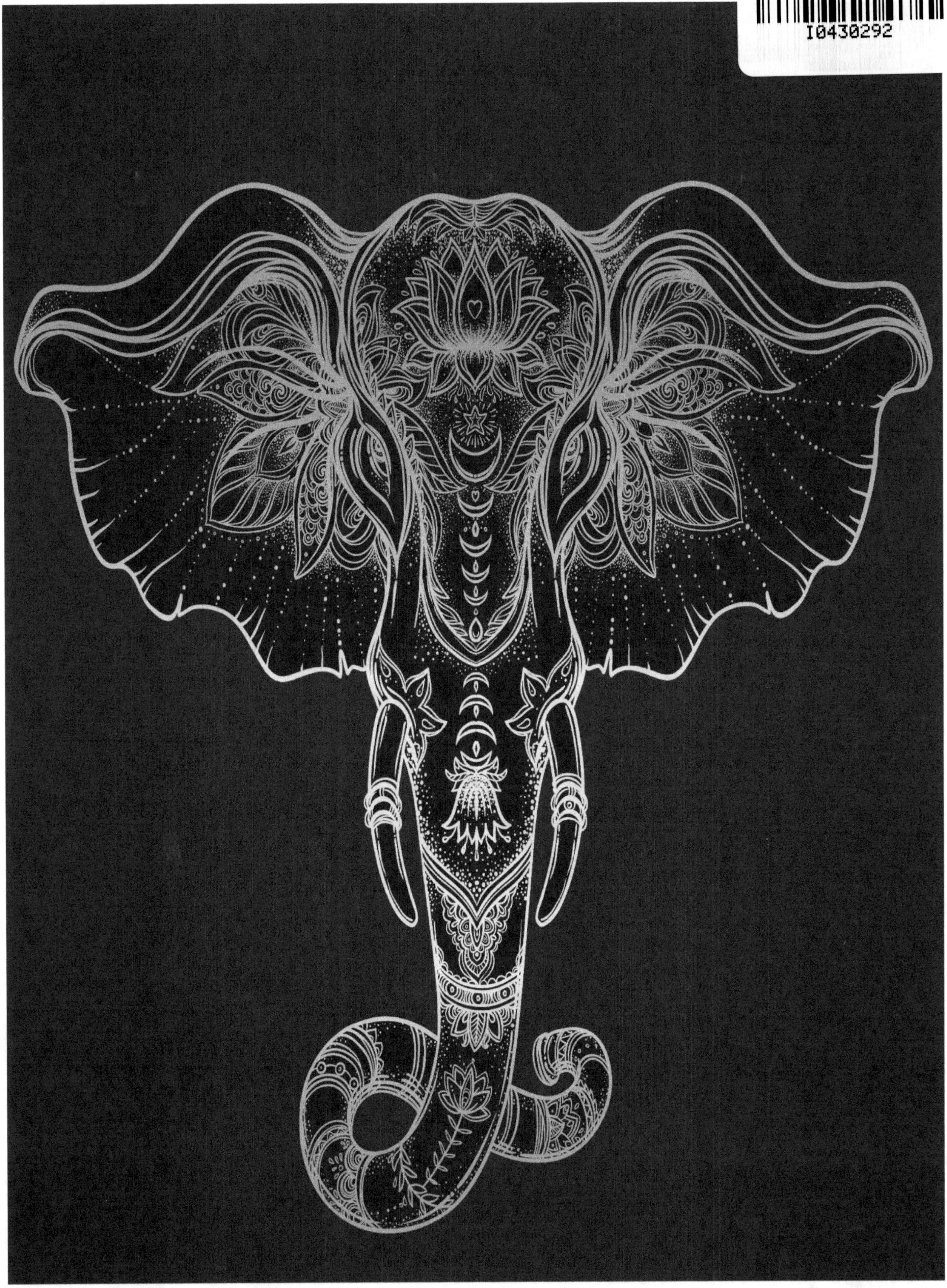

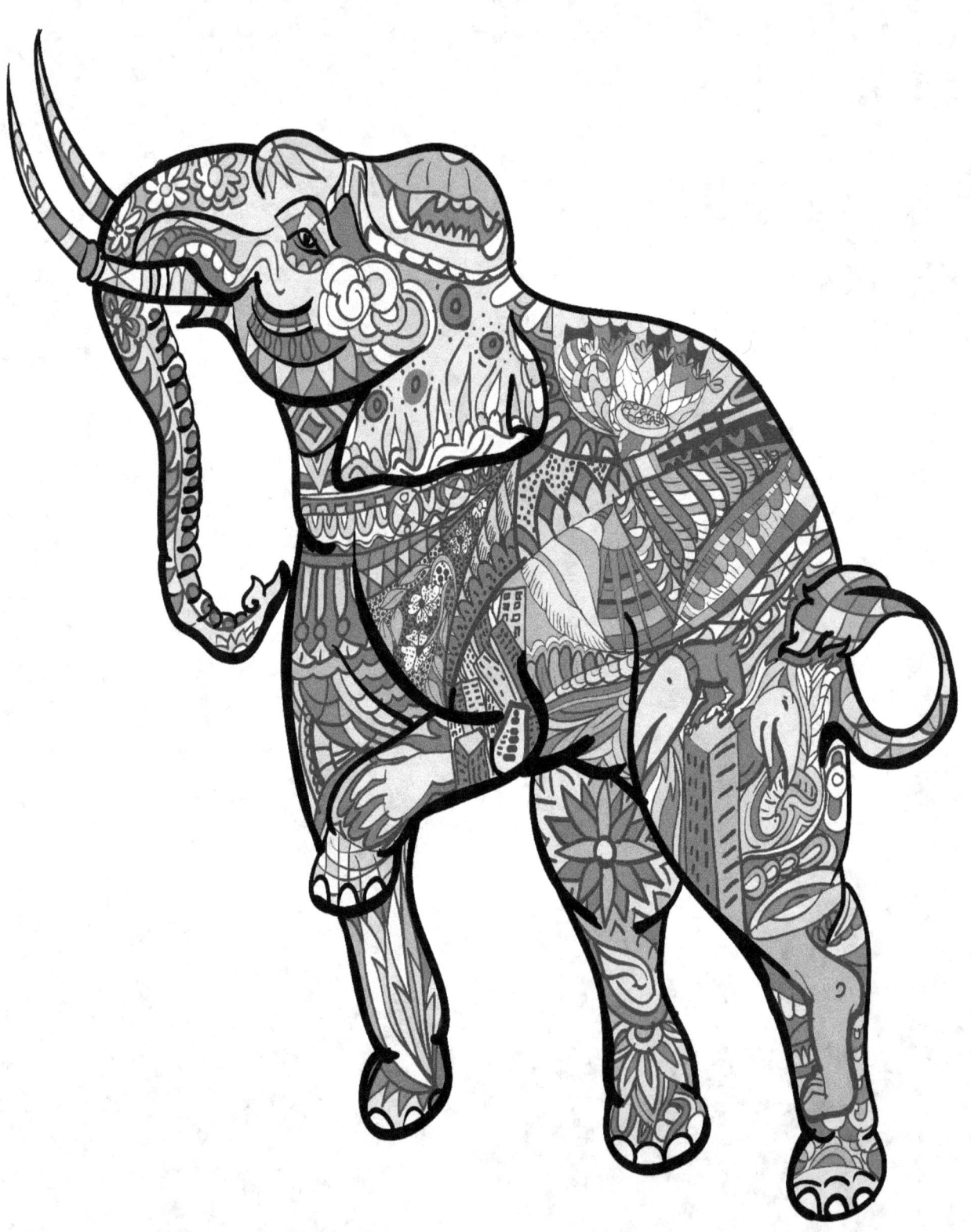

FANTASTIC ELEPHANTS COLORING BOOK

COPYRIGHT © 2022

Dr. Robert K. Wheeler Jr.

All Rights Reserved

Reproduction in any format is only allowed with written permission from the author.

ISBN 9798370842108

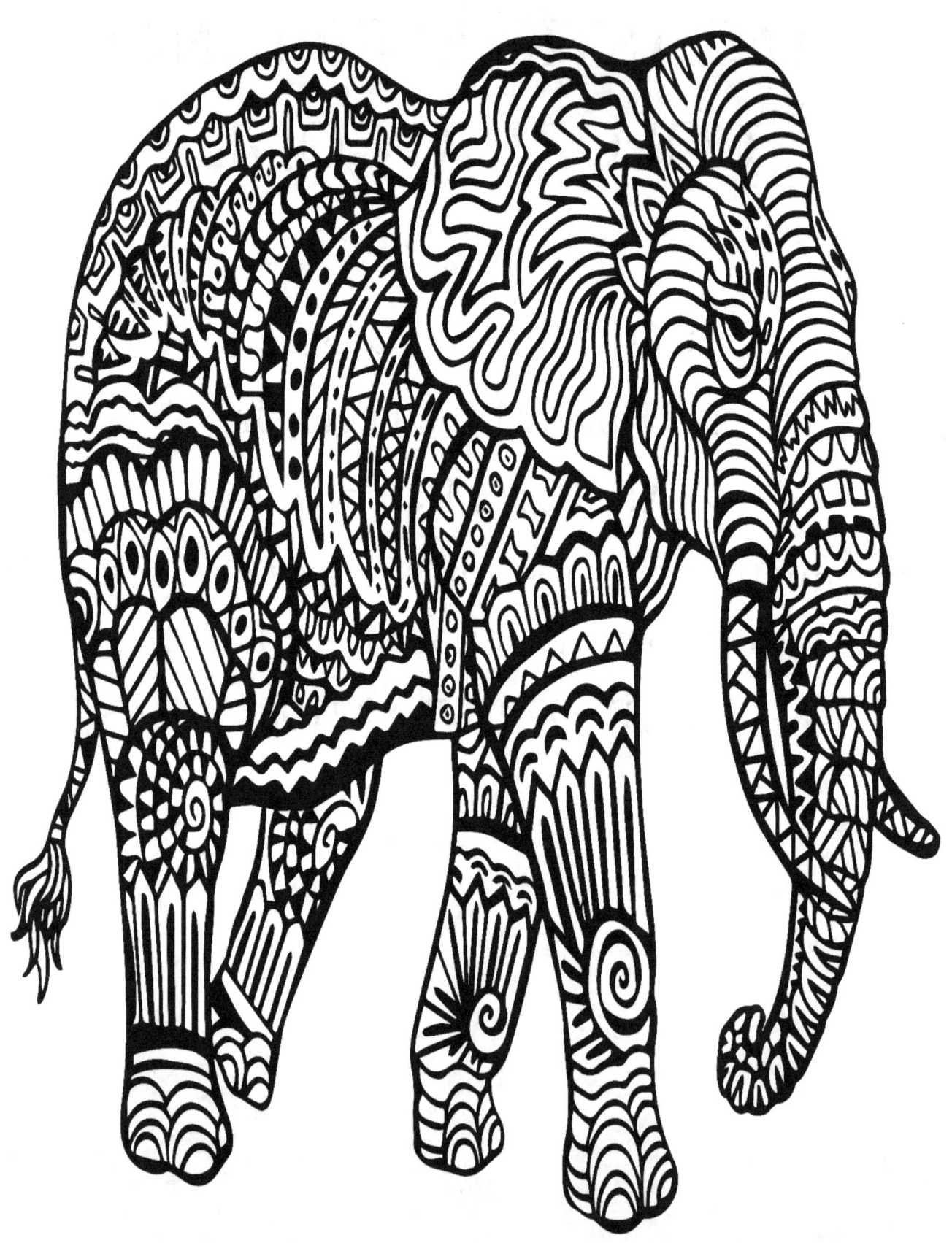

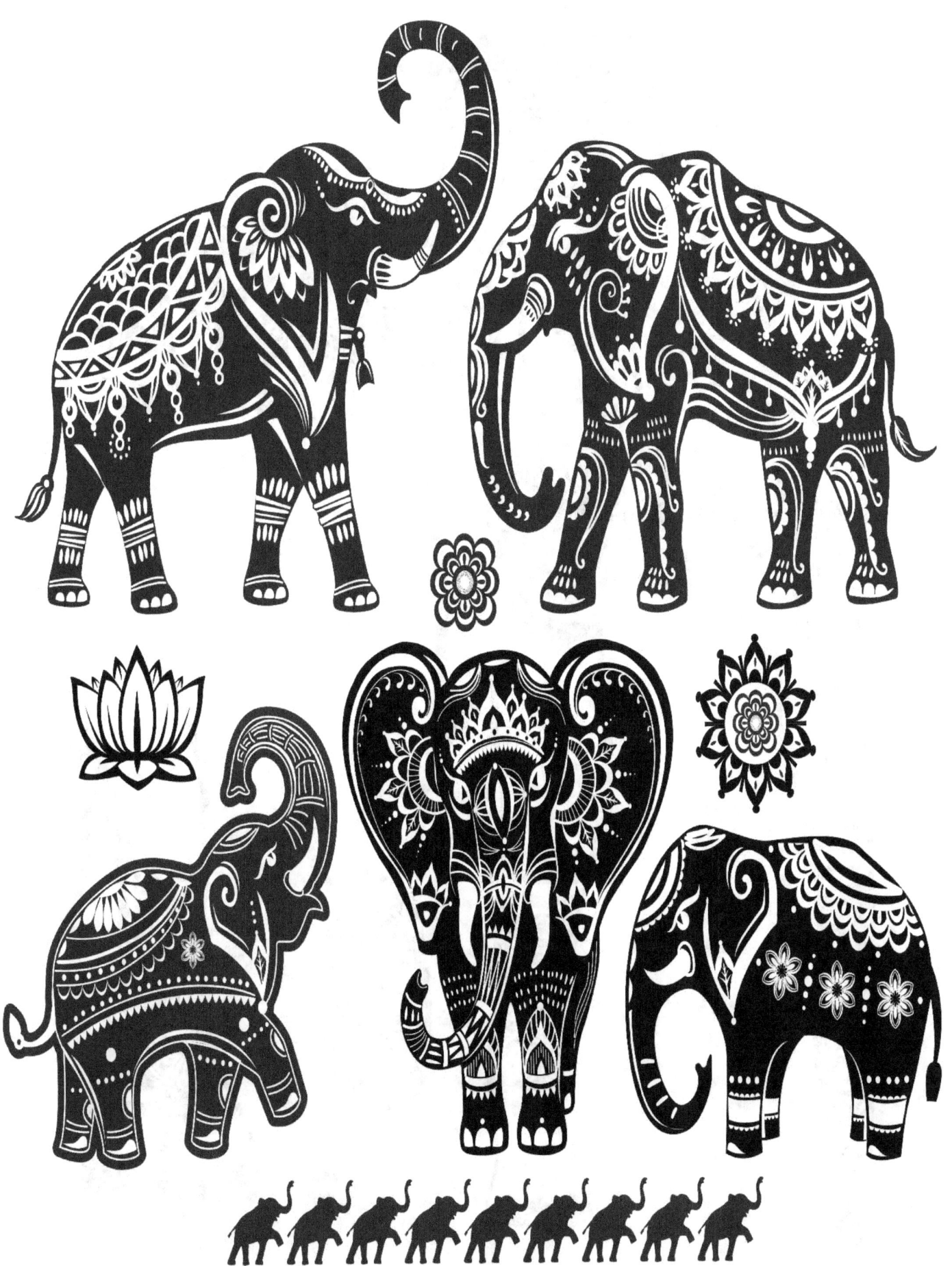

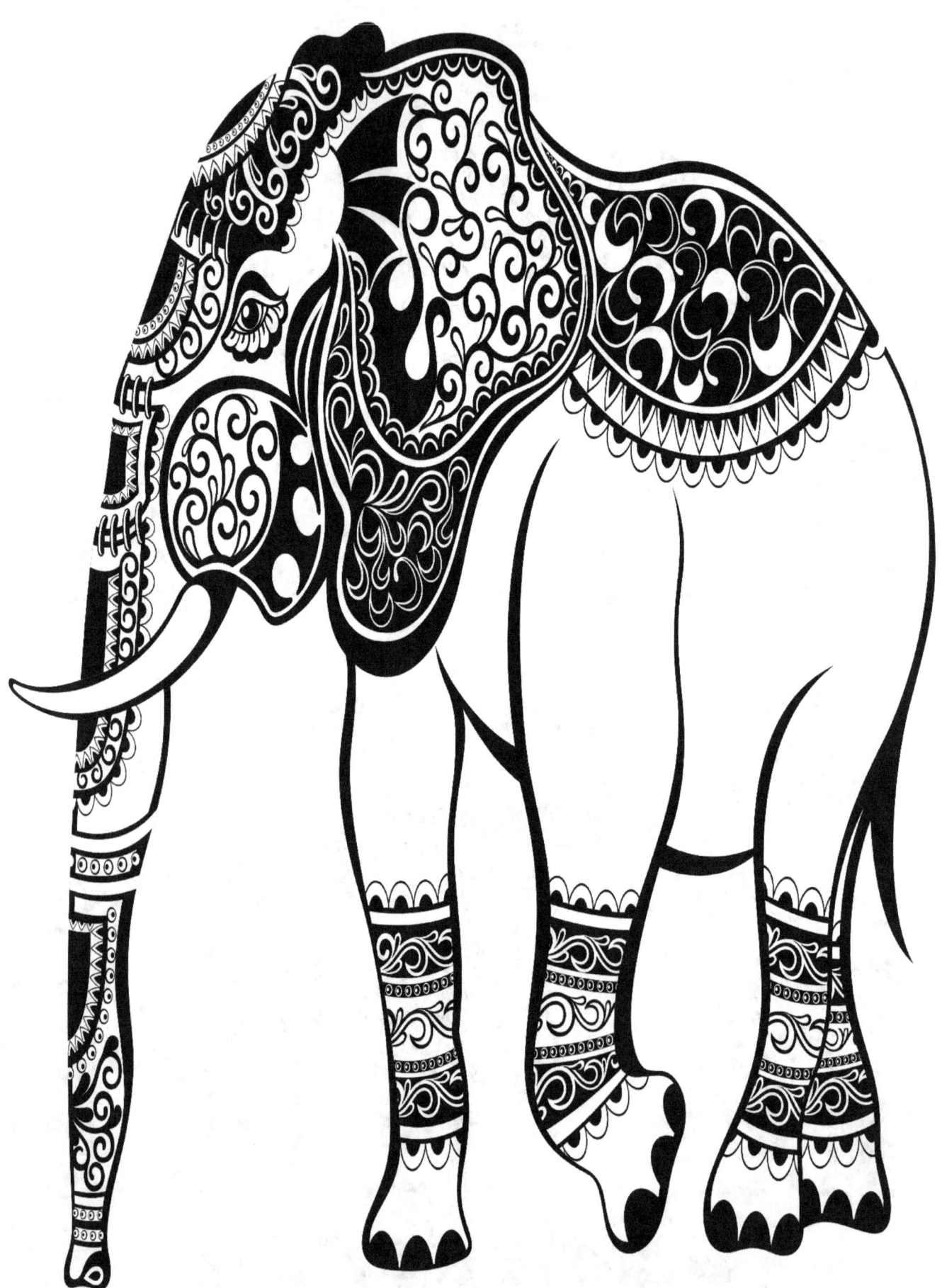

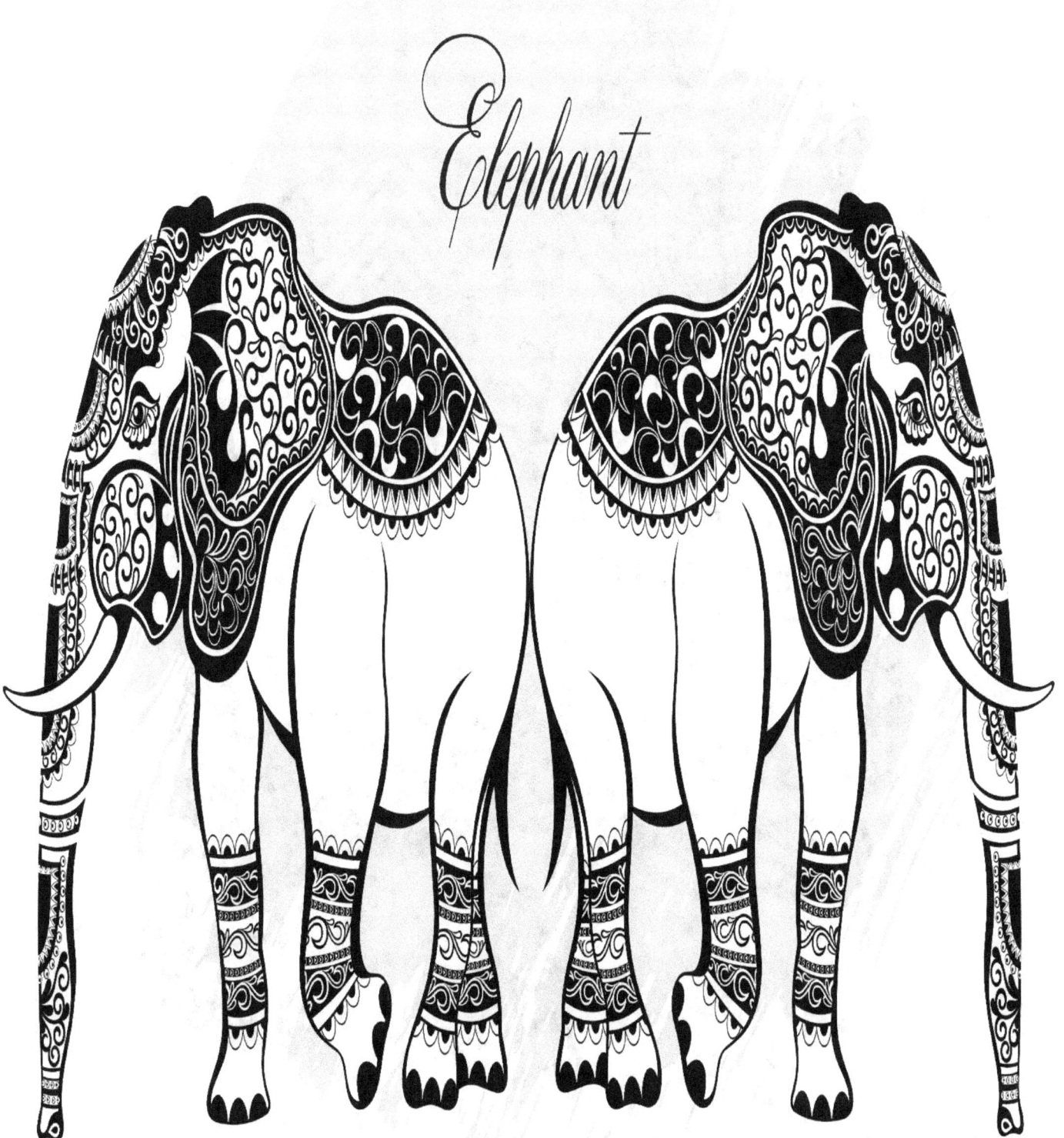

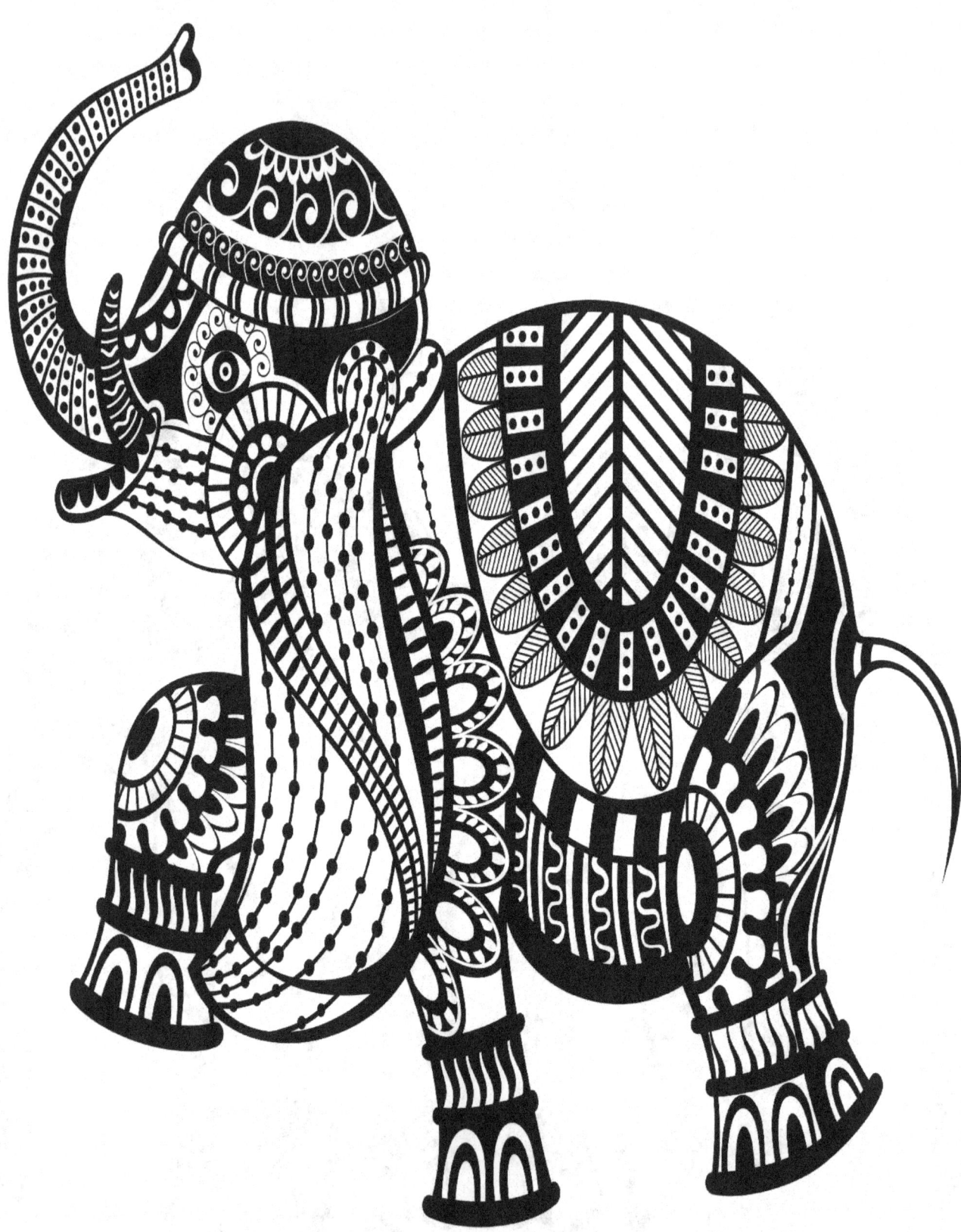

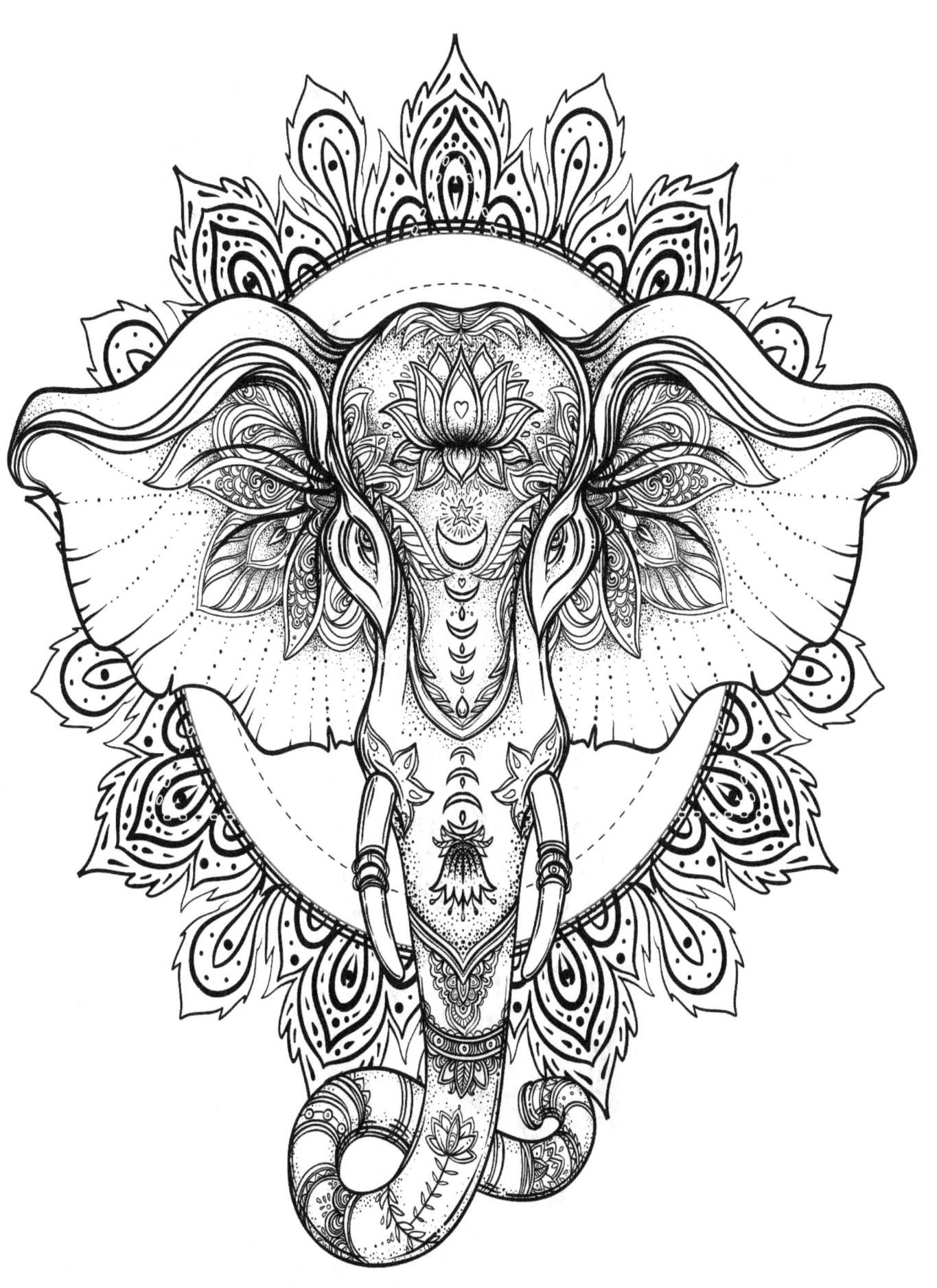

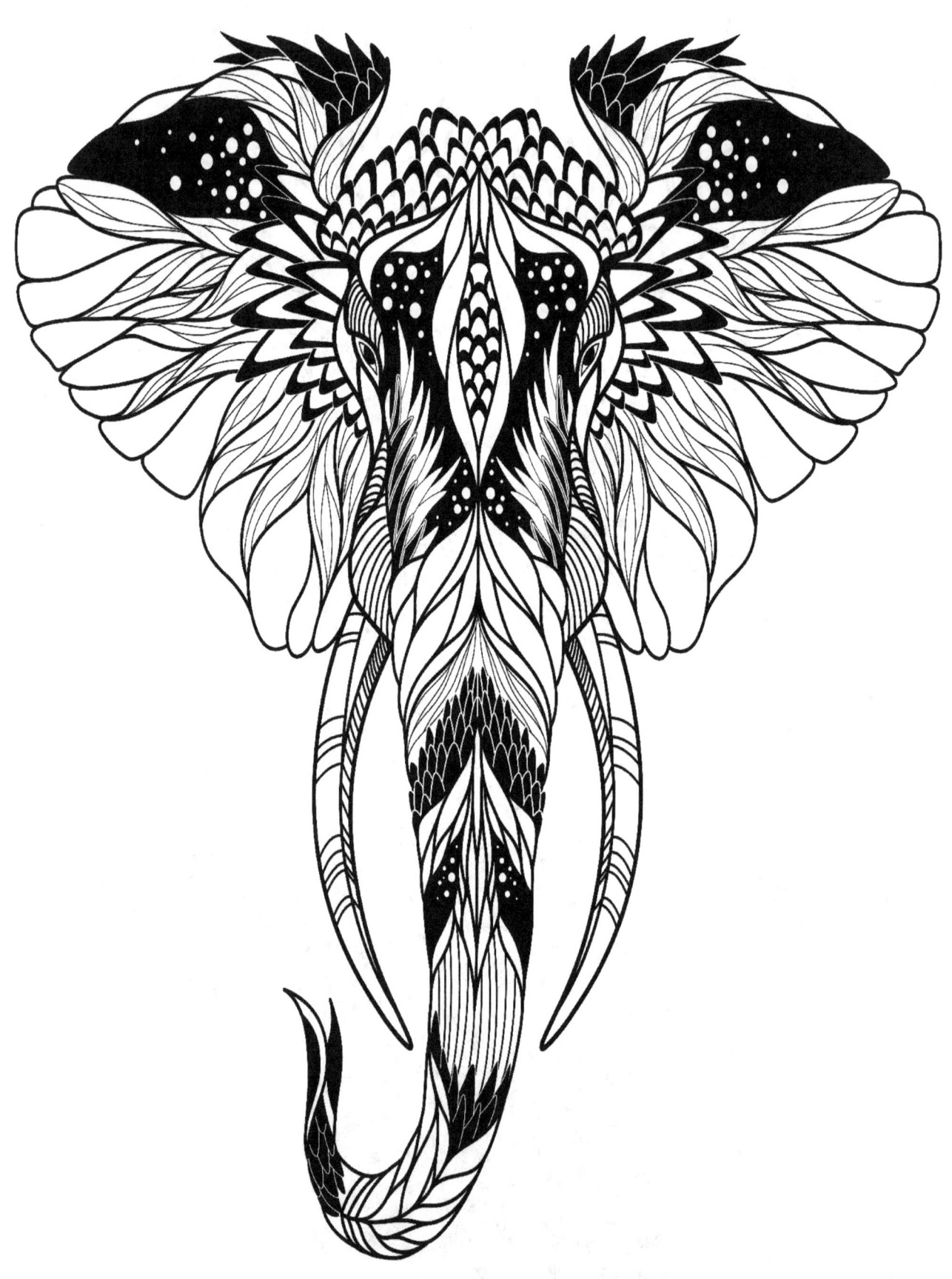

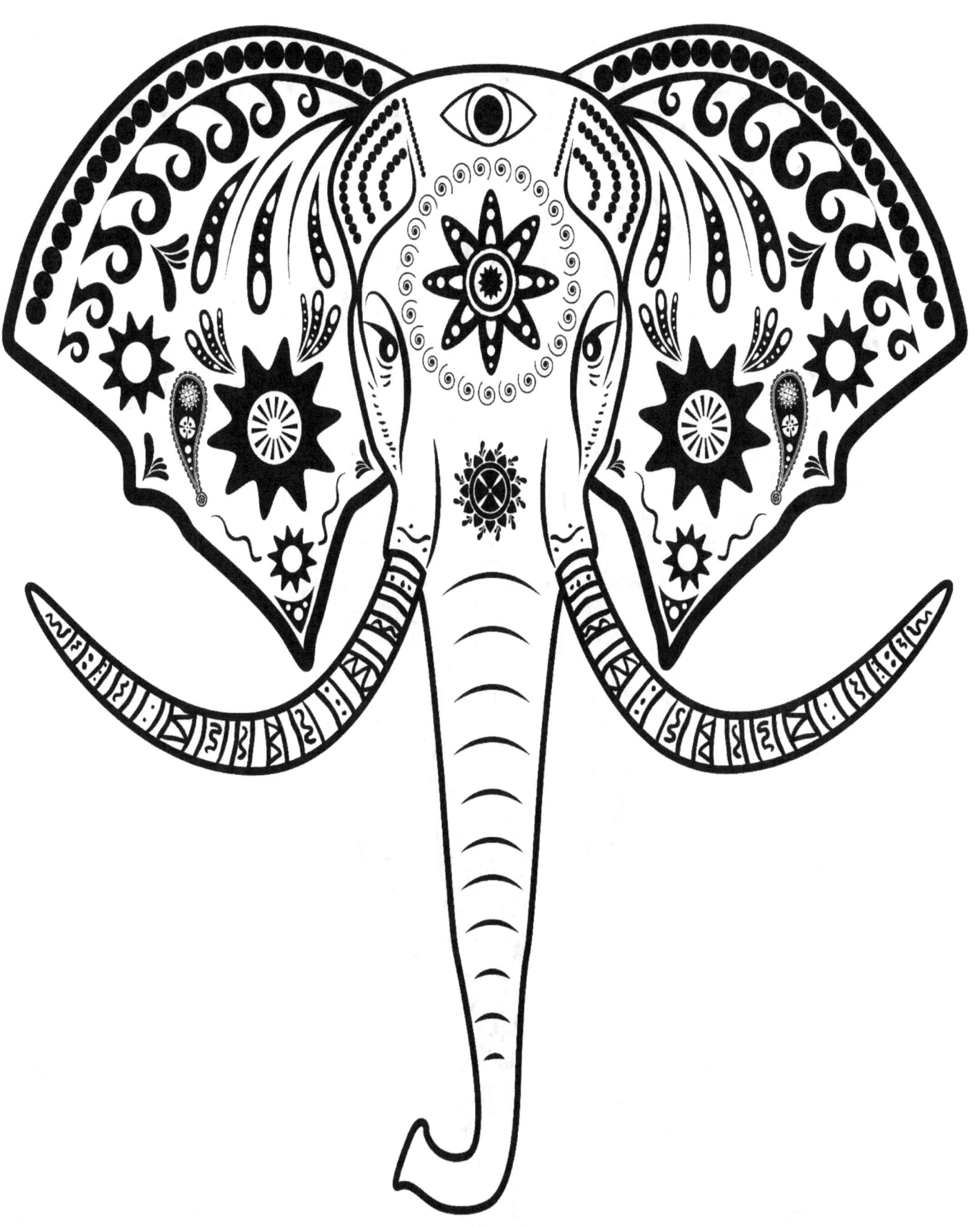

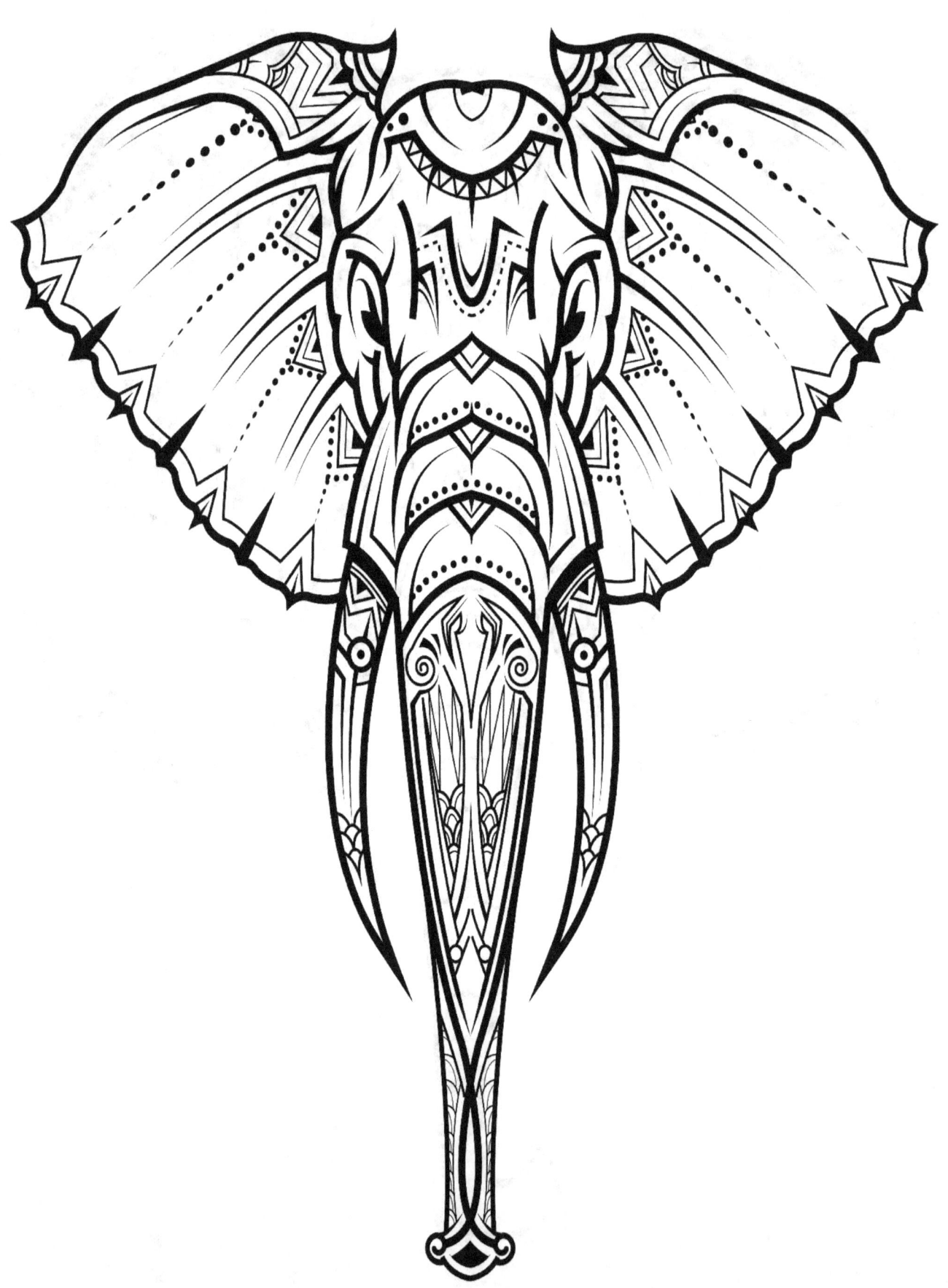

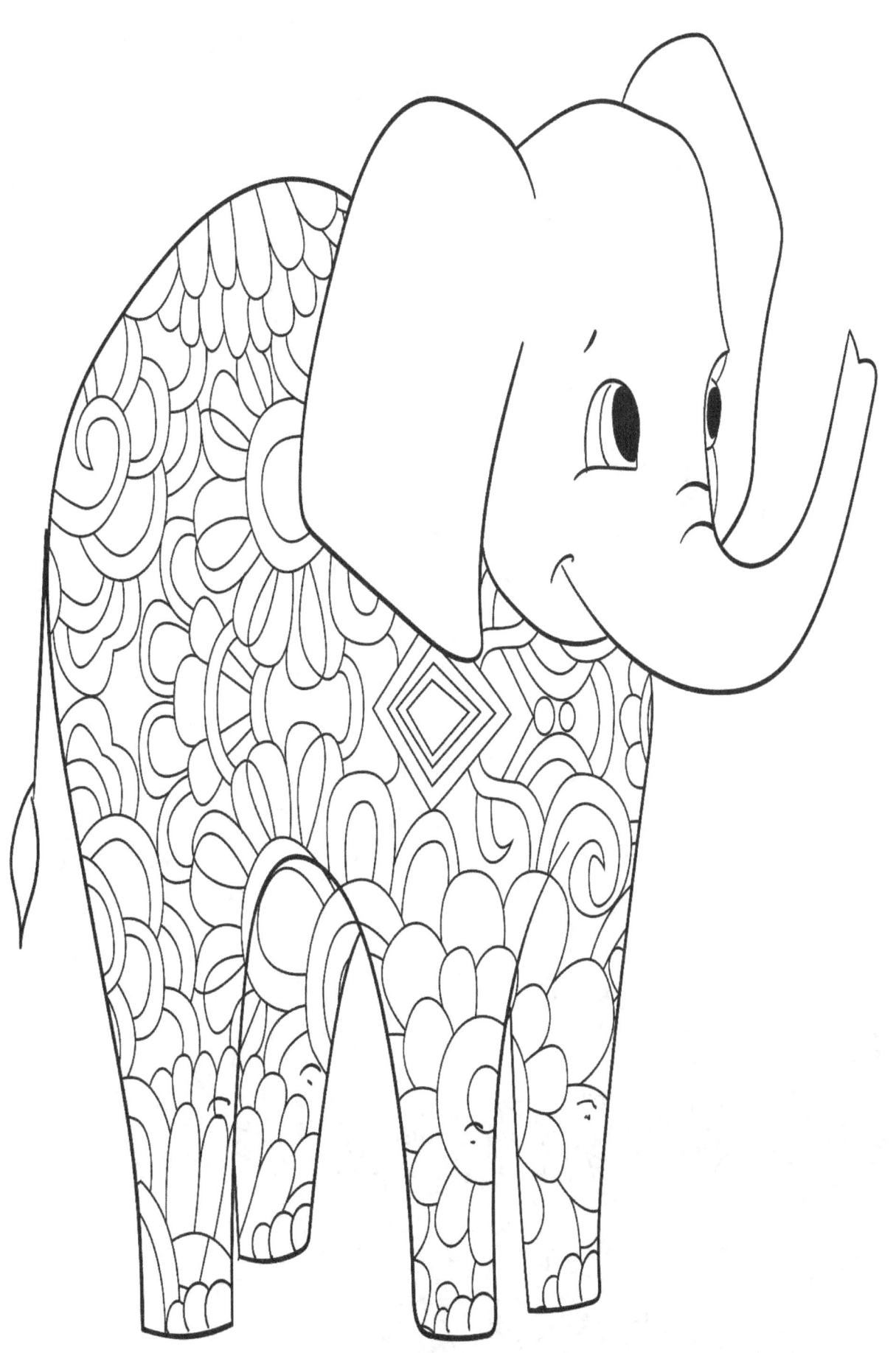

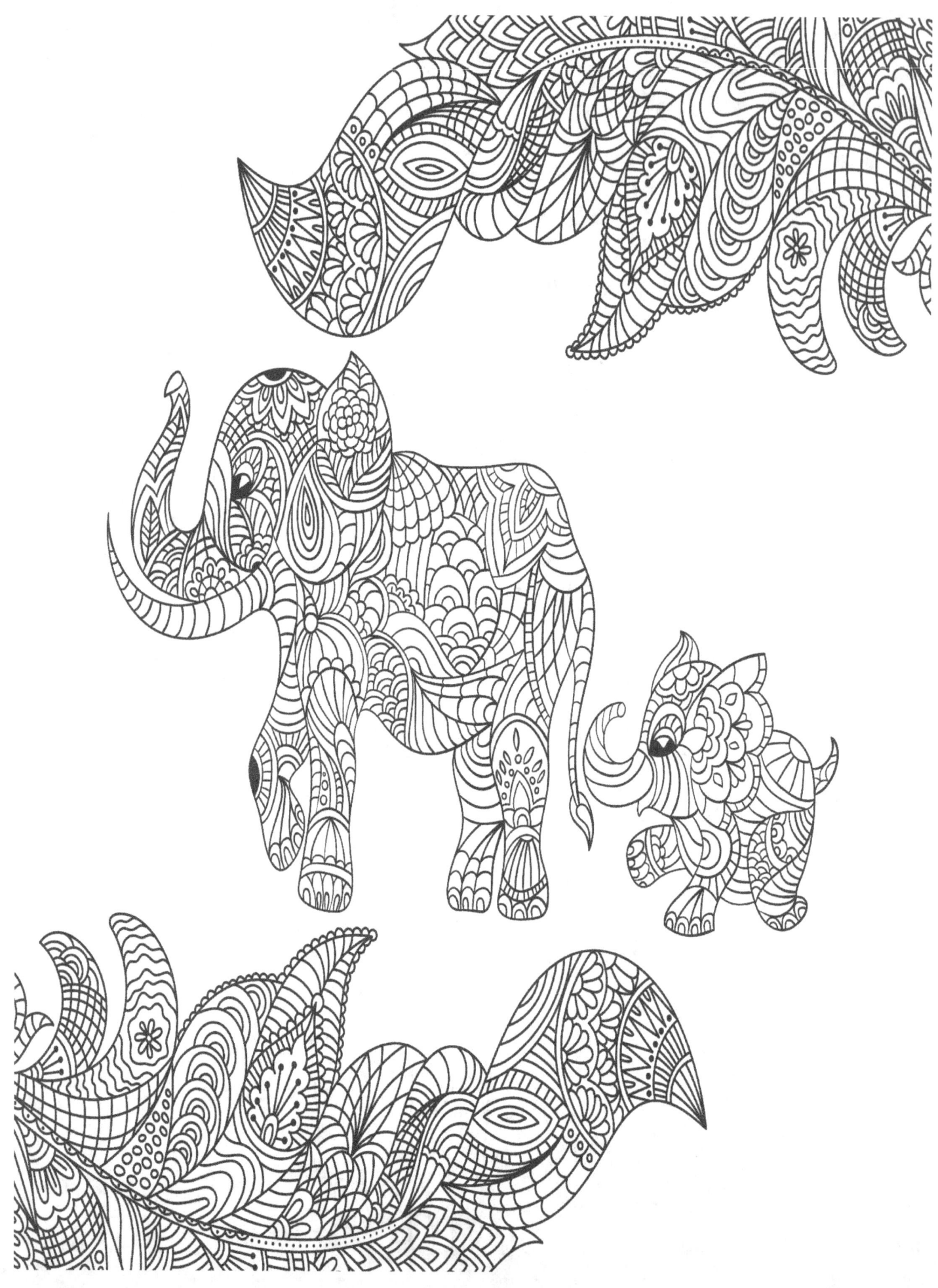

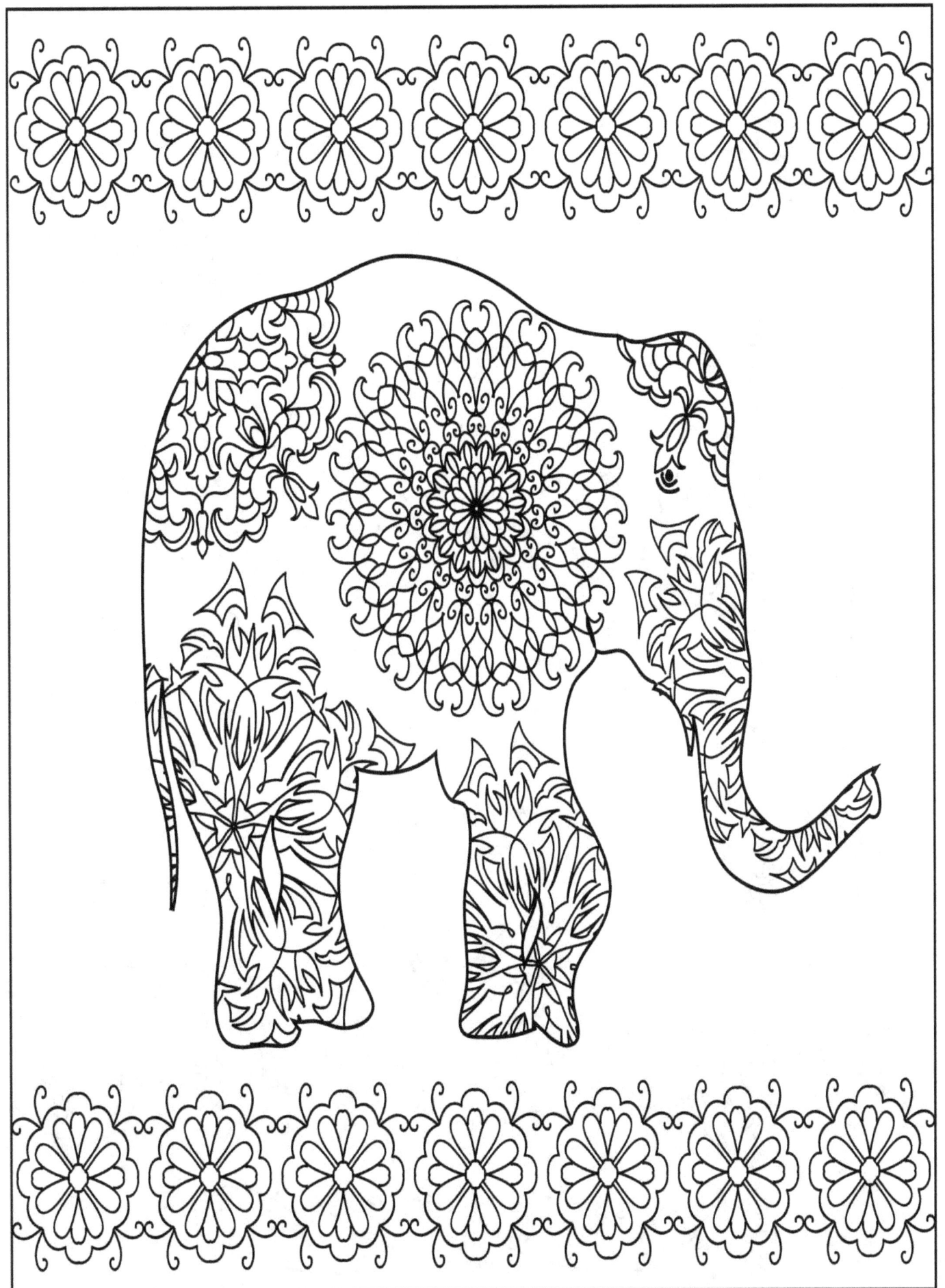

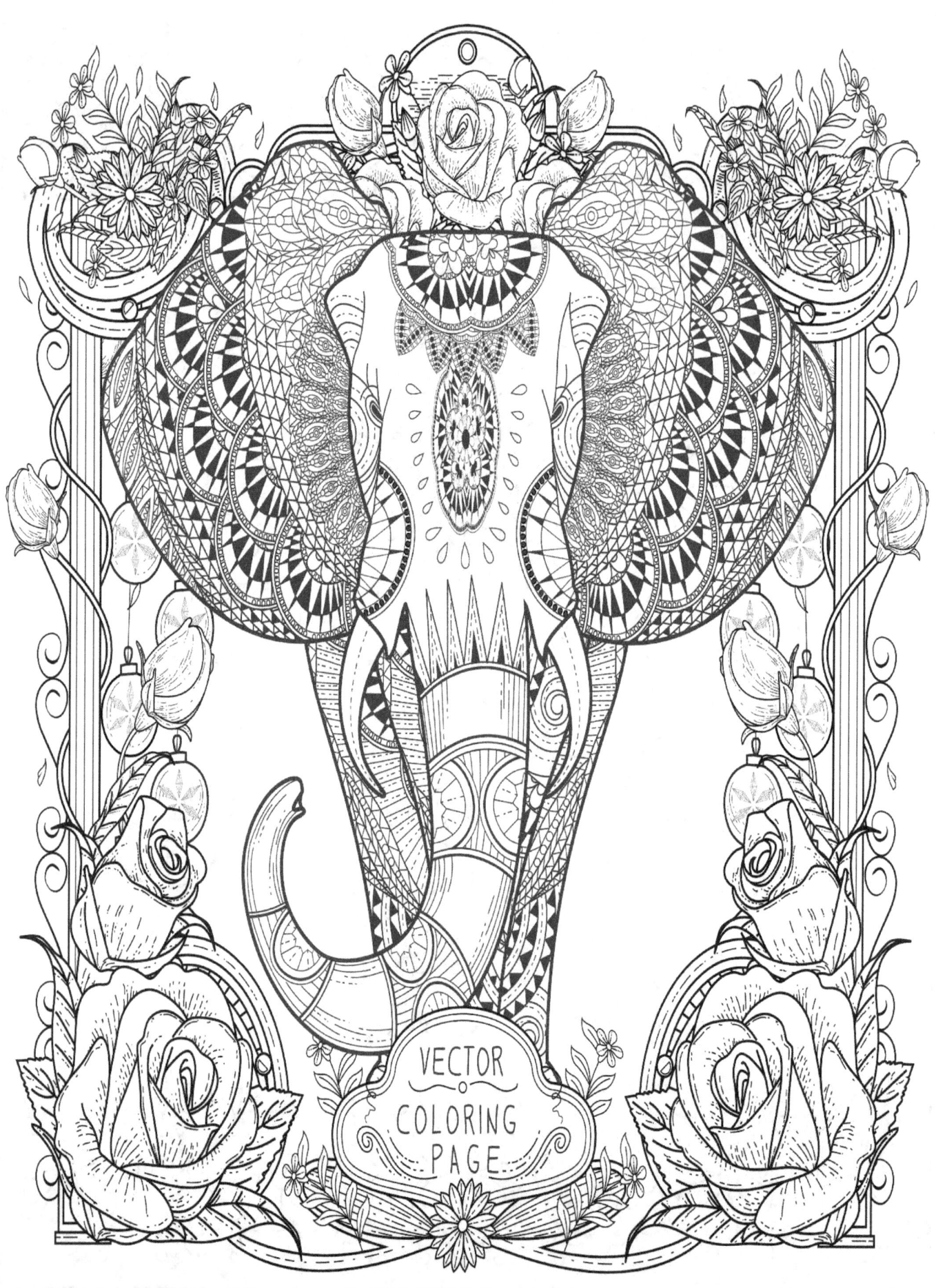

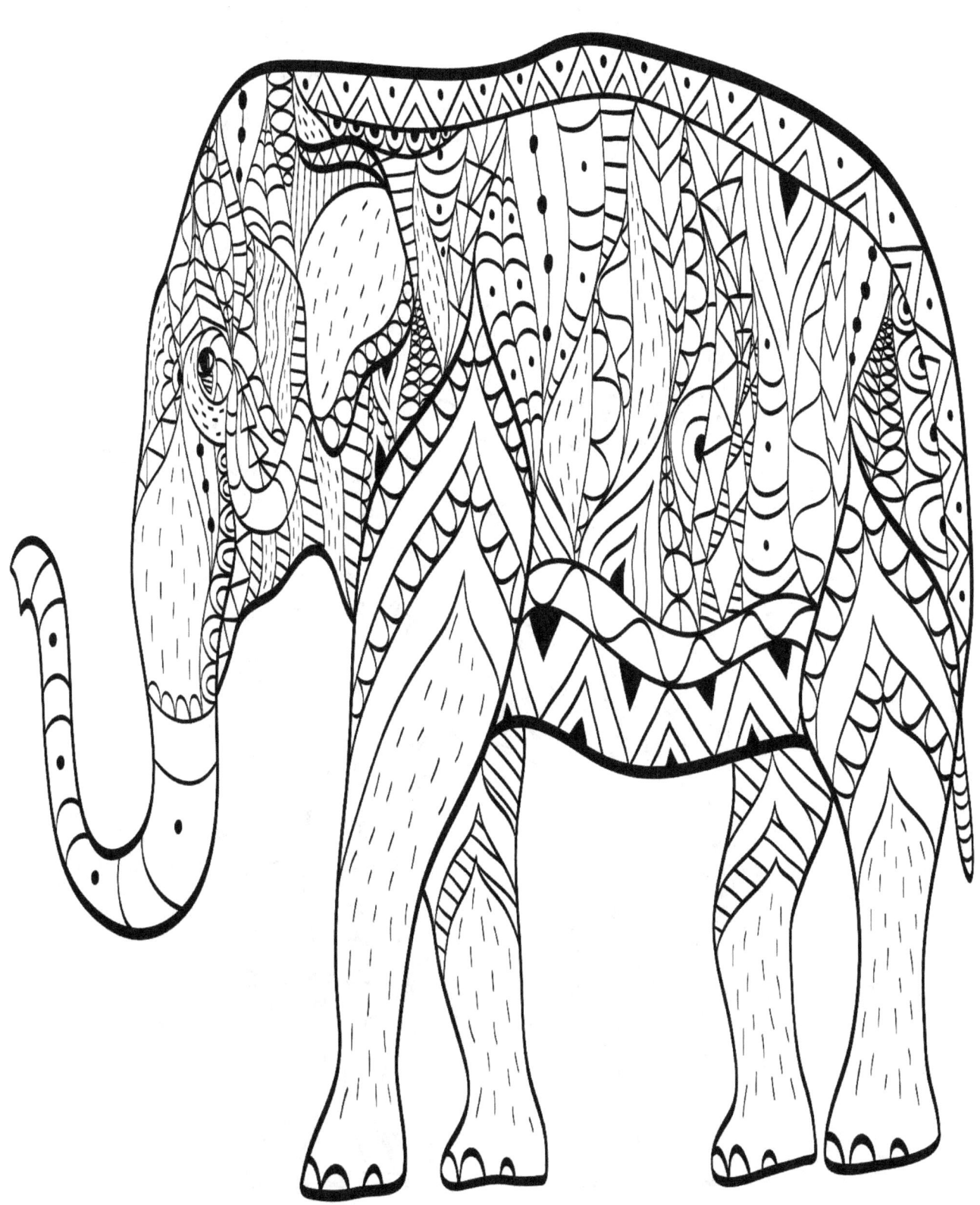

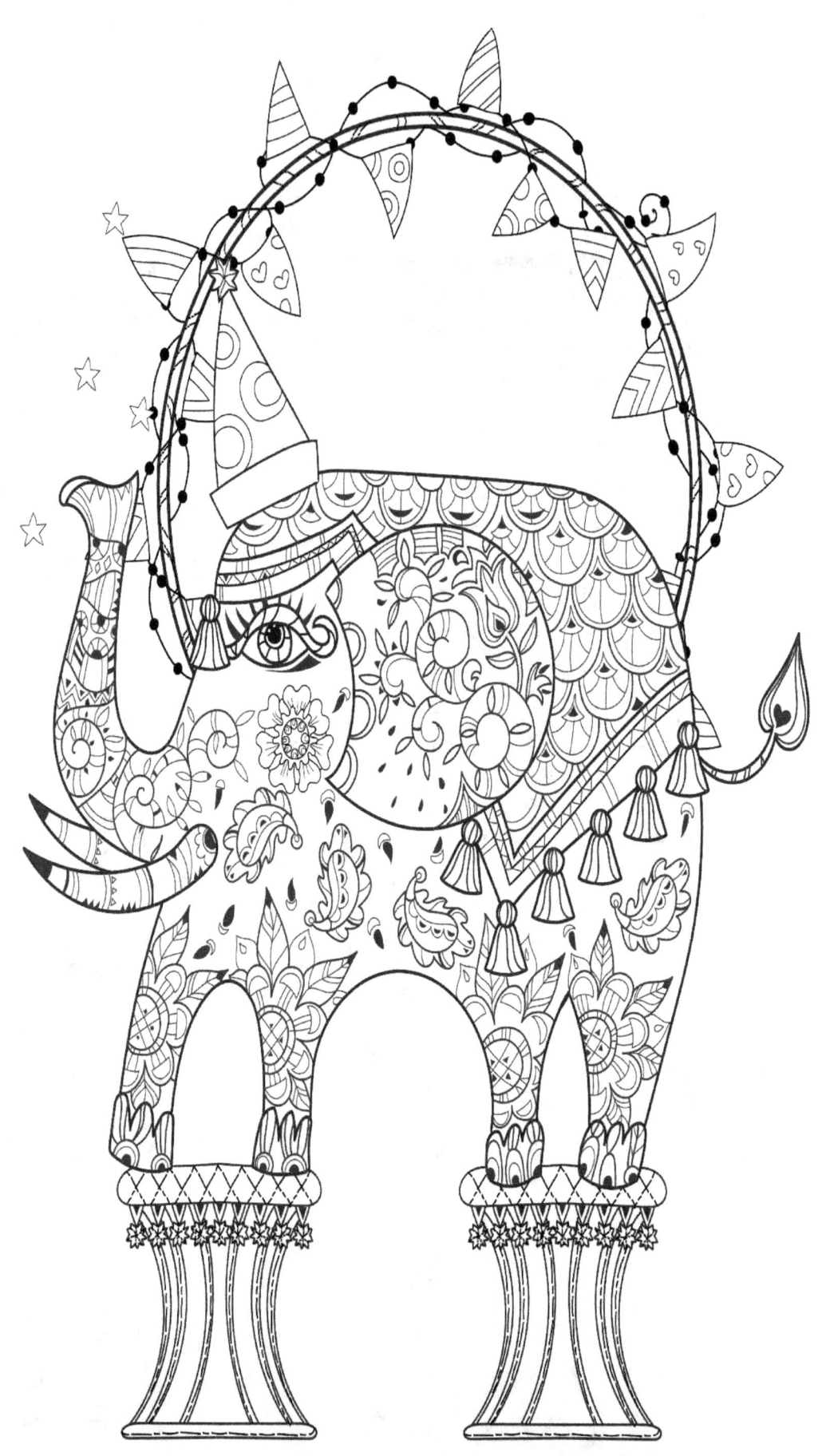

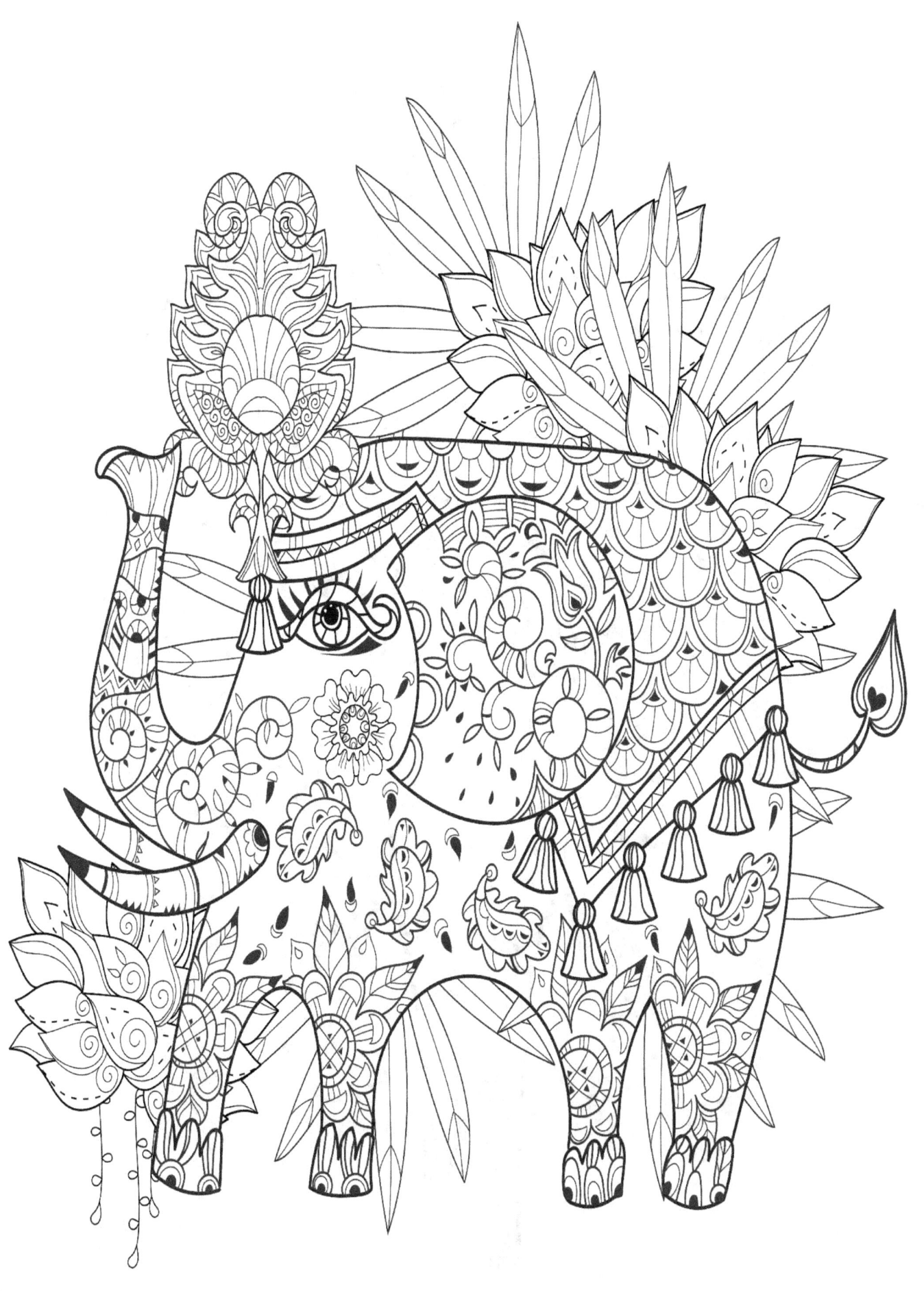

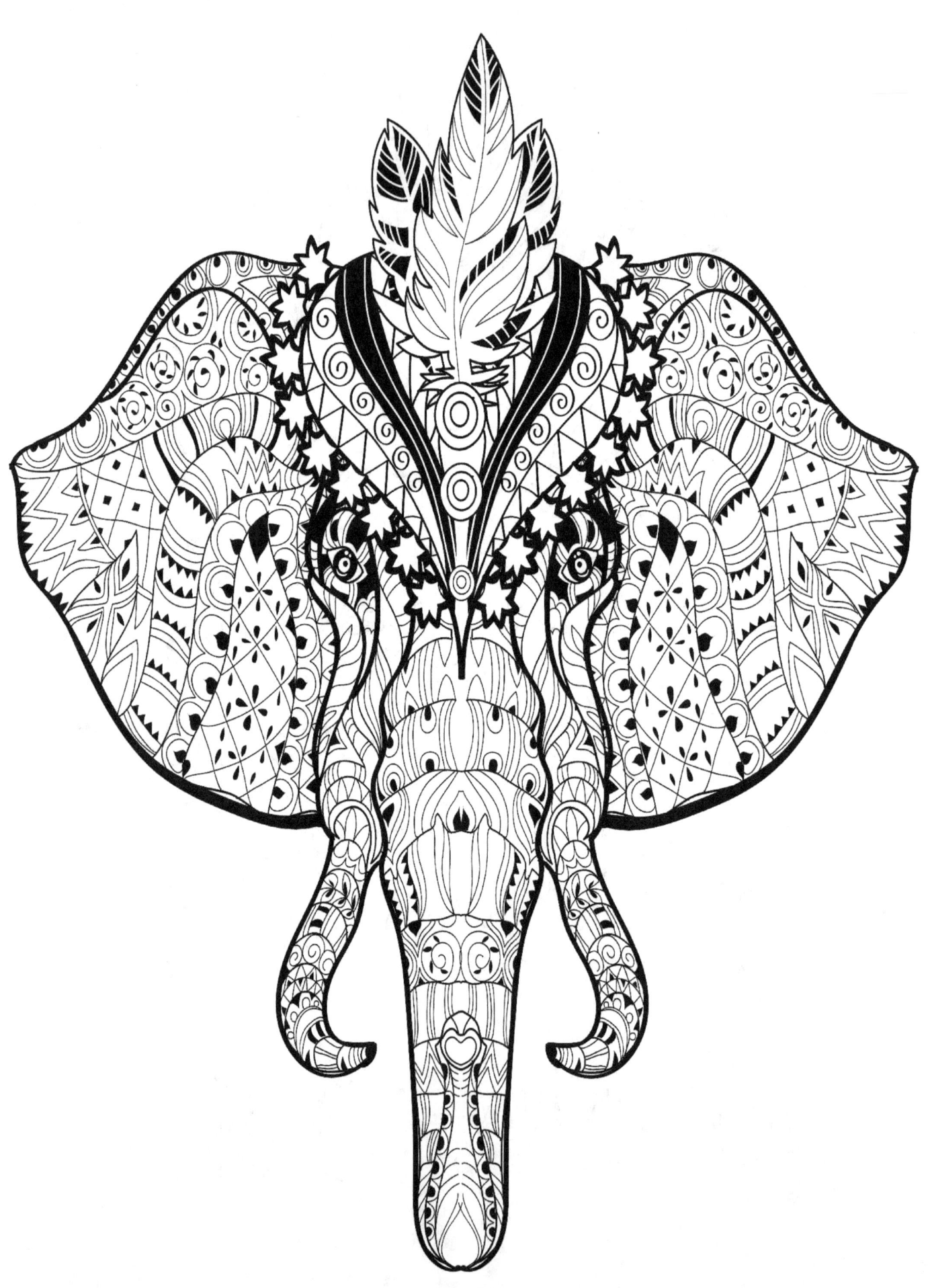

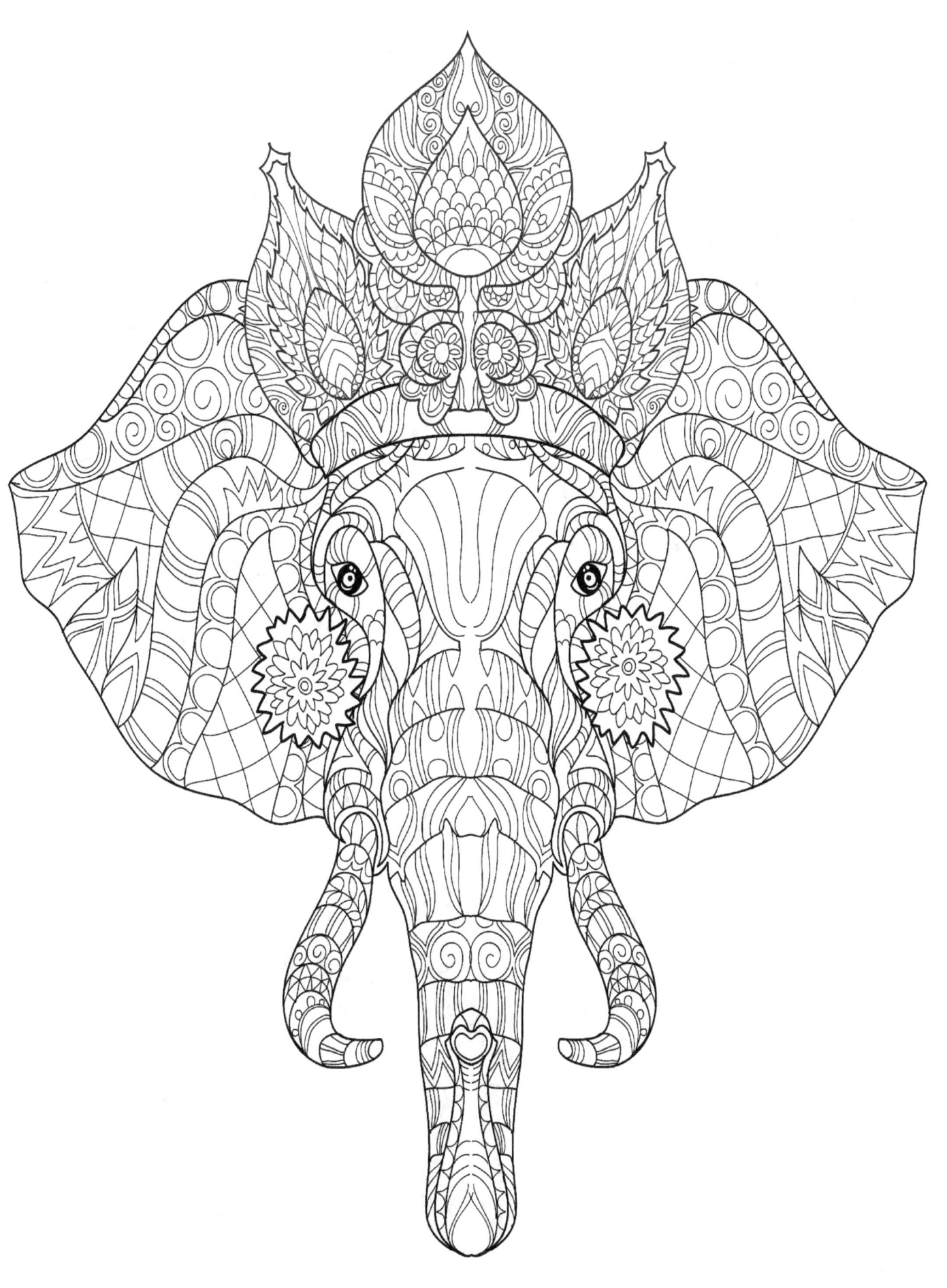

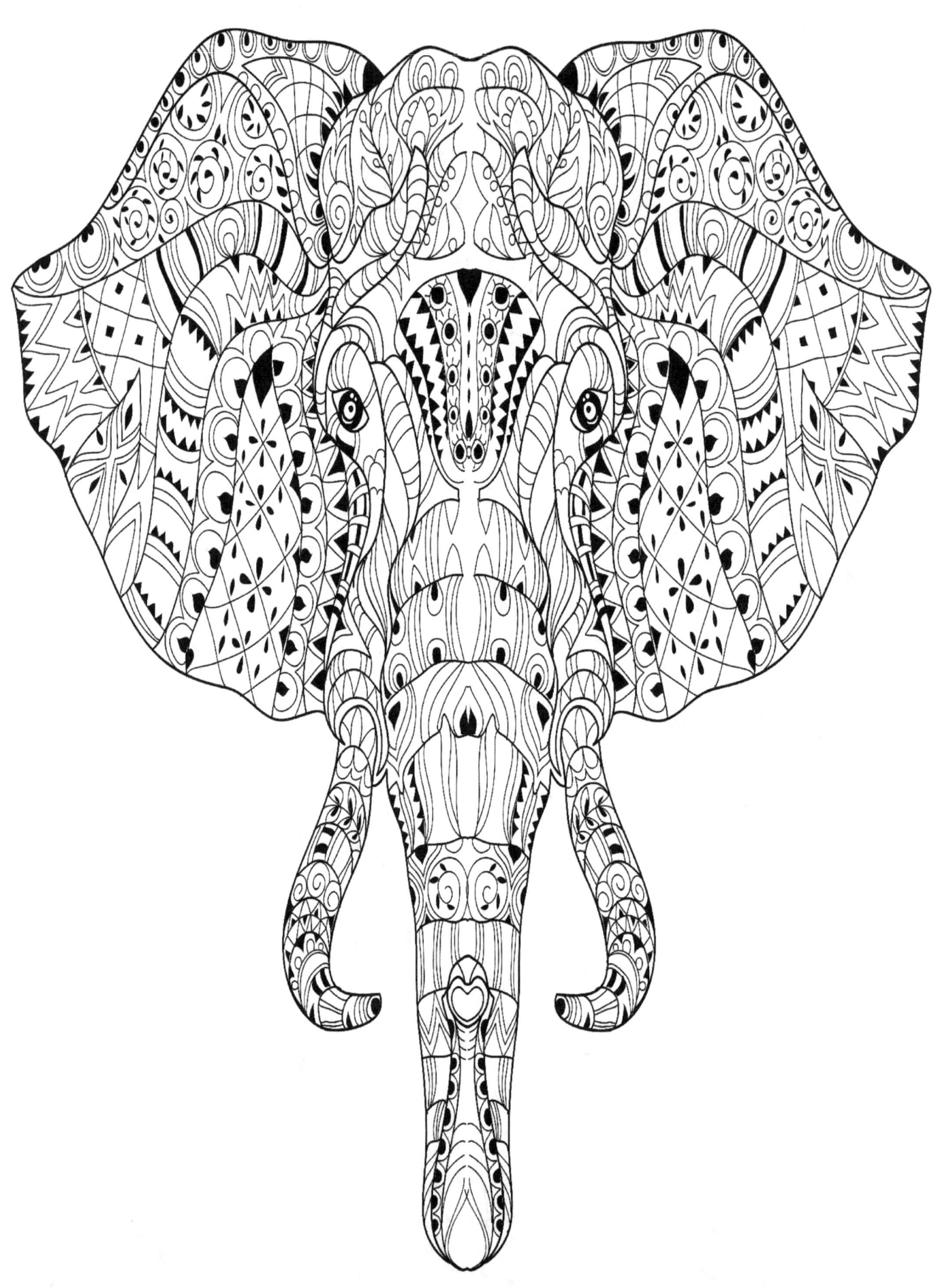

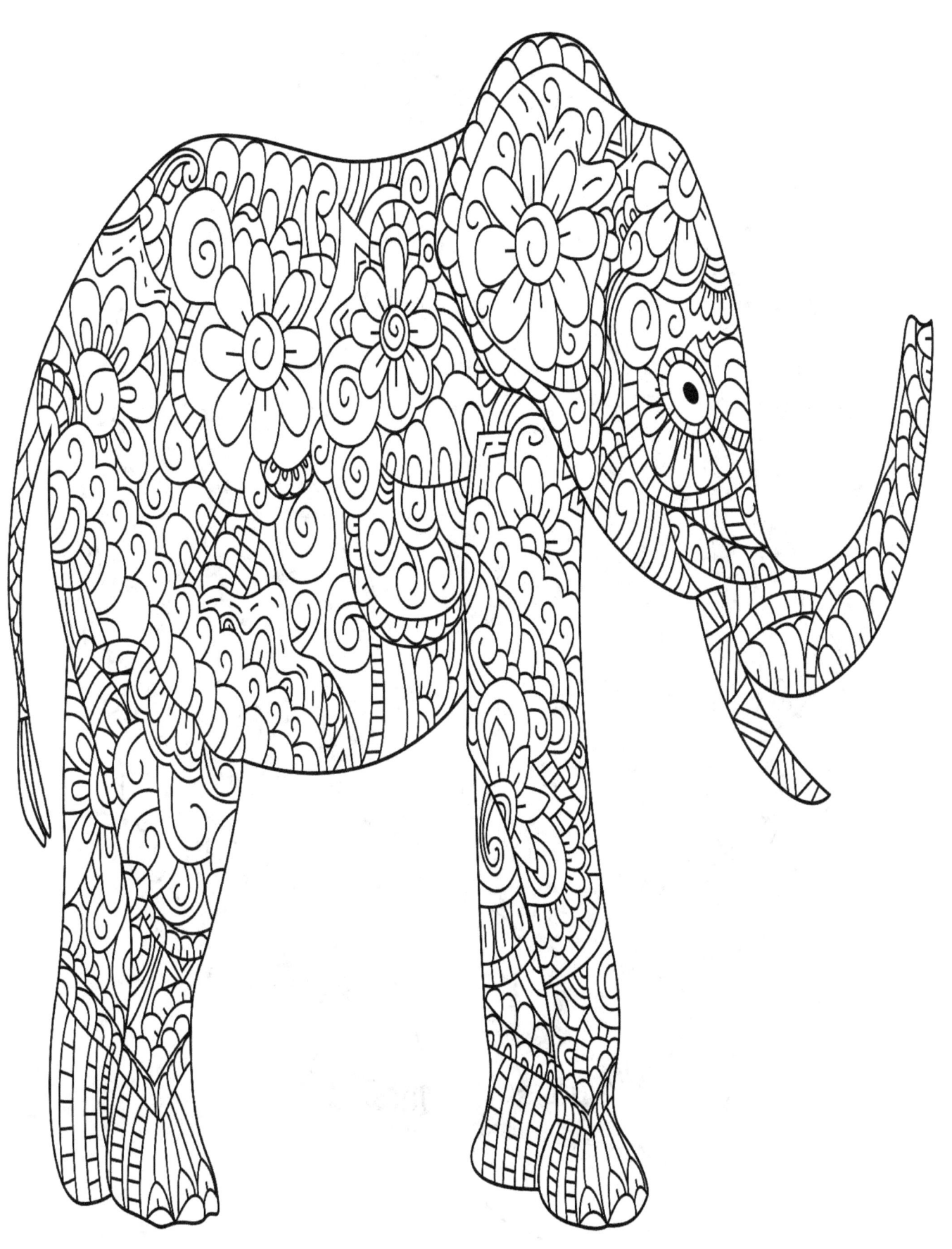

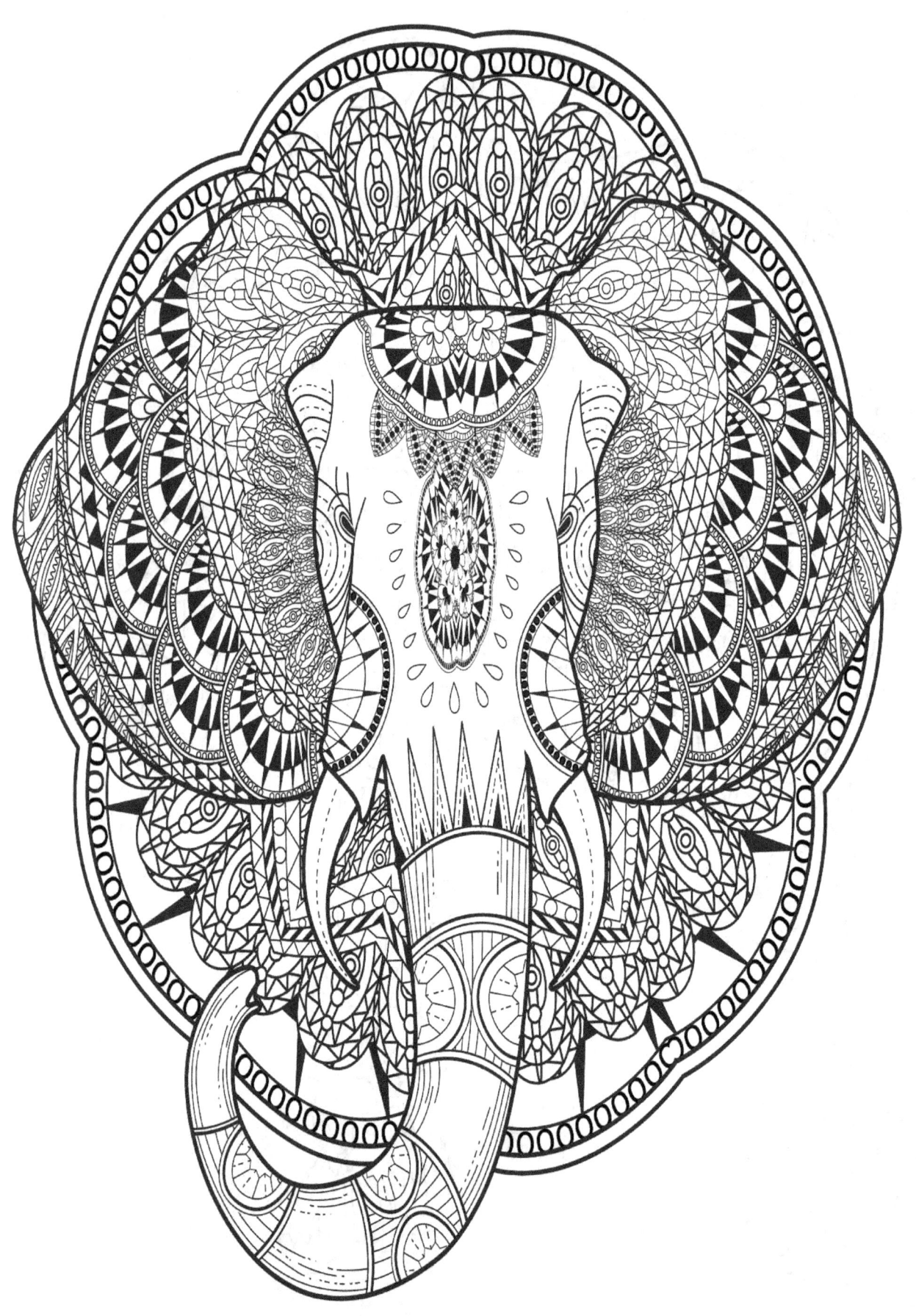

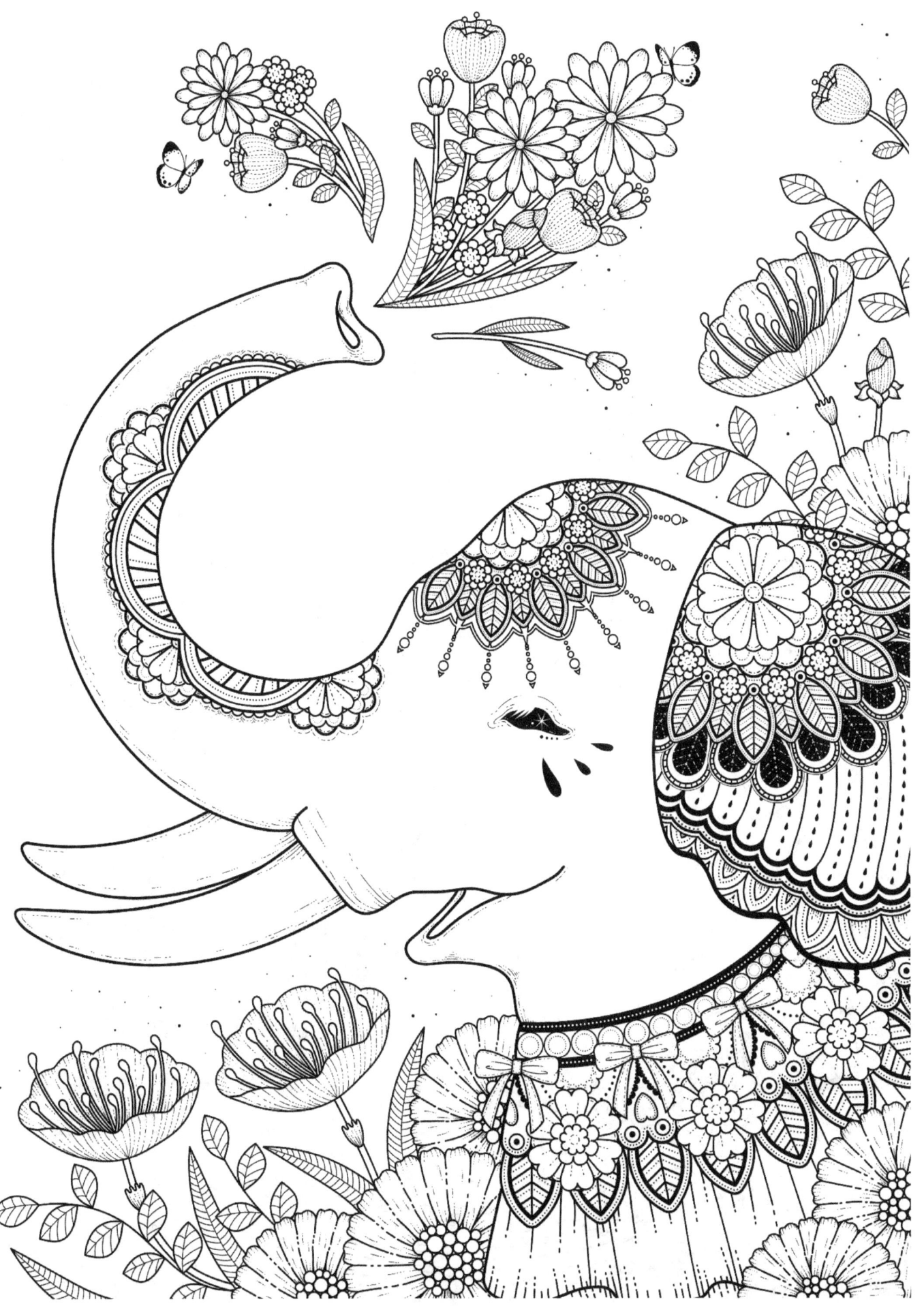

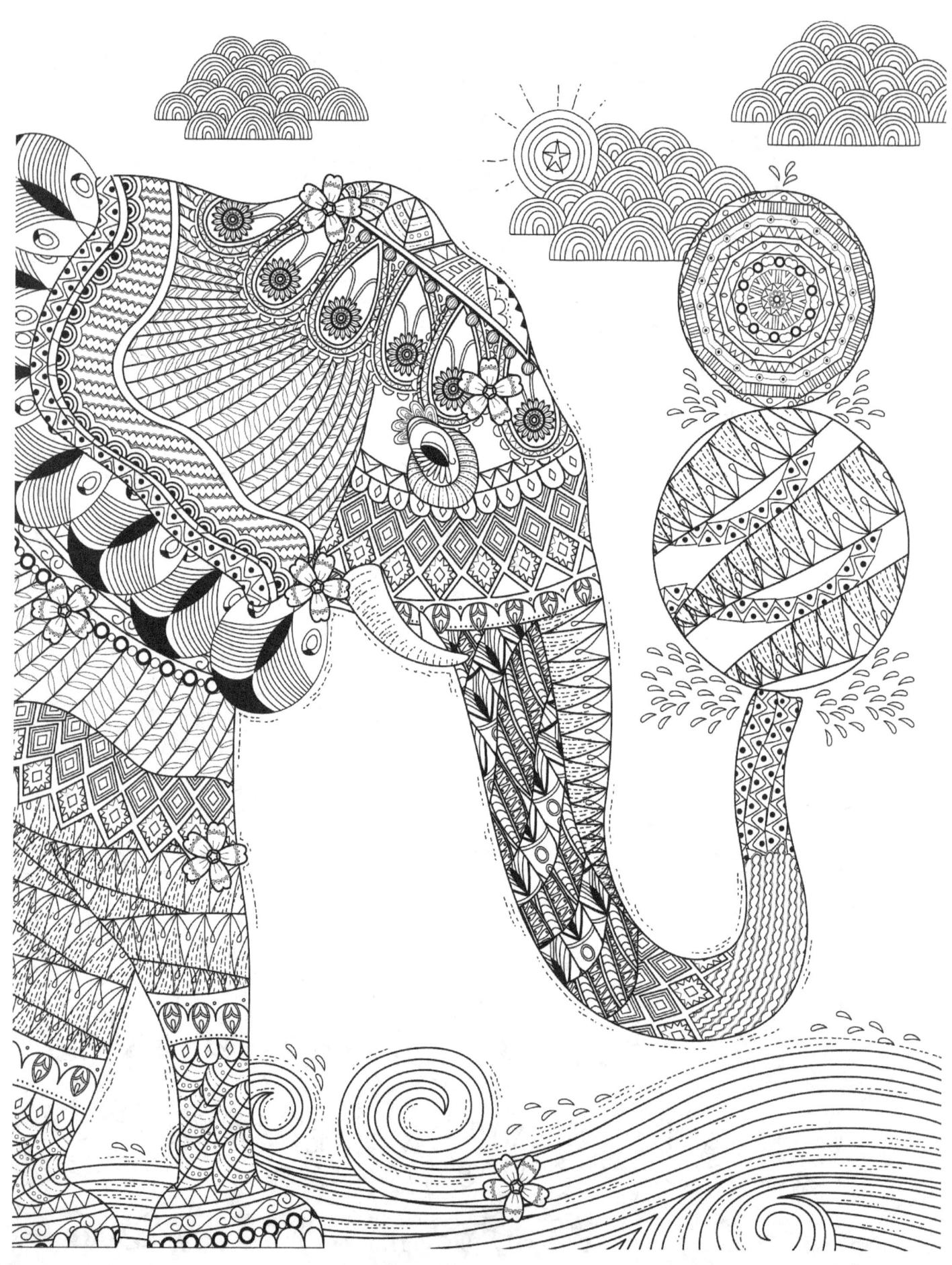

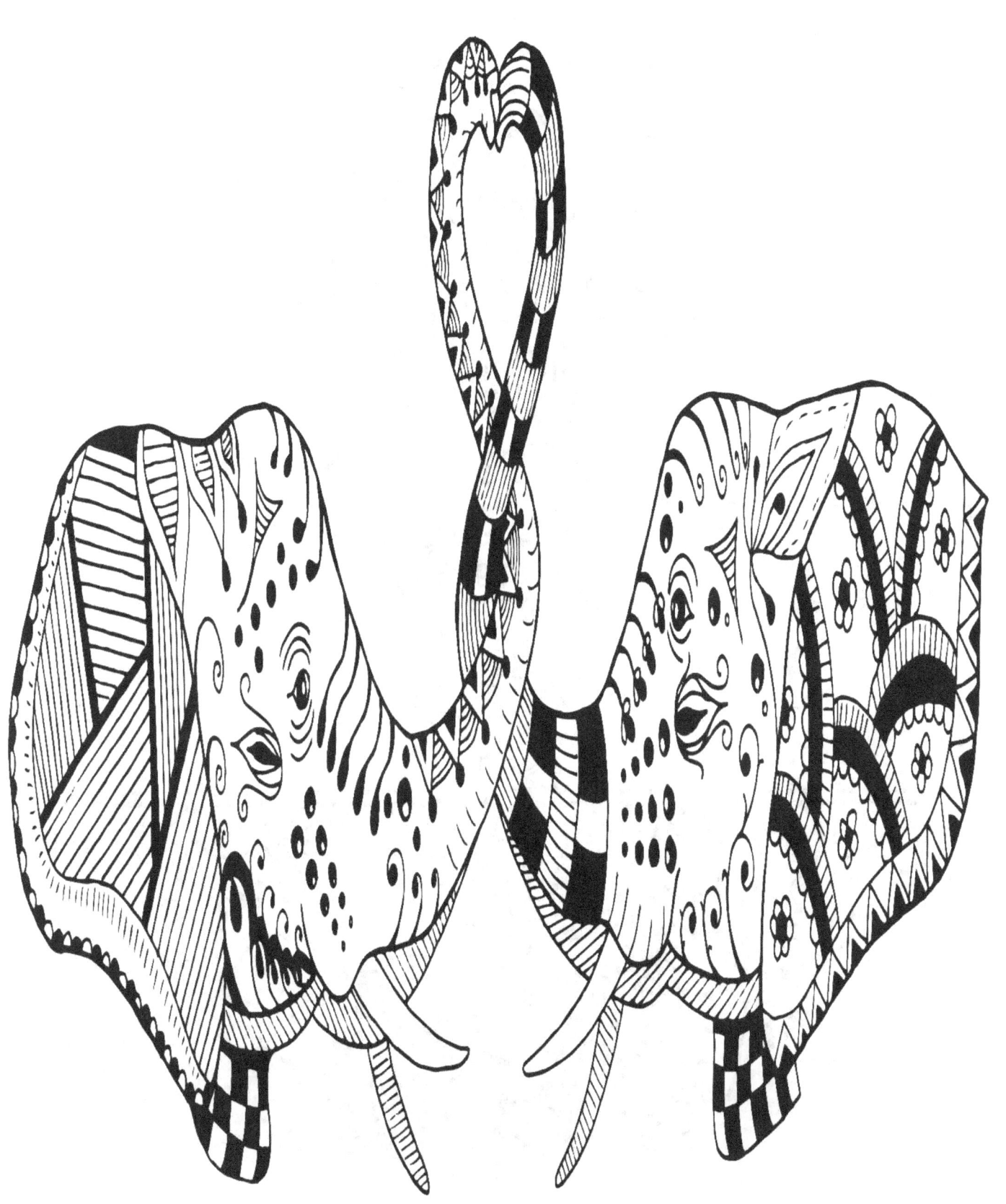

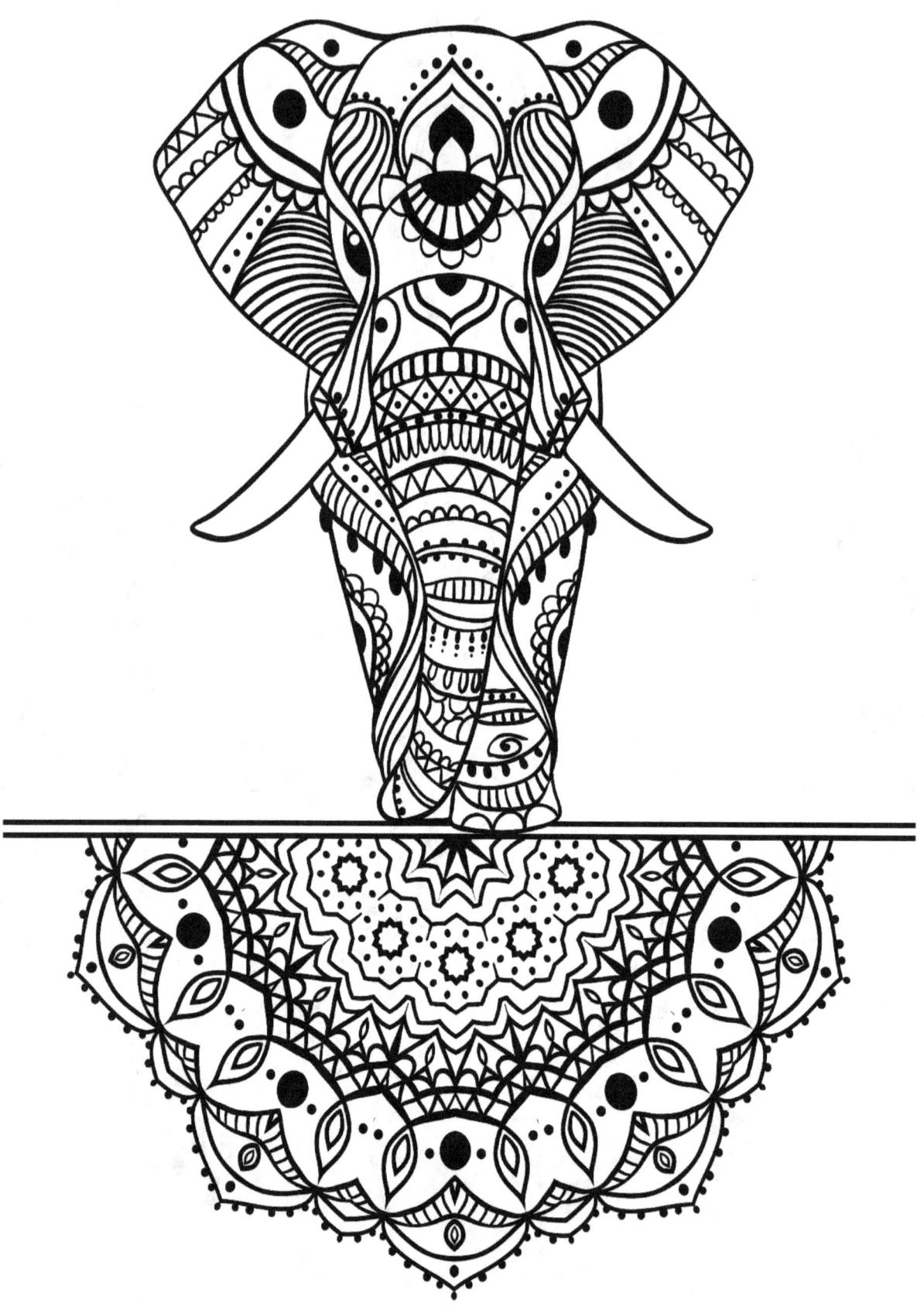

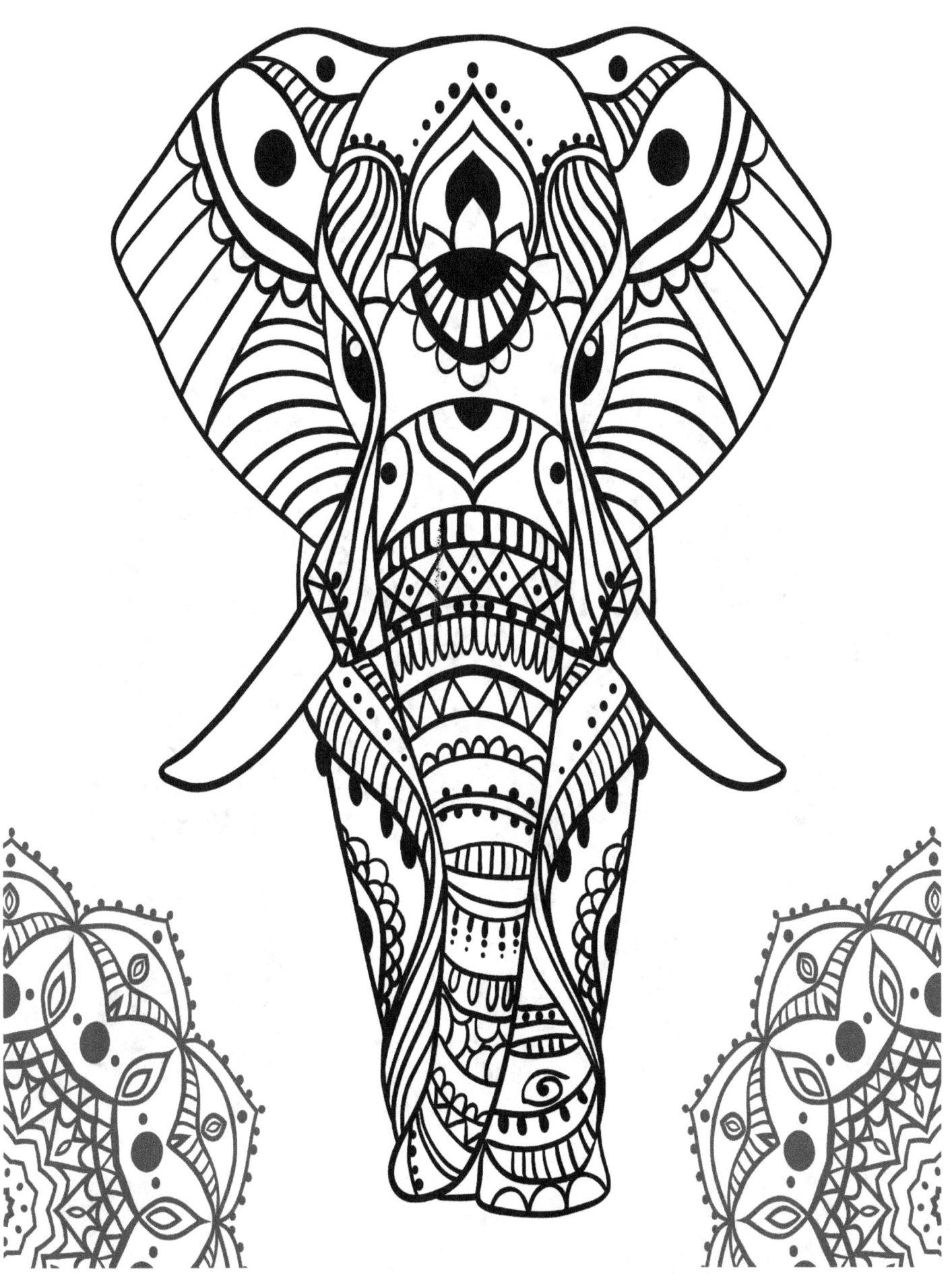

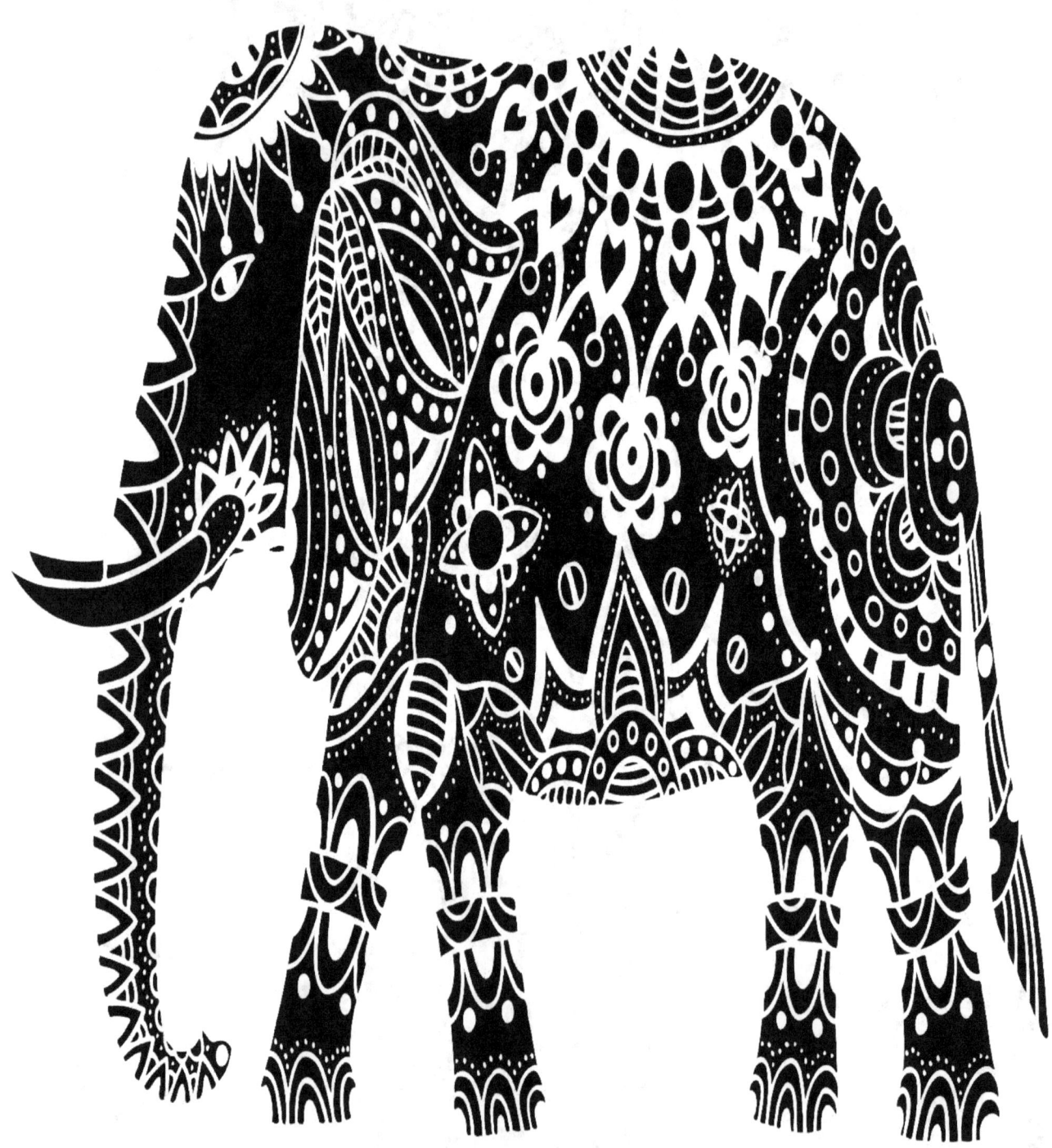

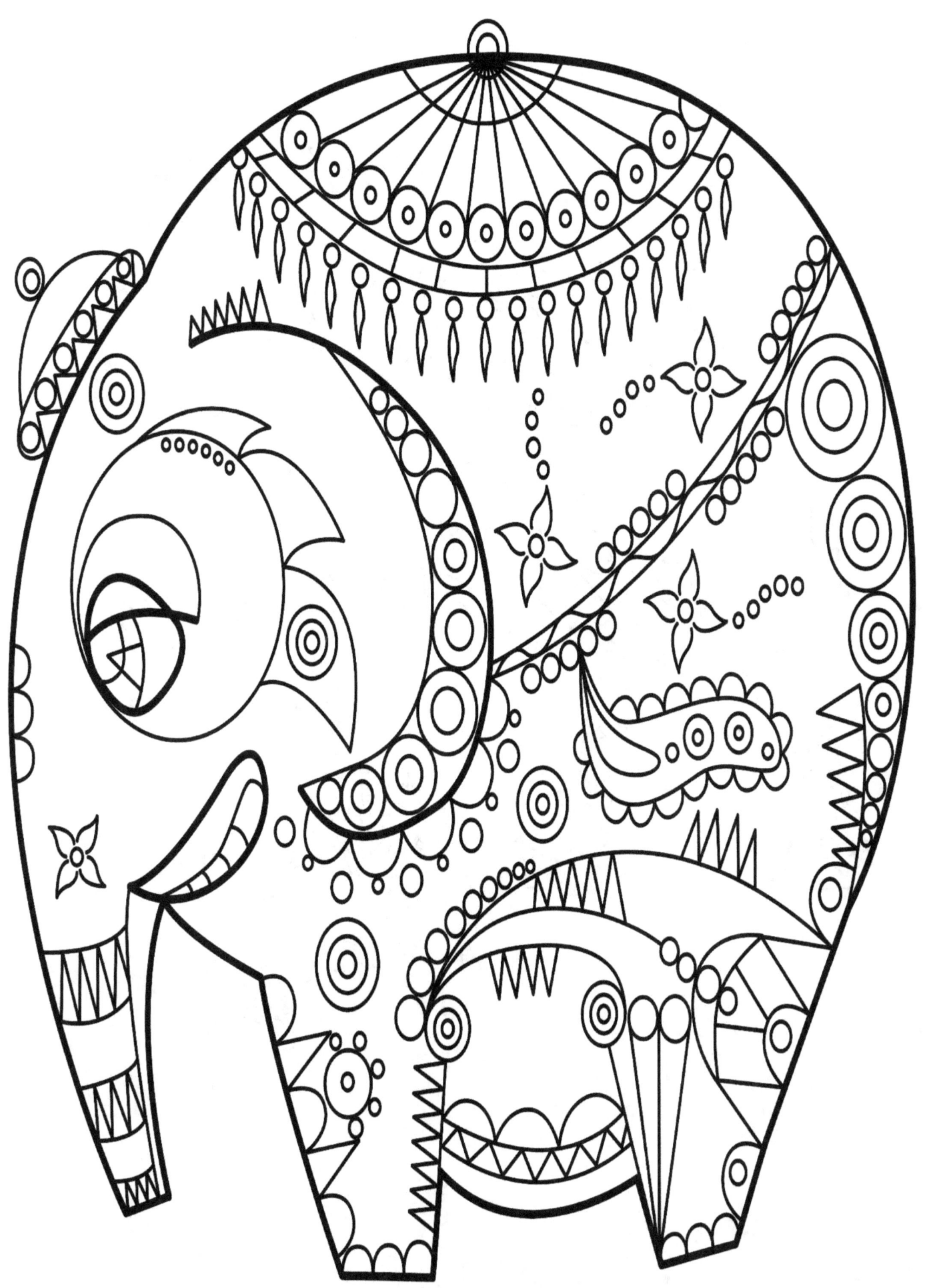

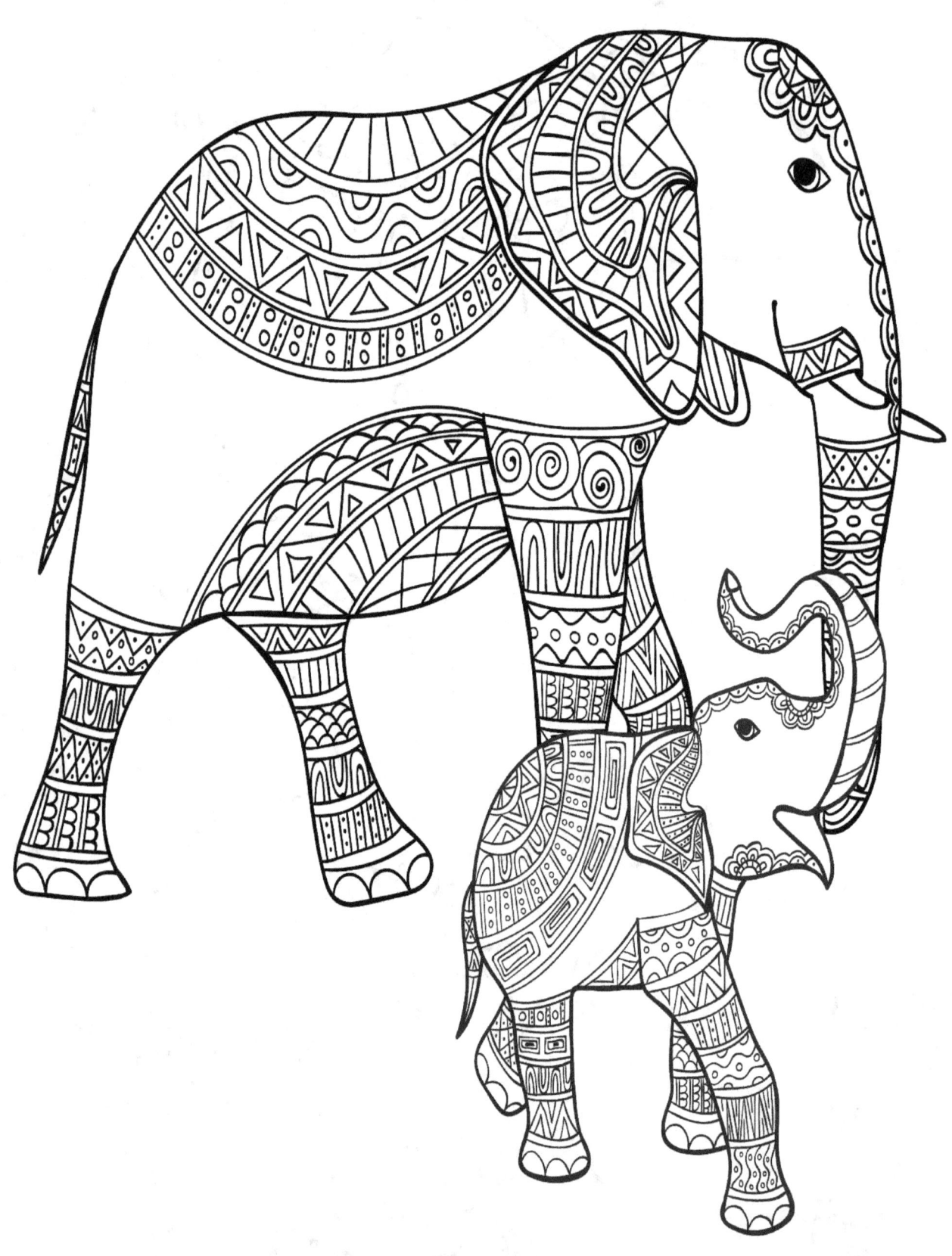

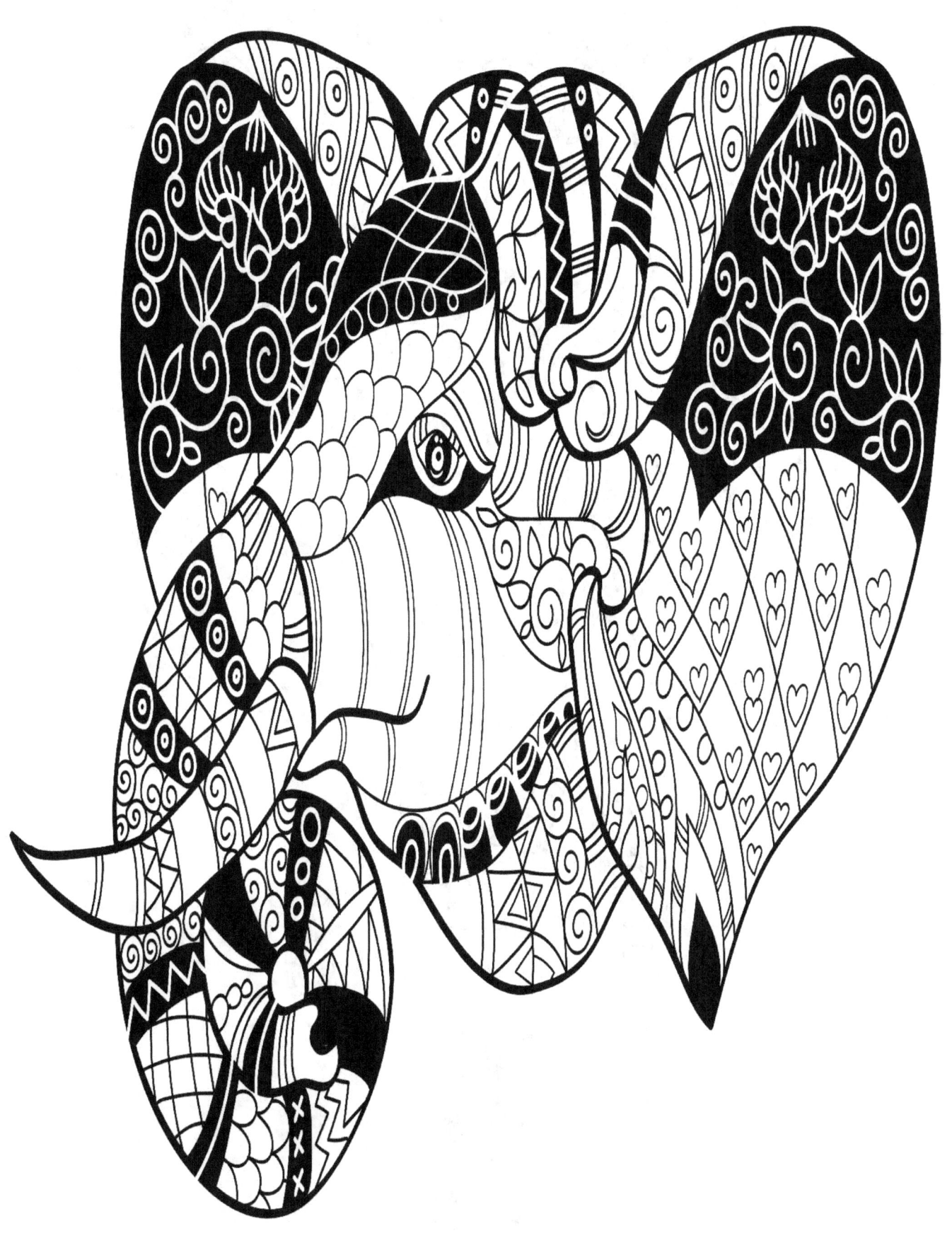

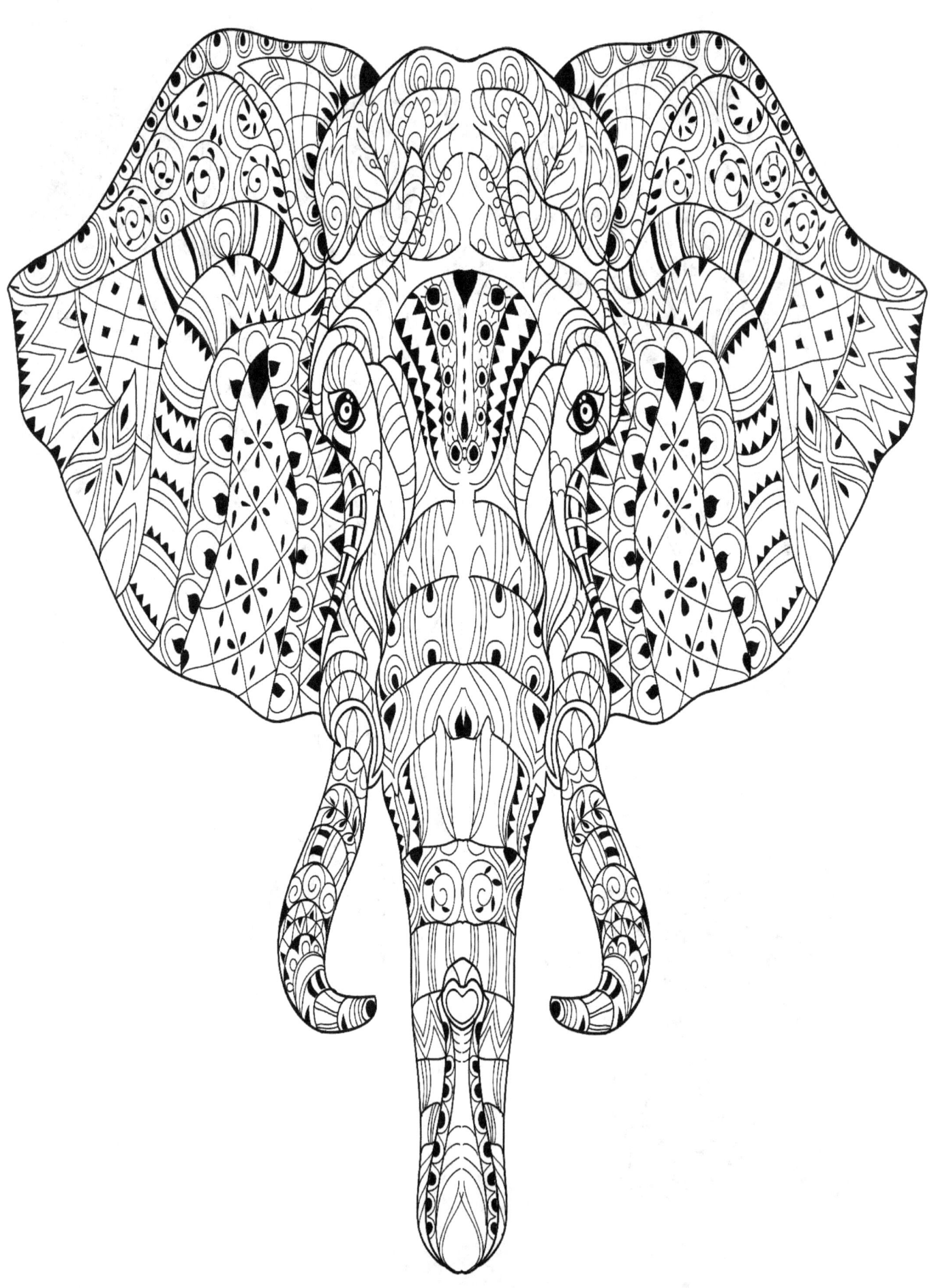

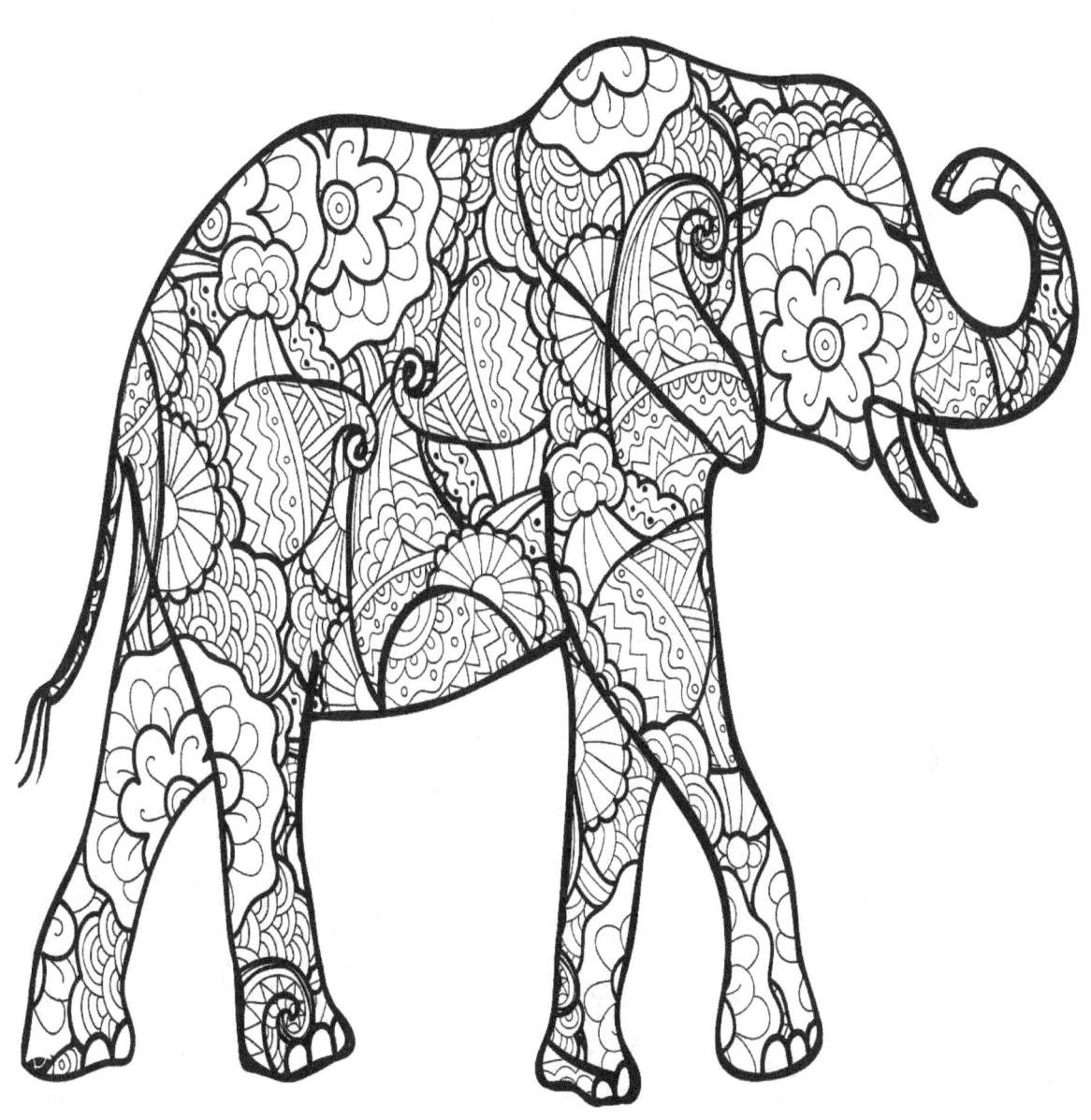

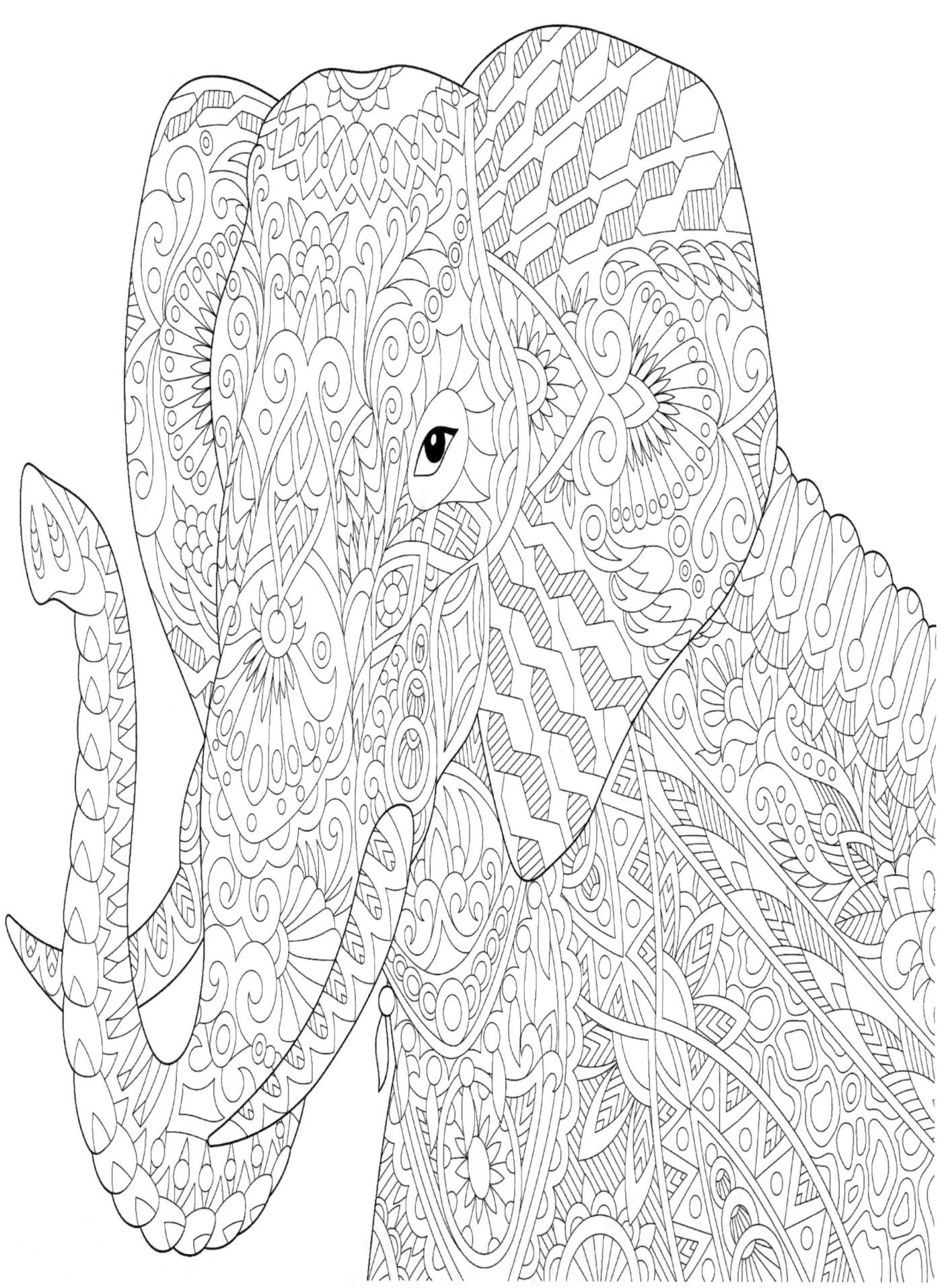

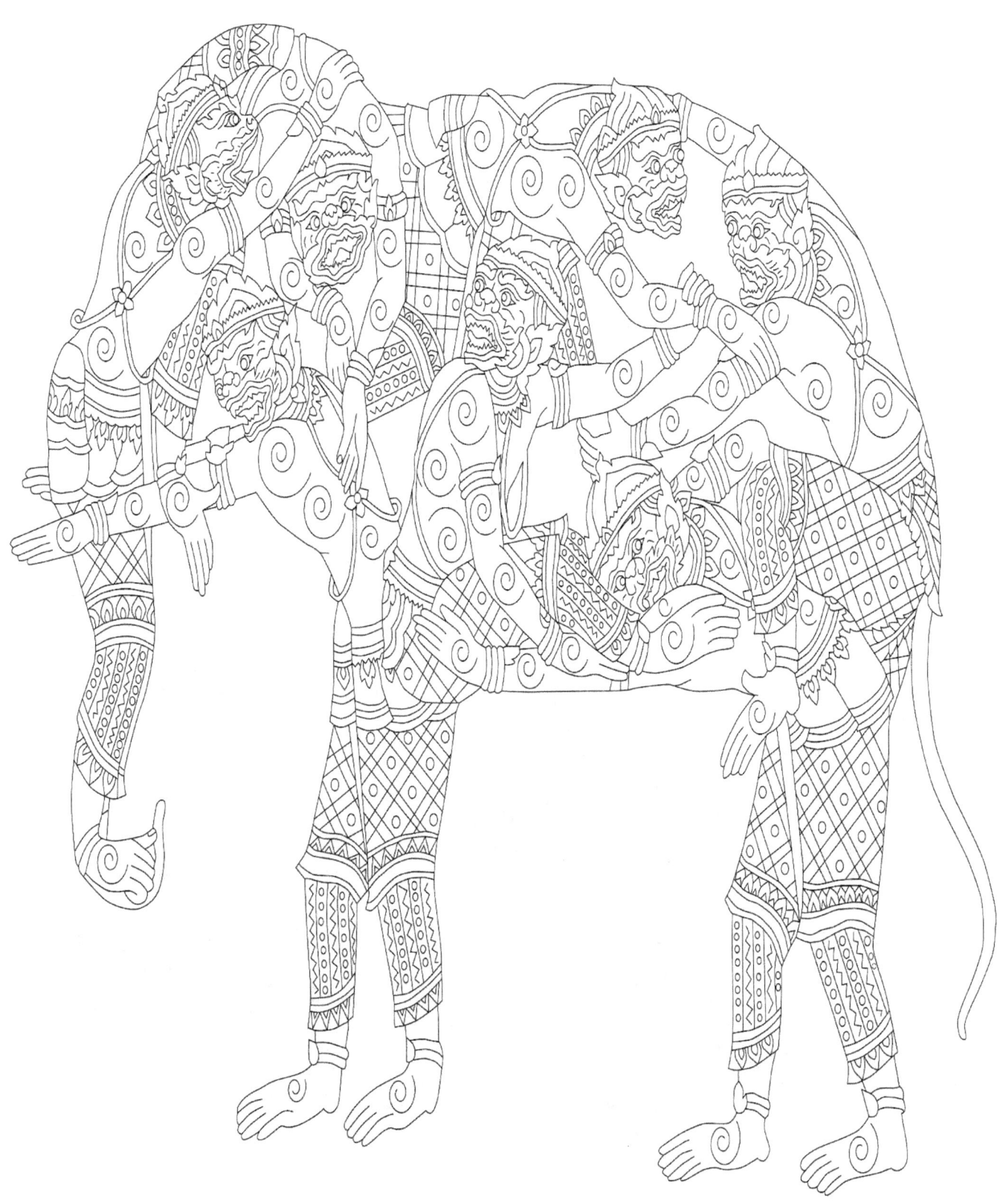

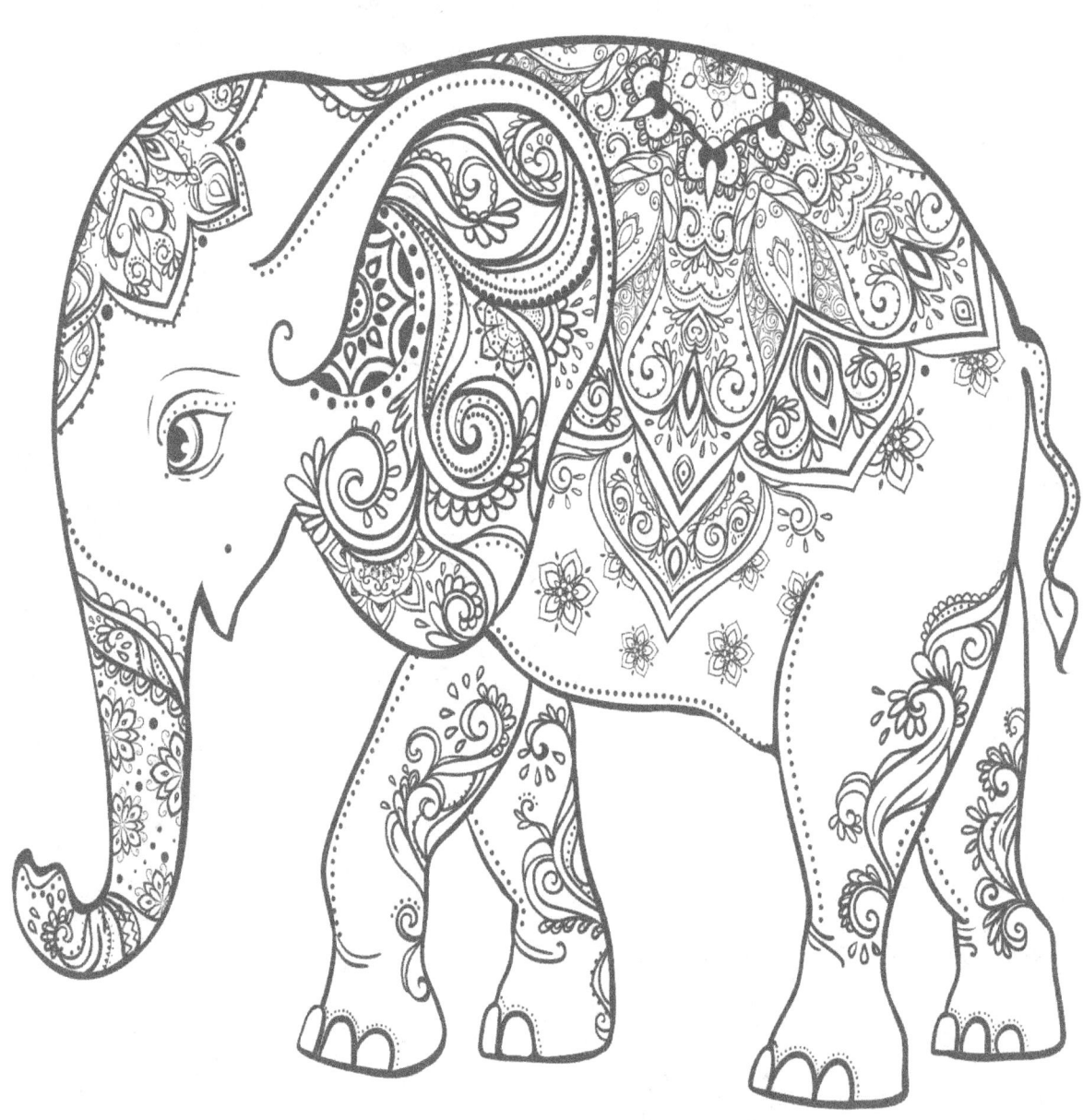

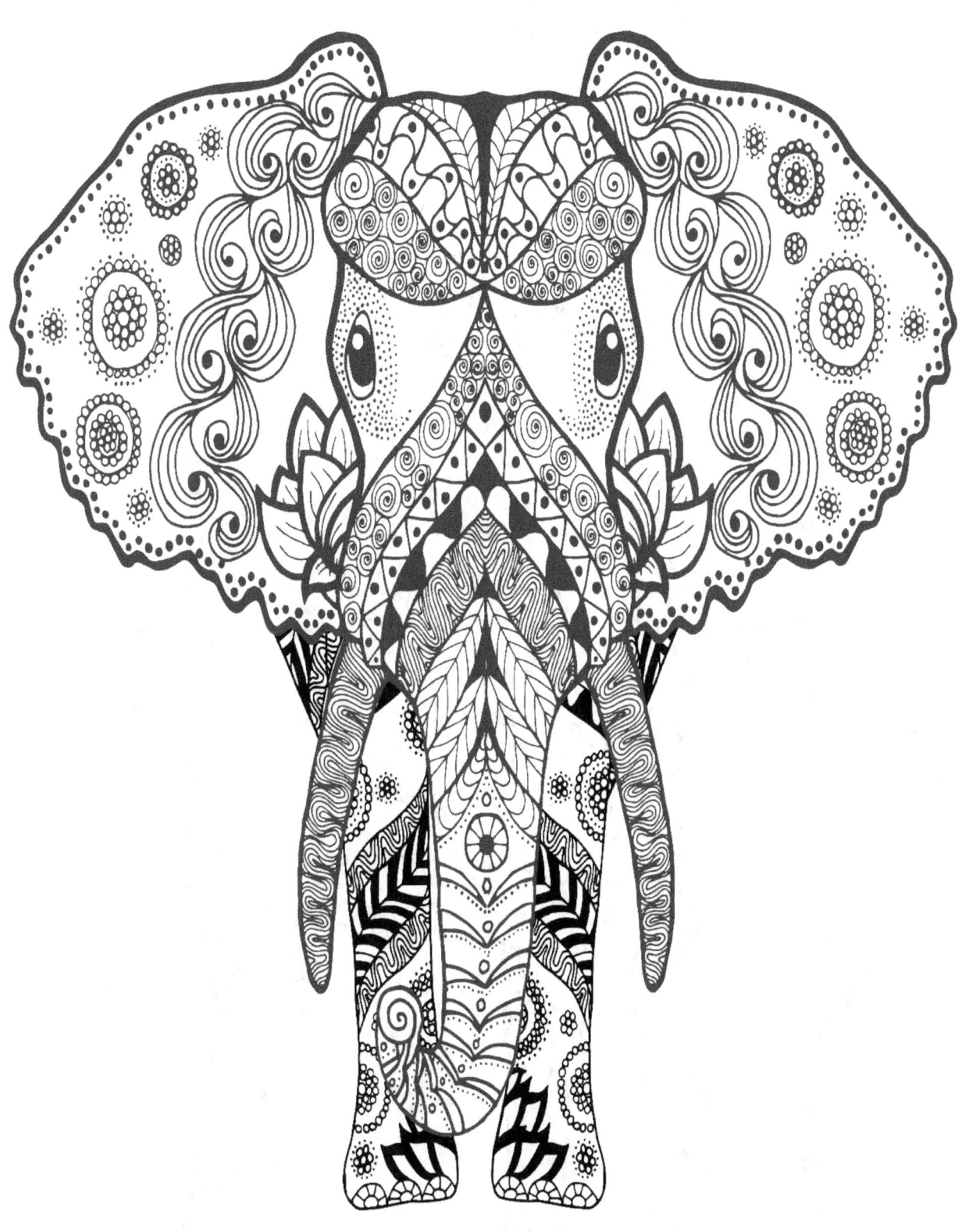

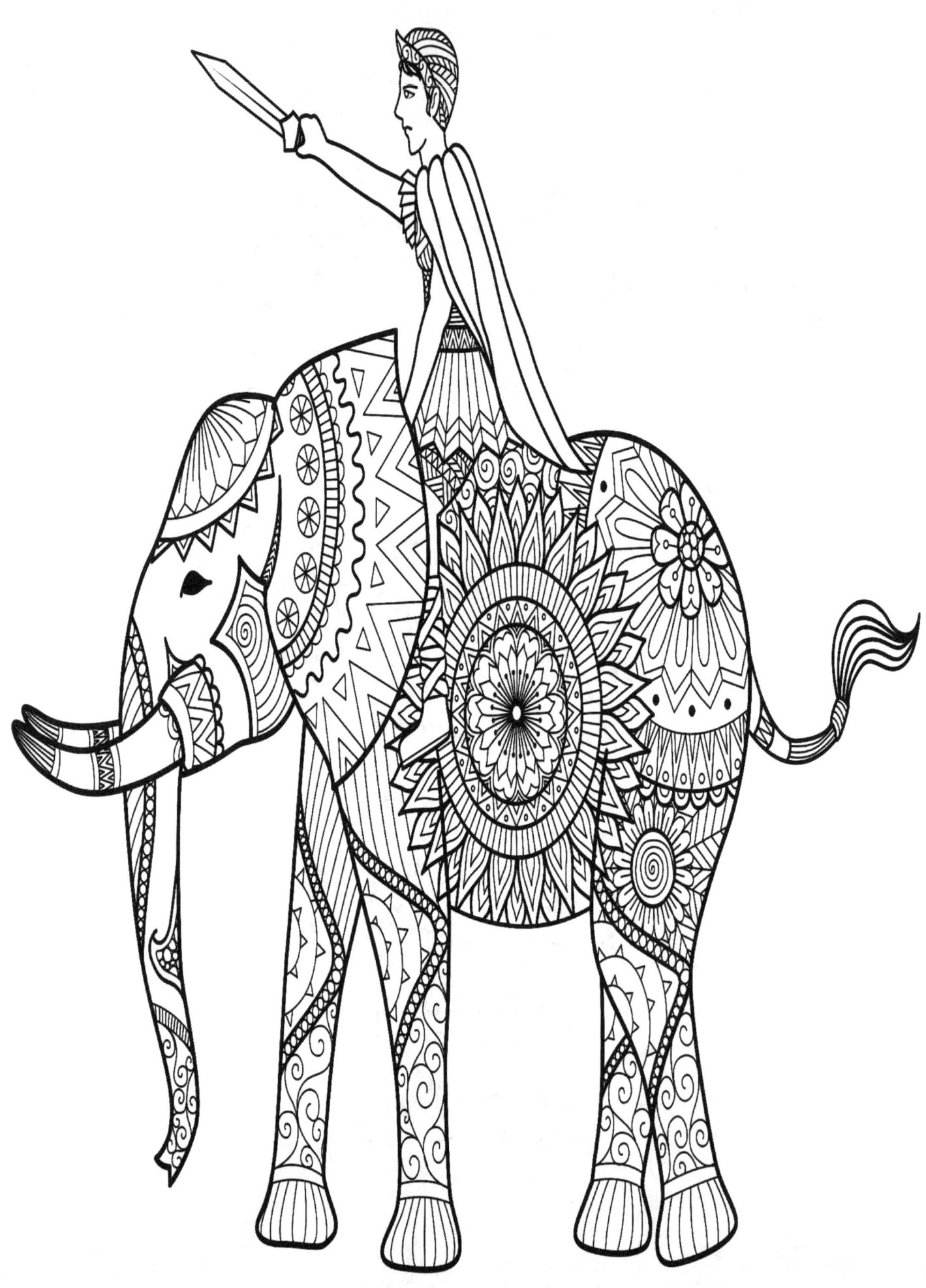

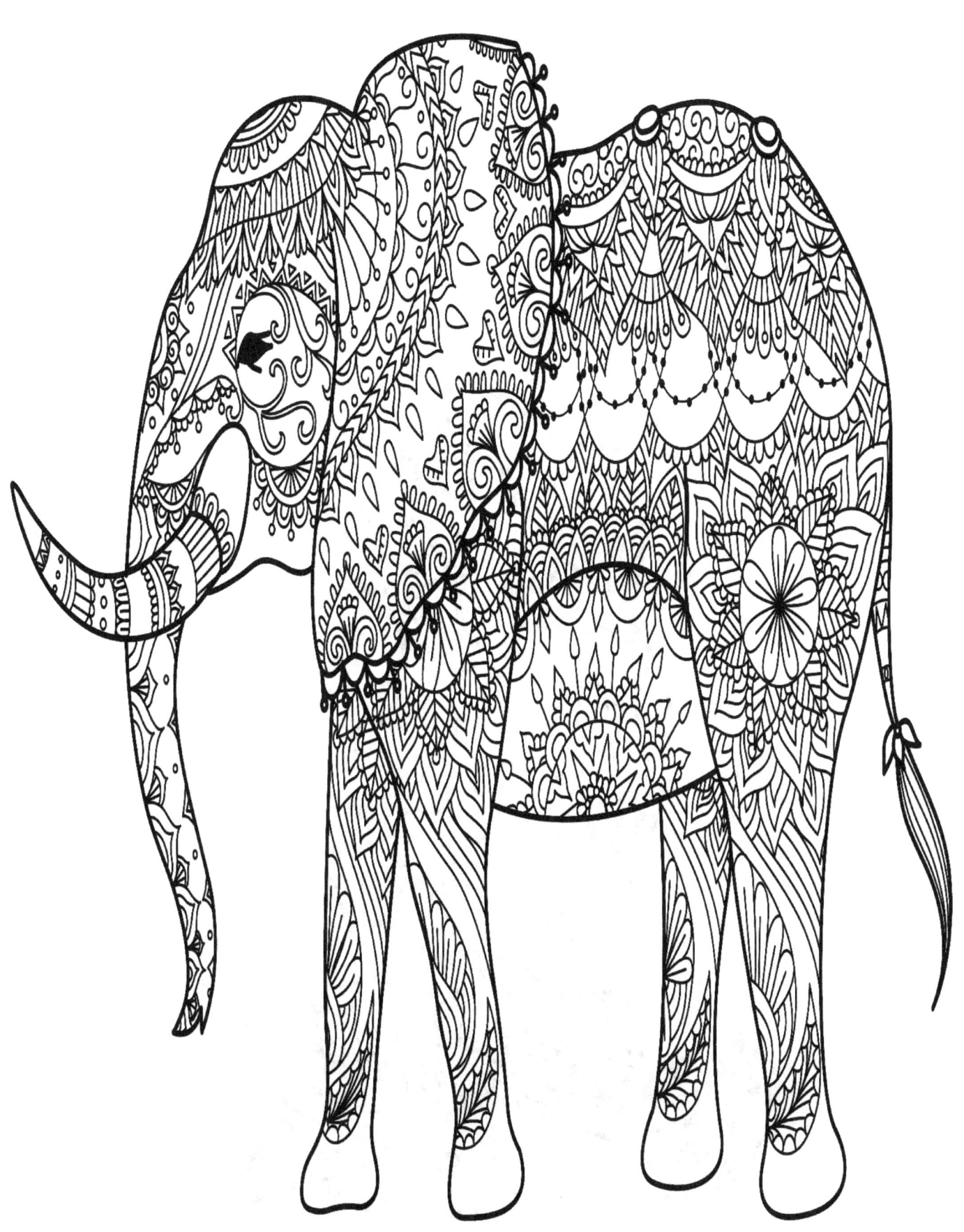

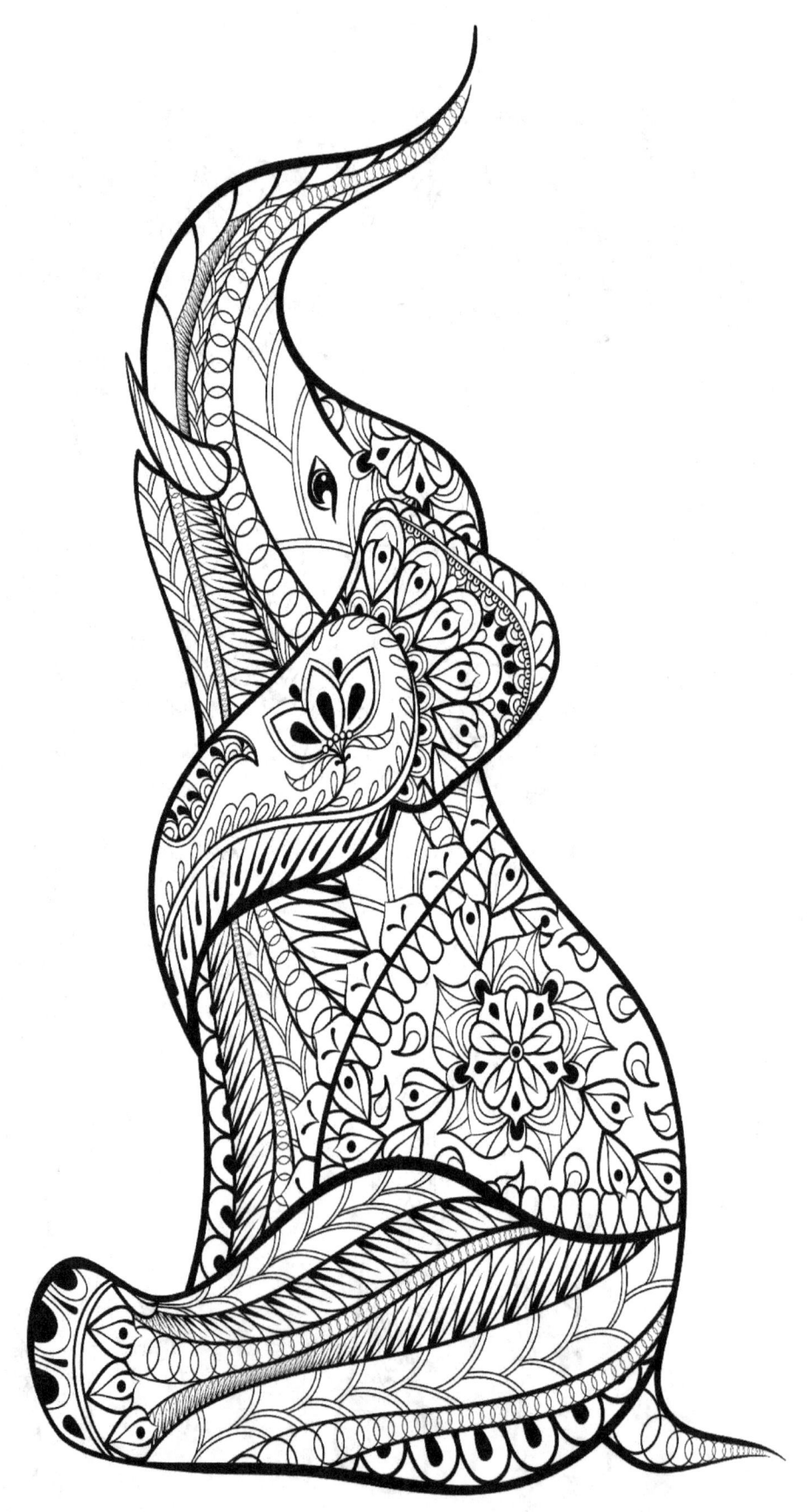

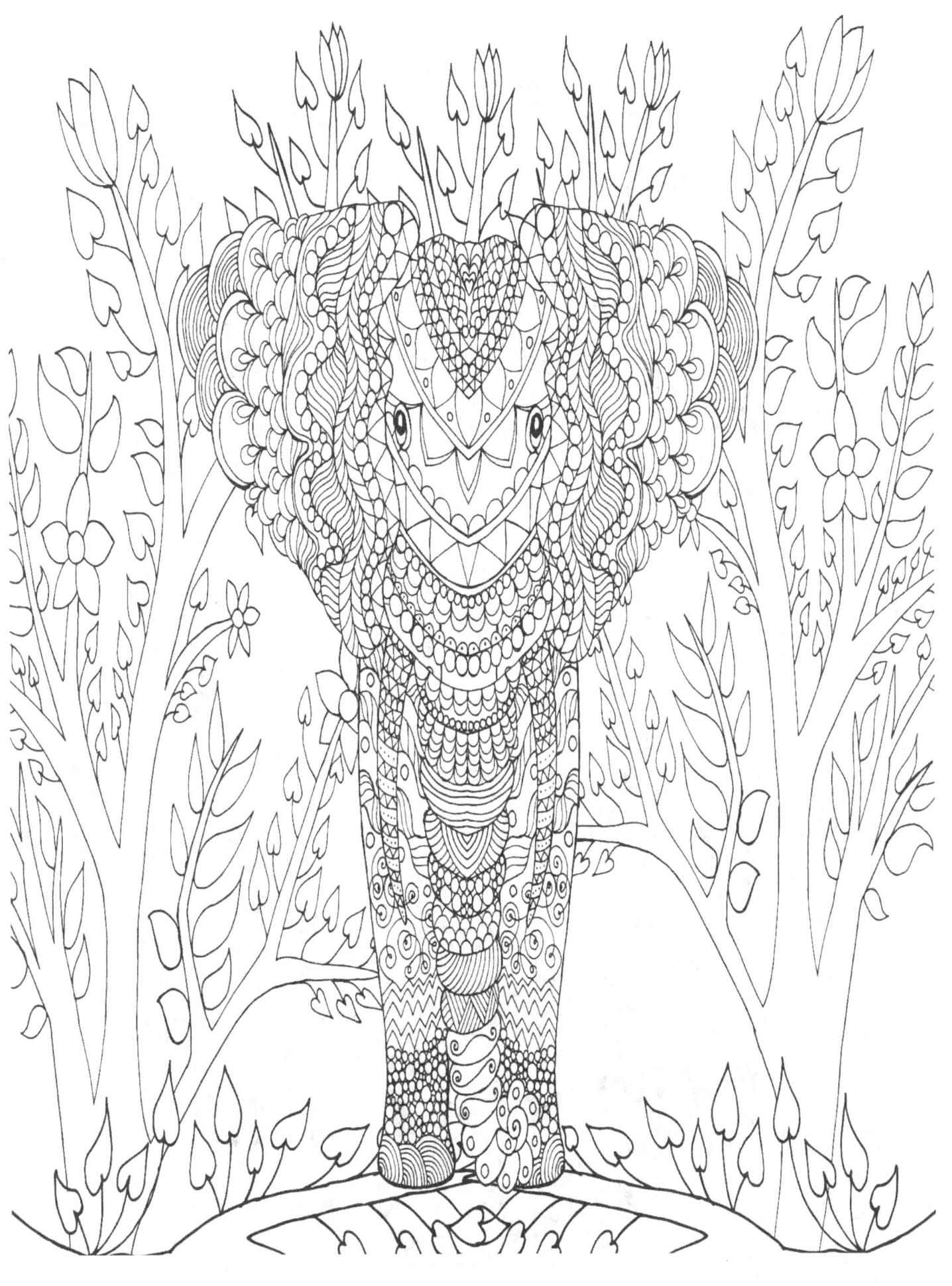

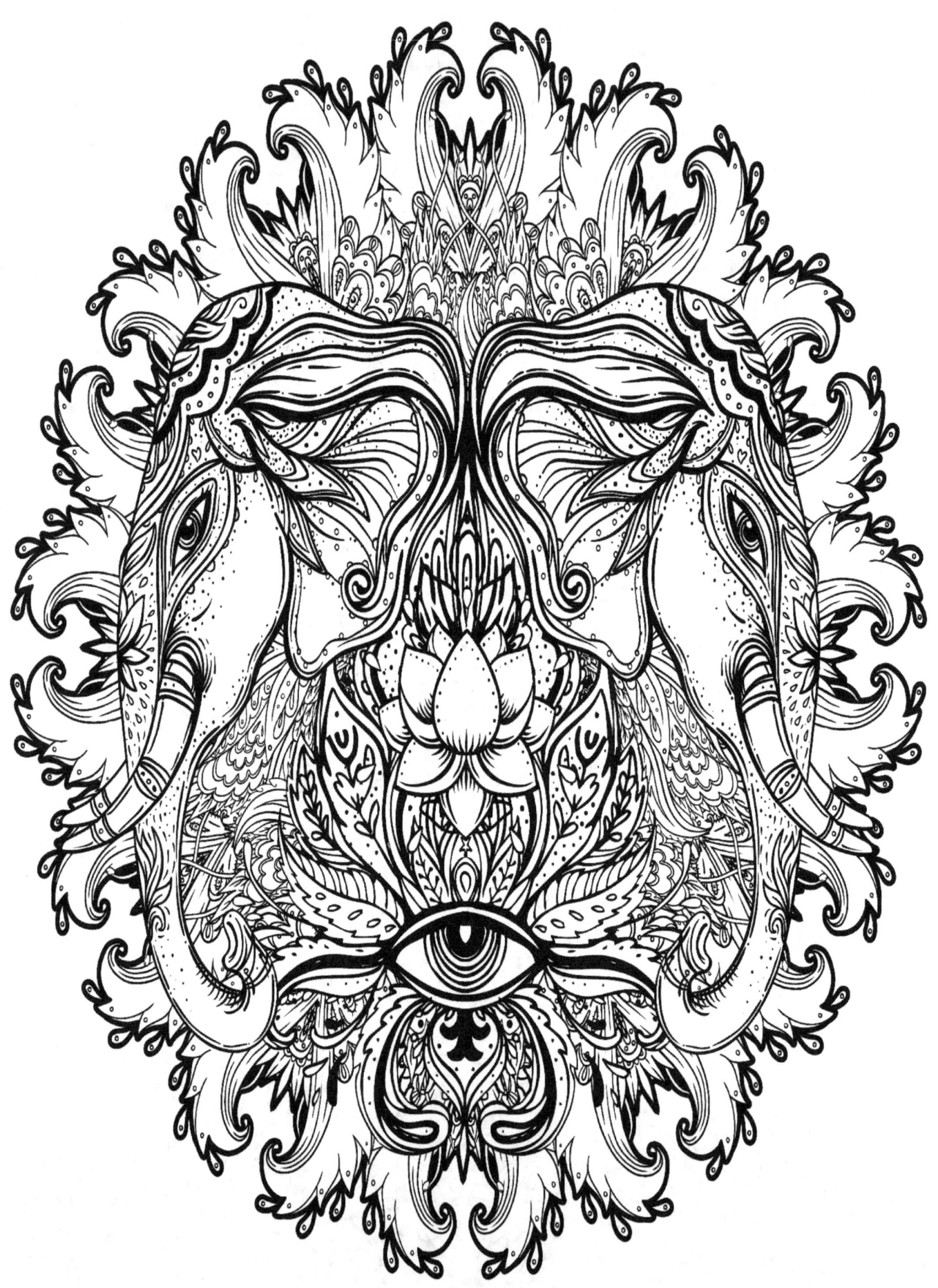

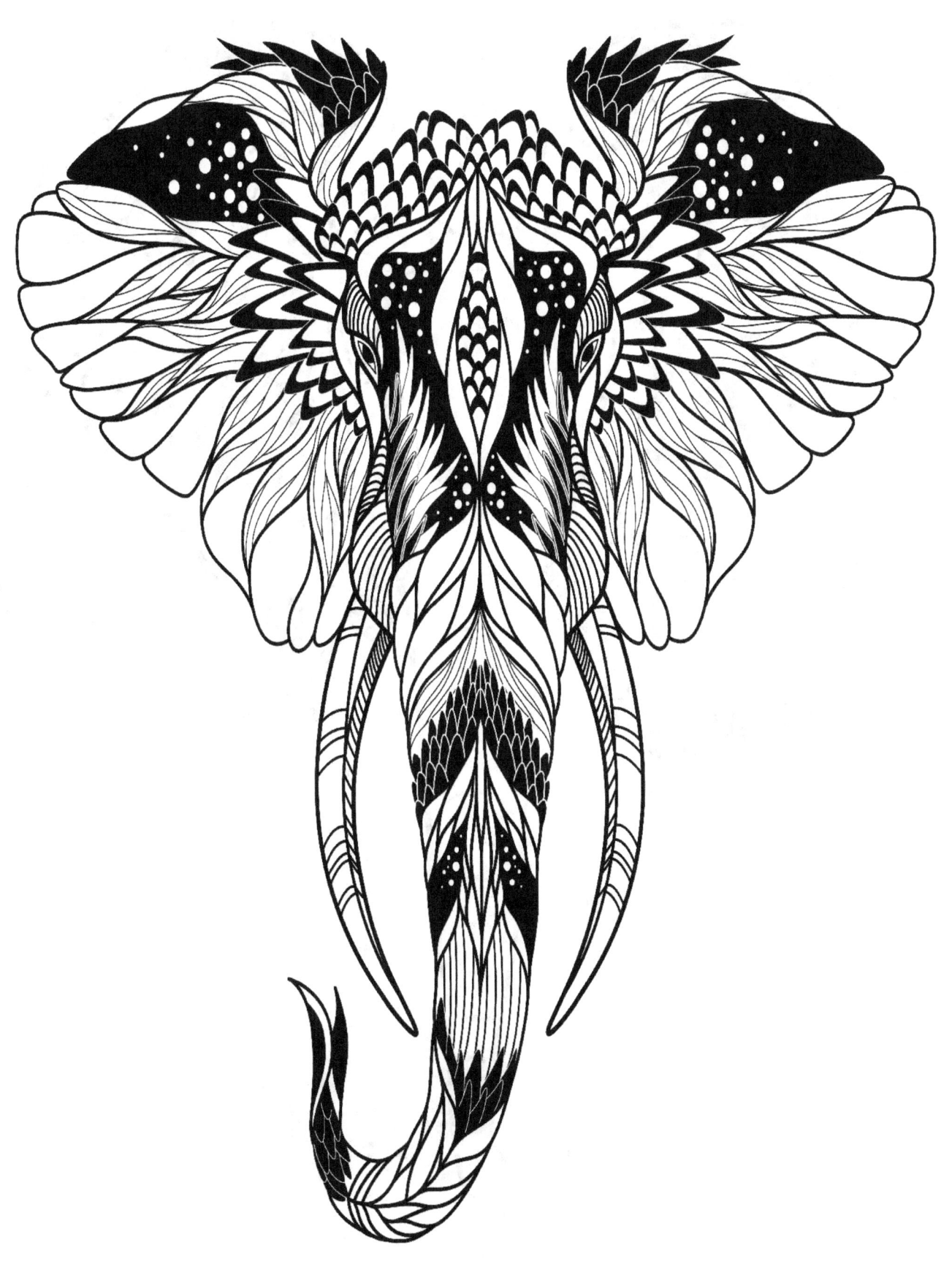

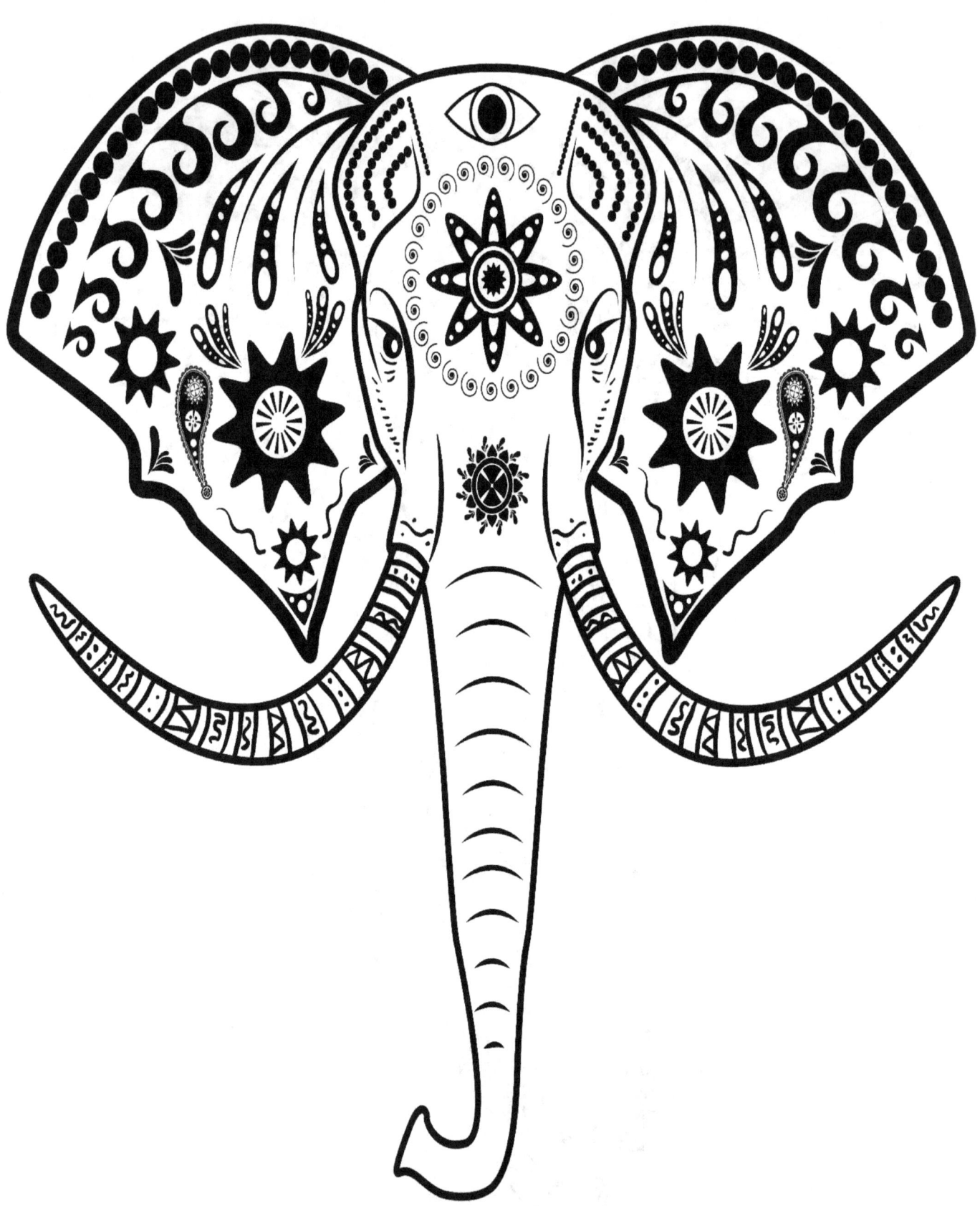

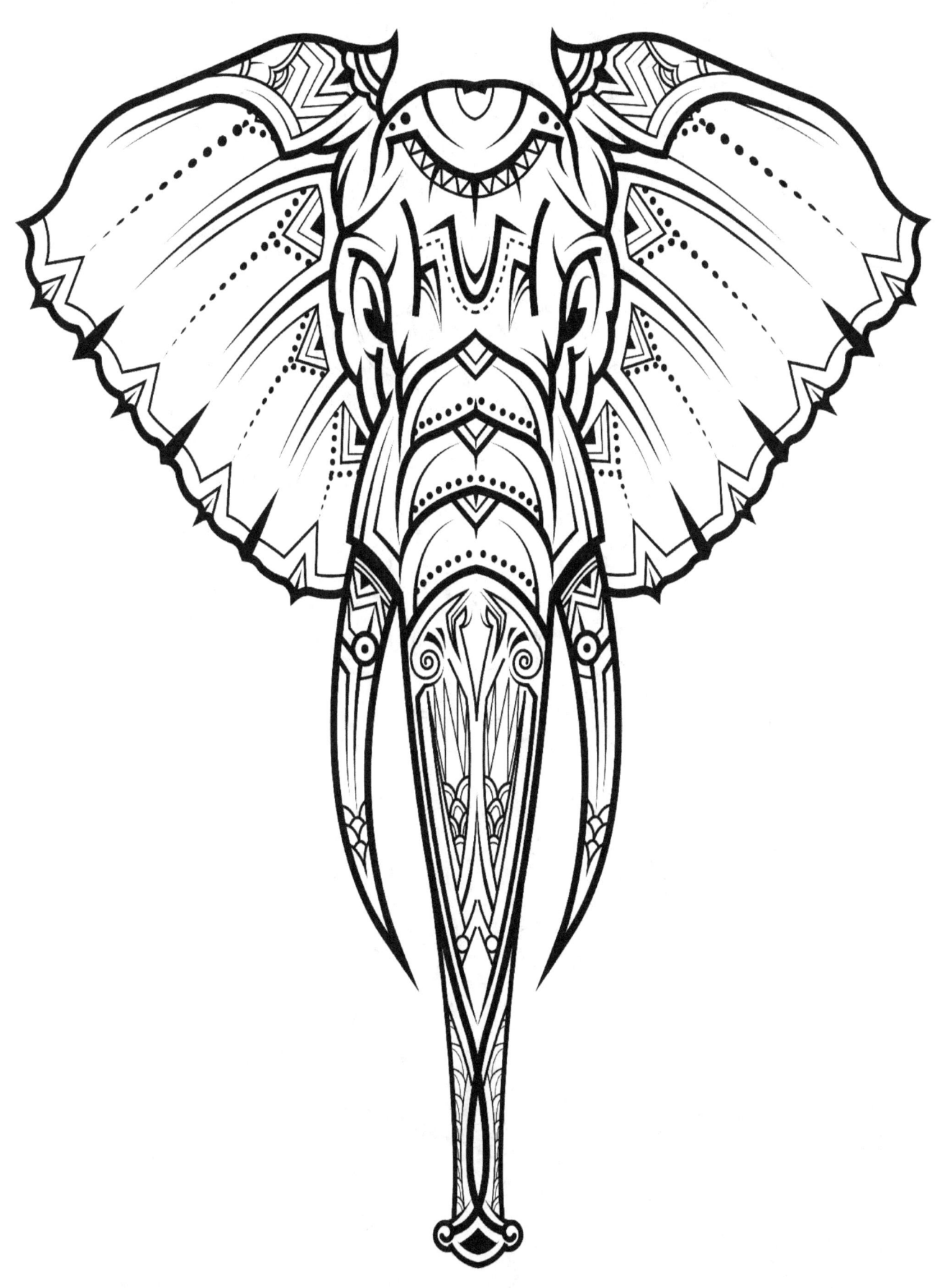

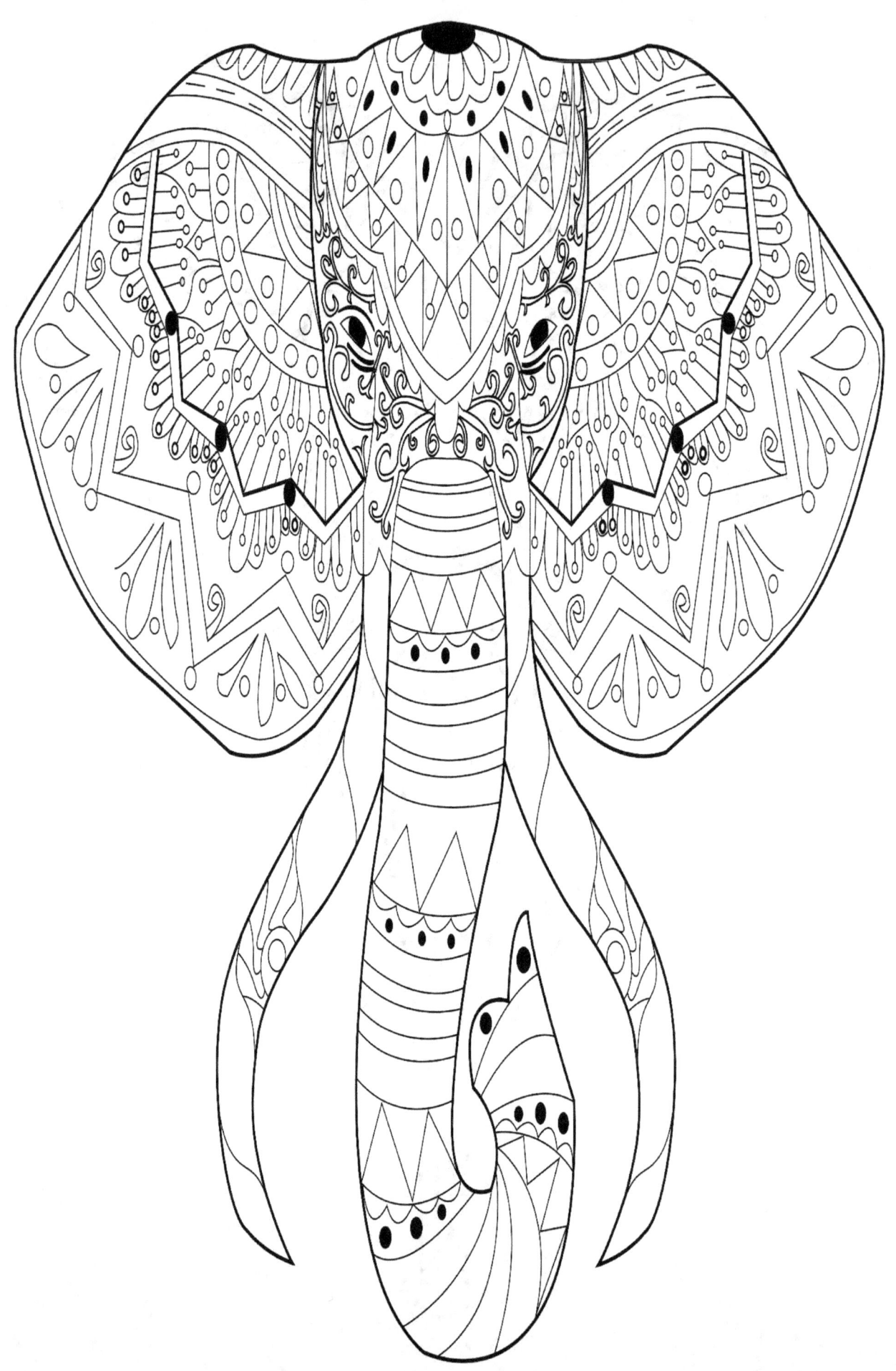

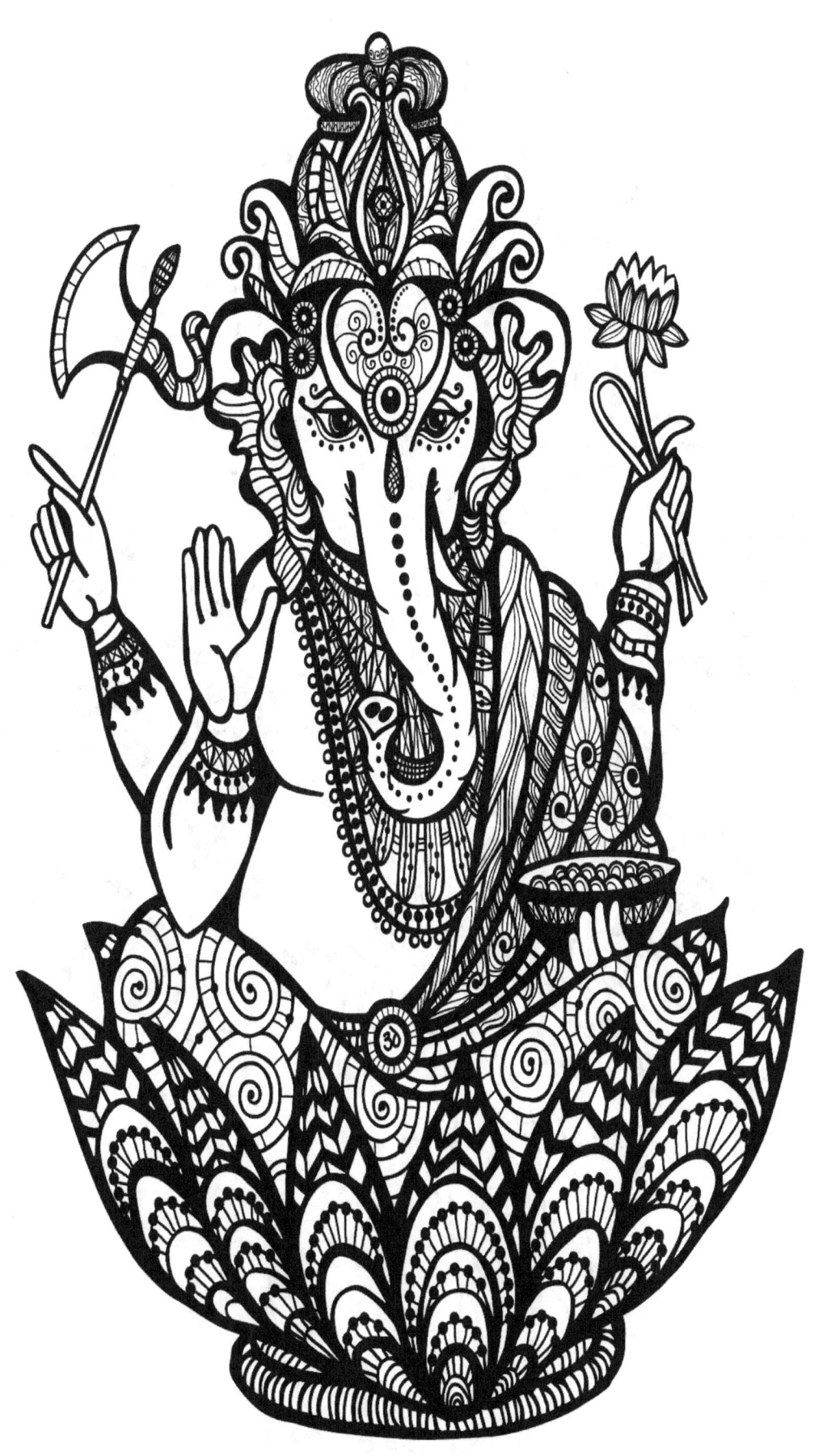

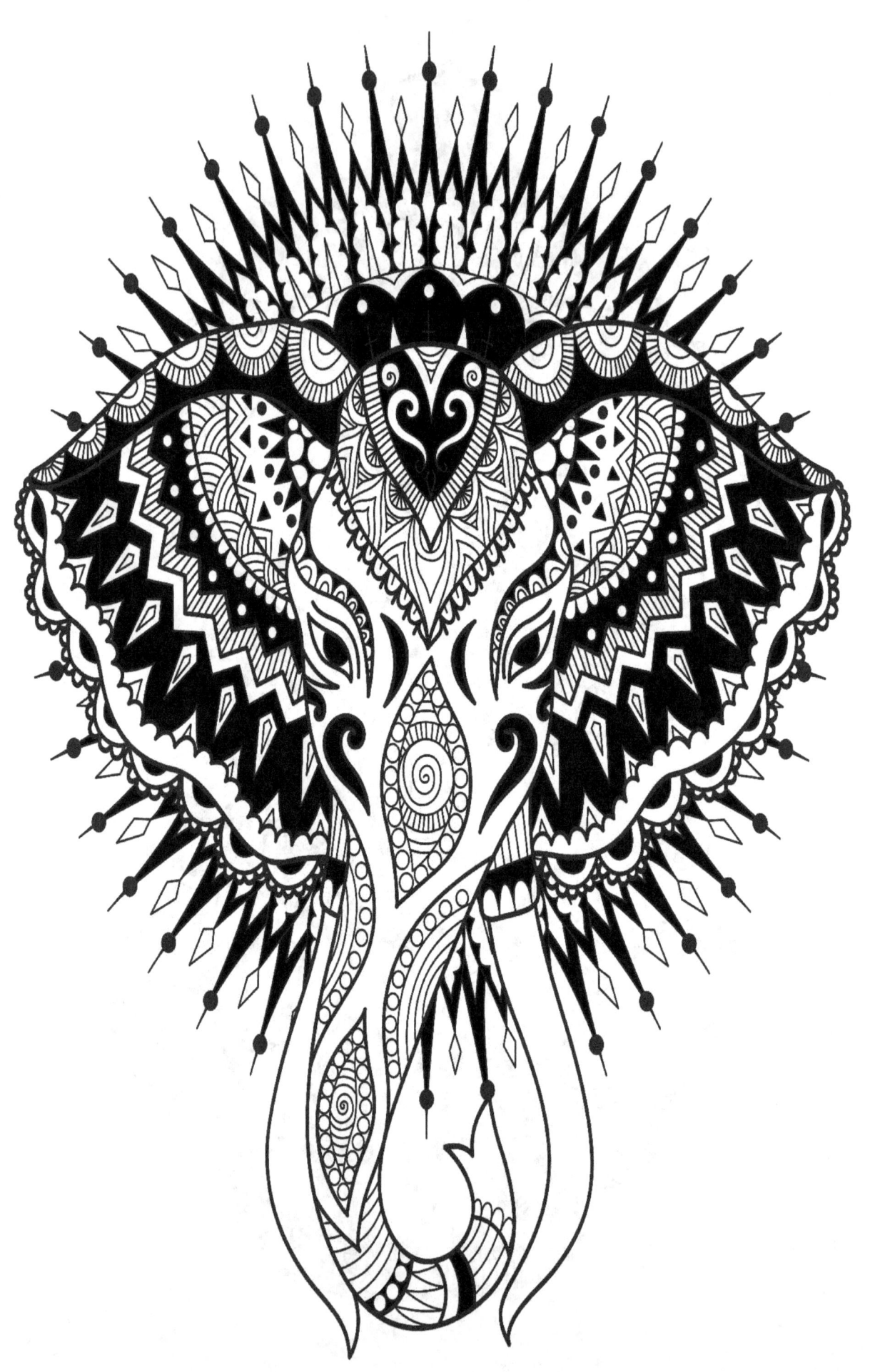

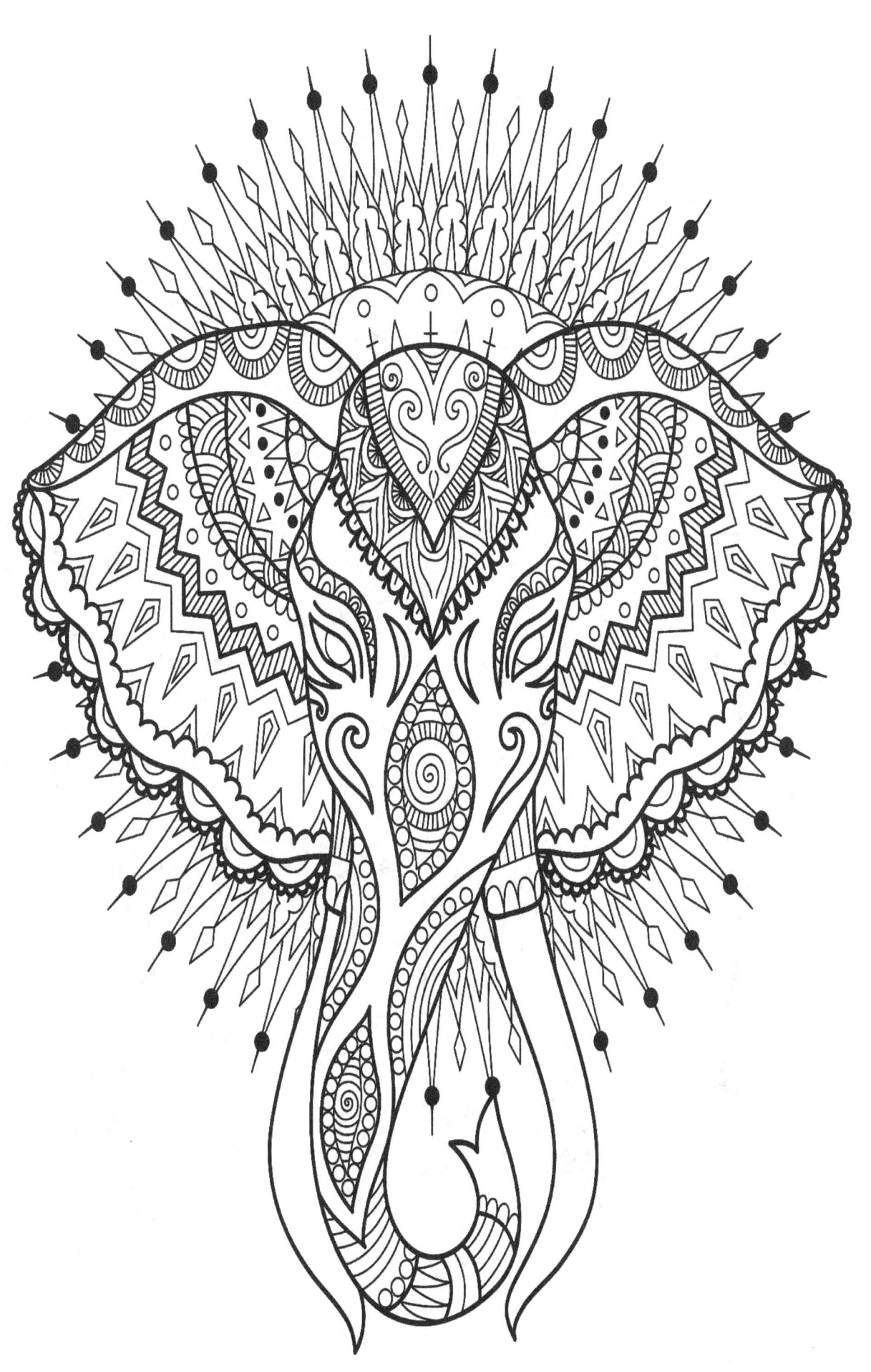

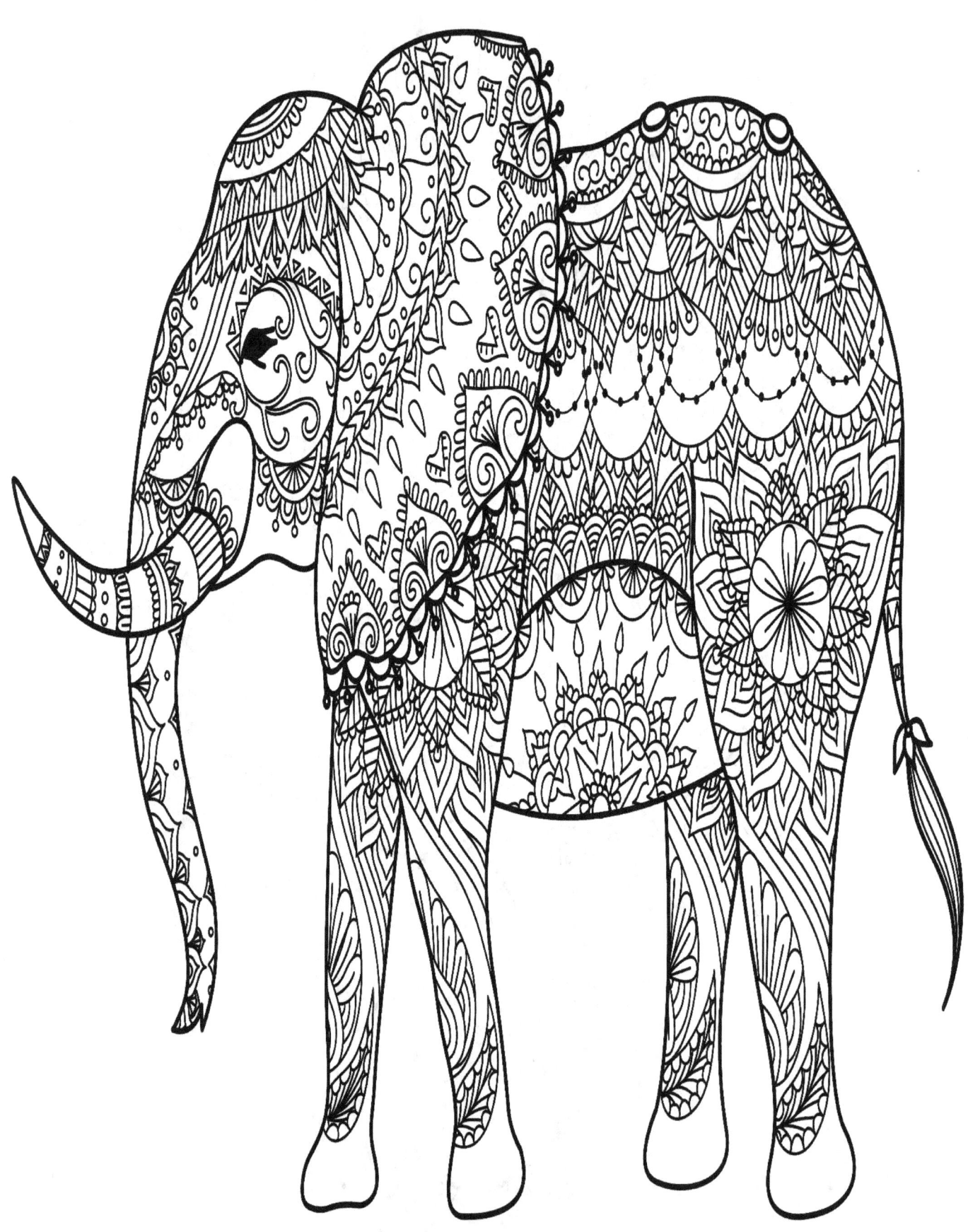

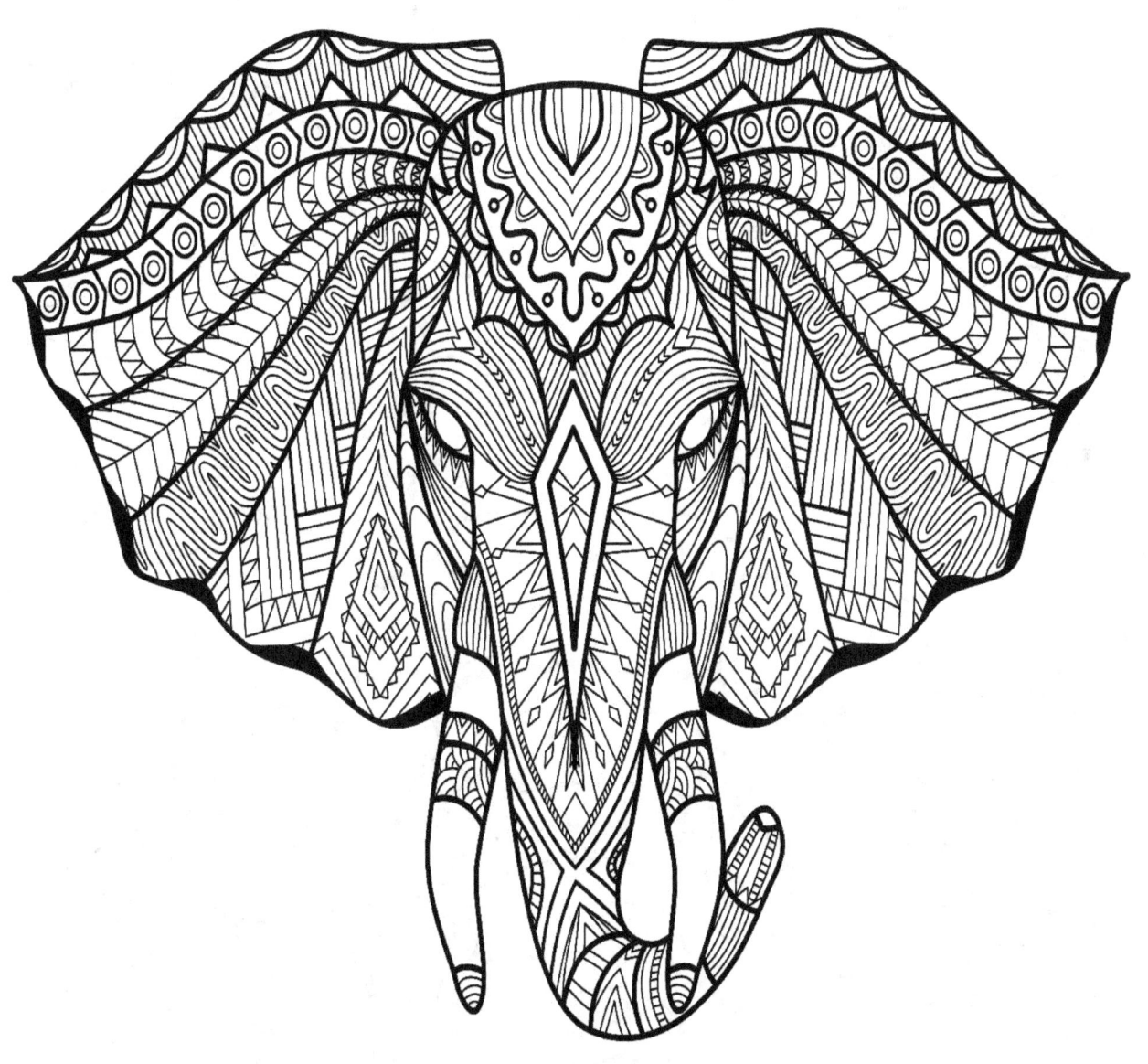

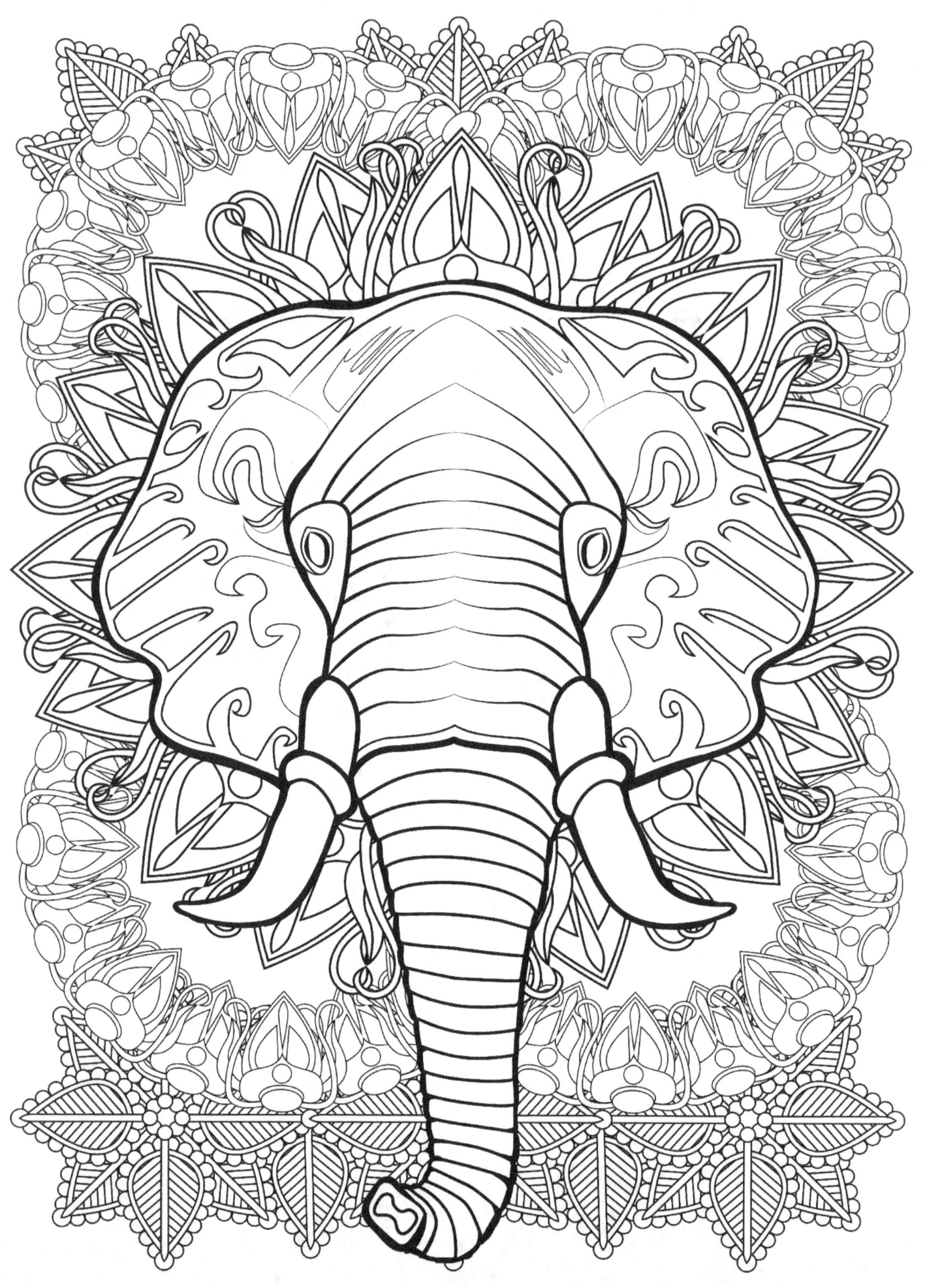

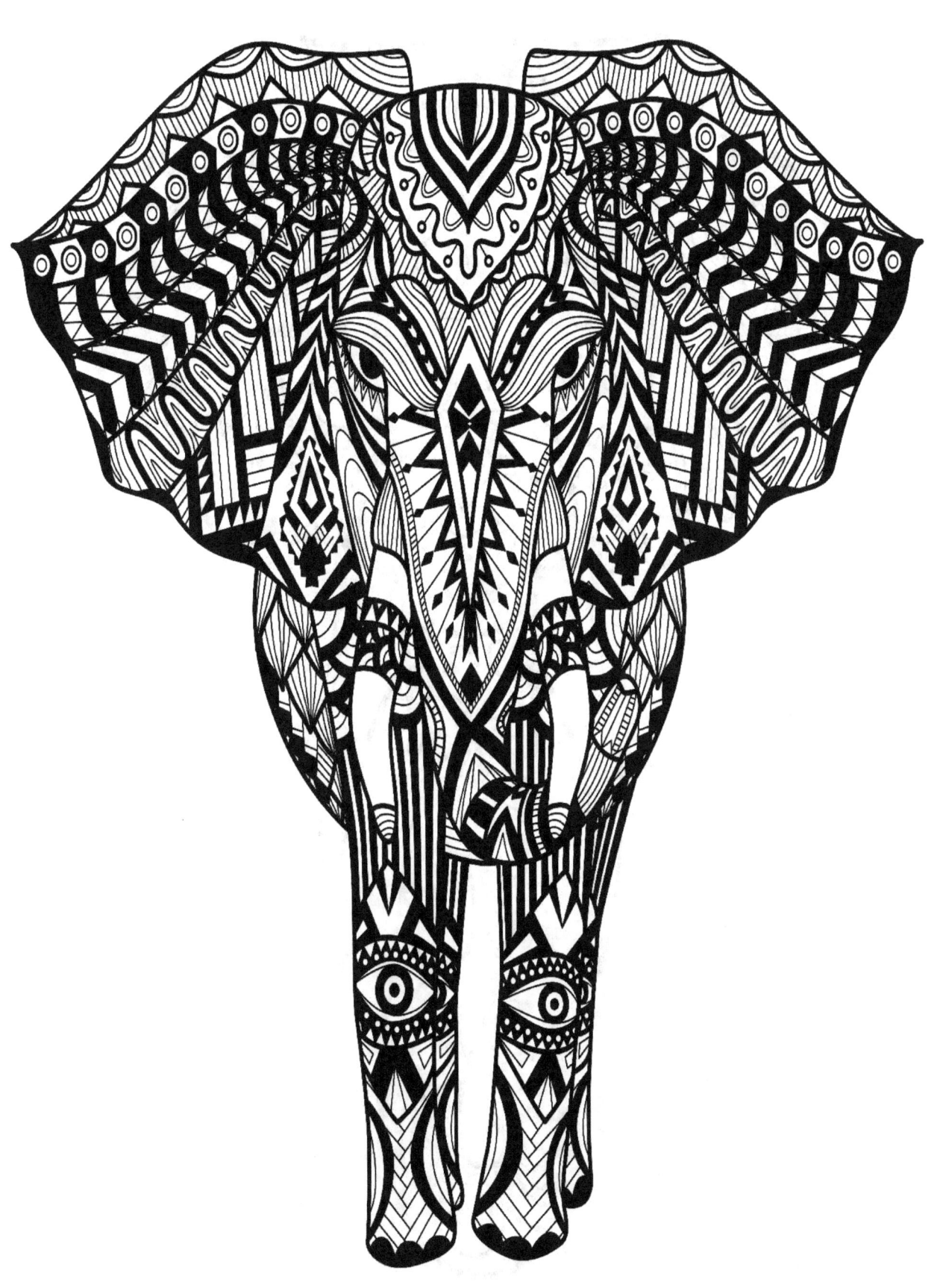

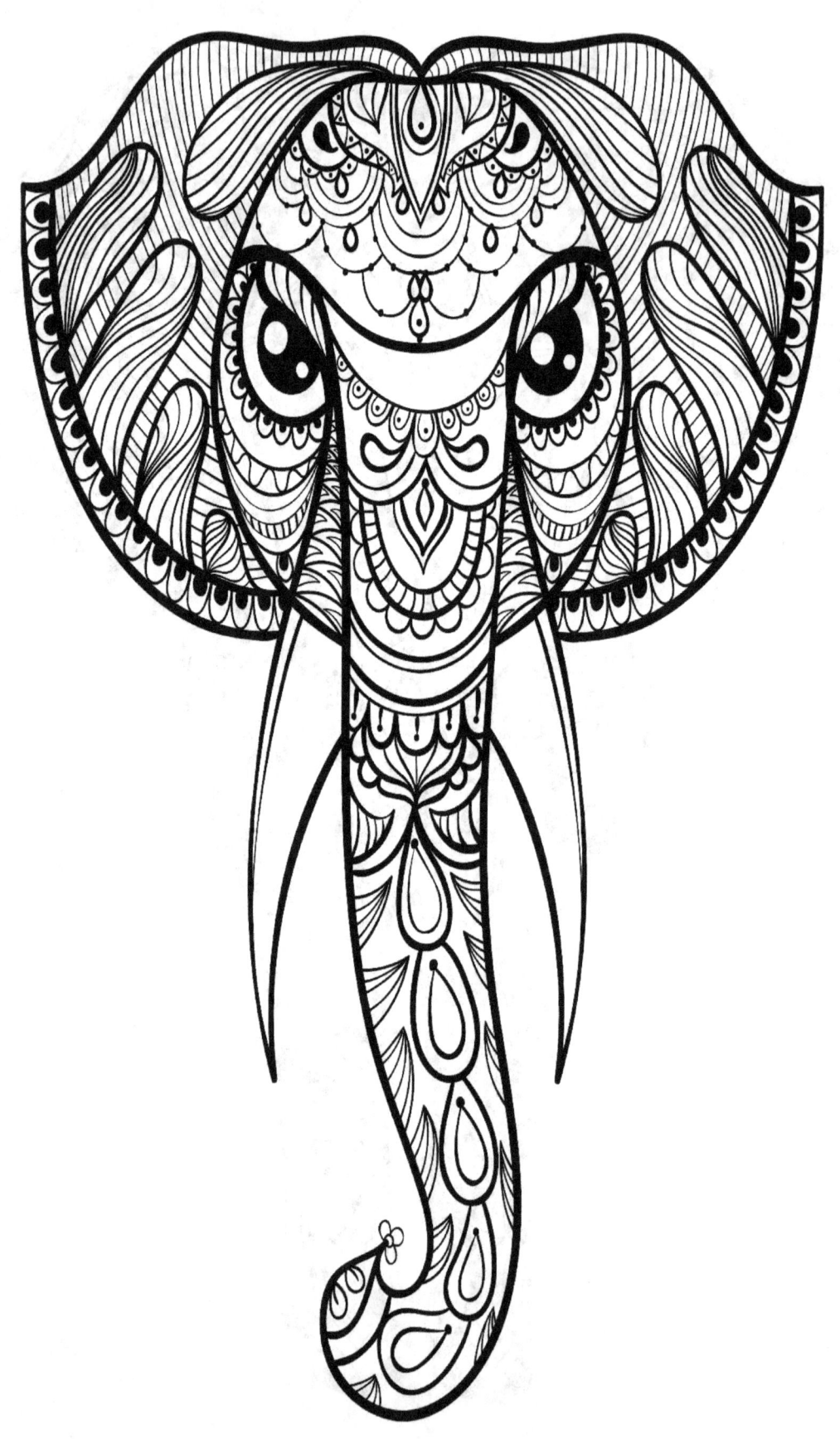

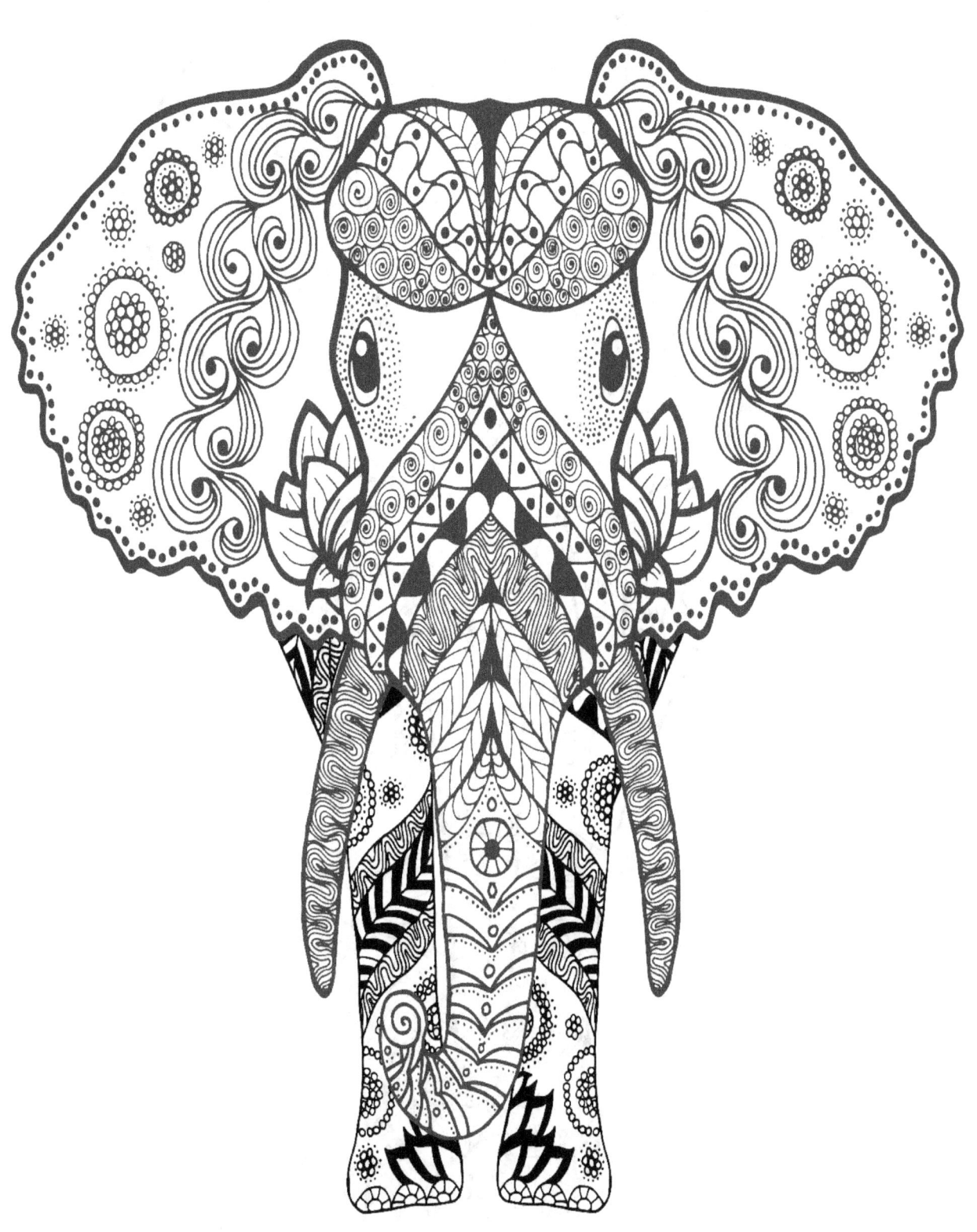

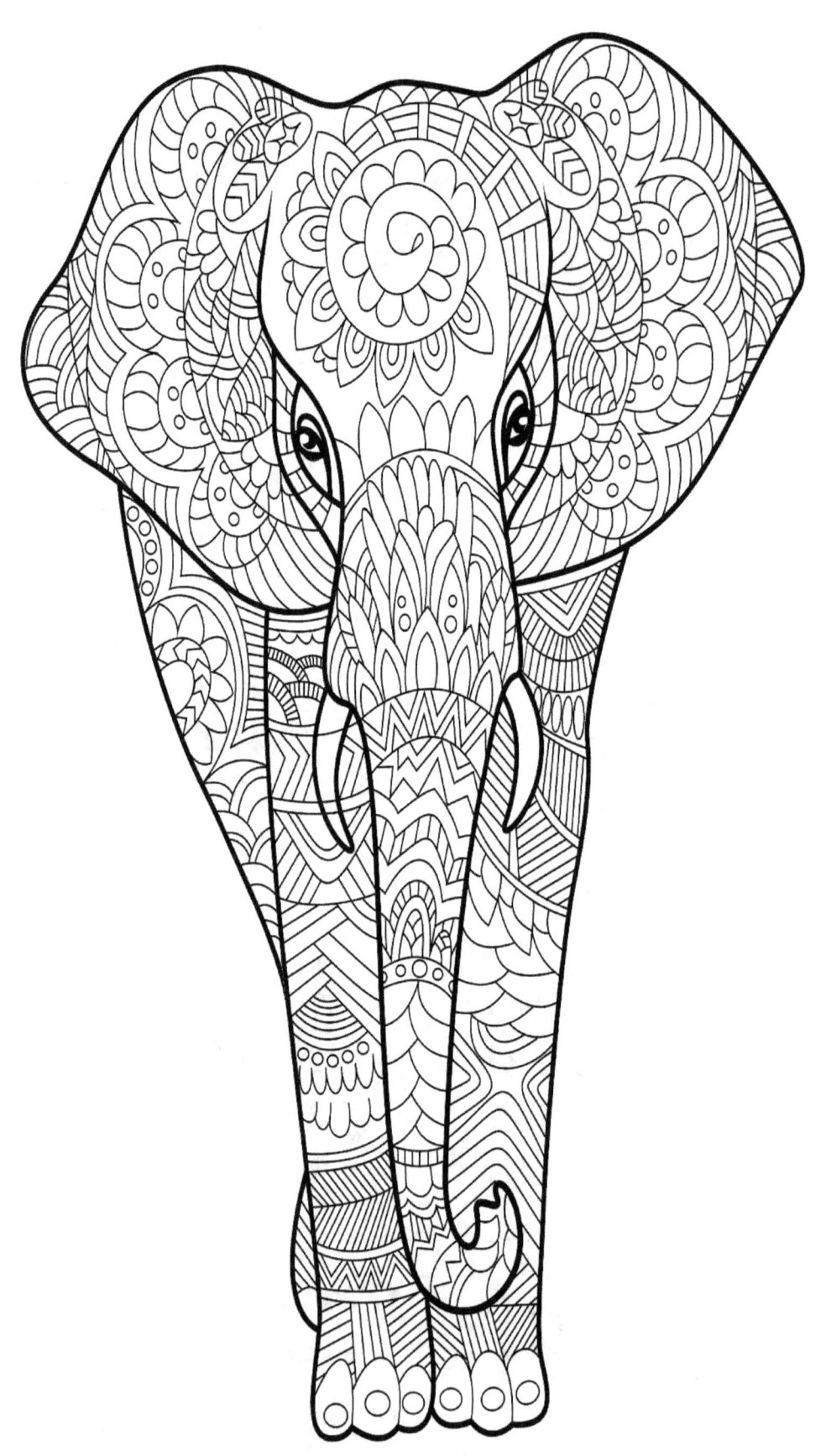

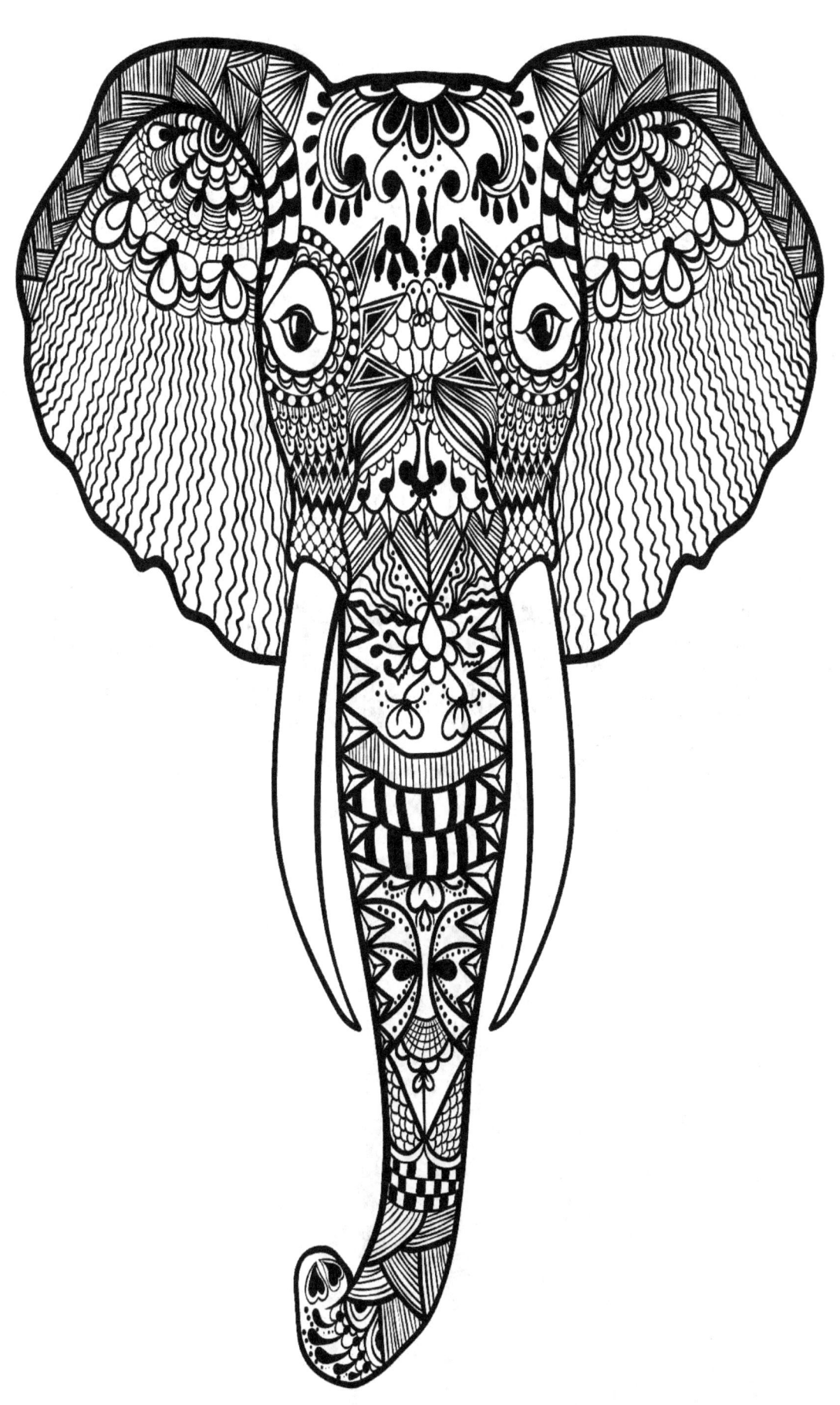

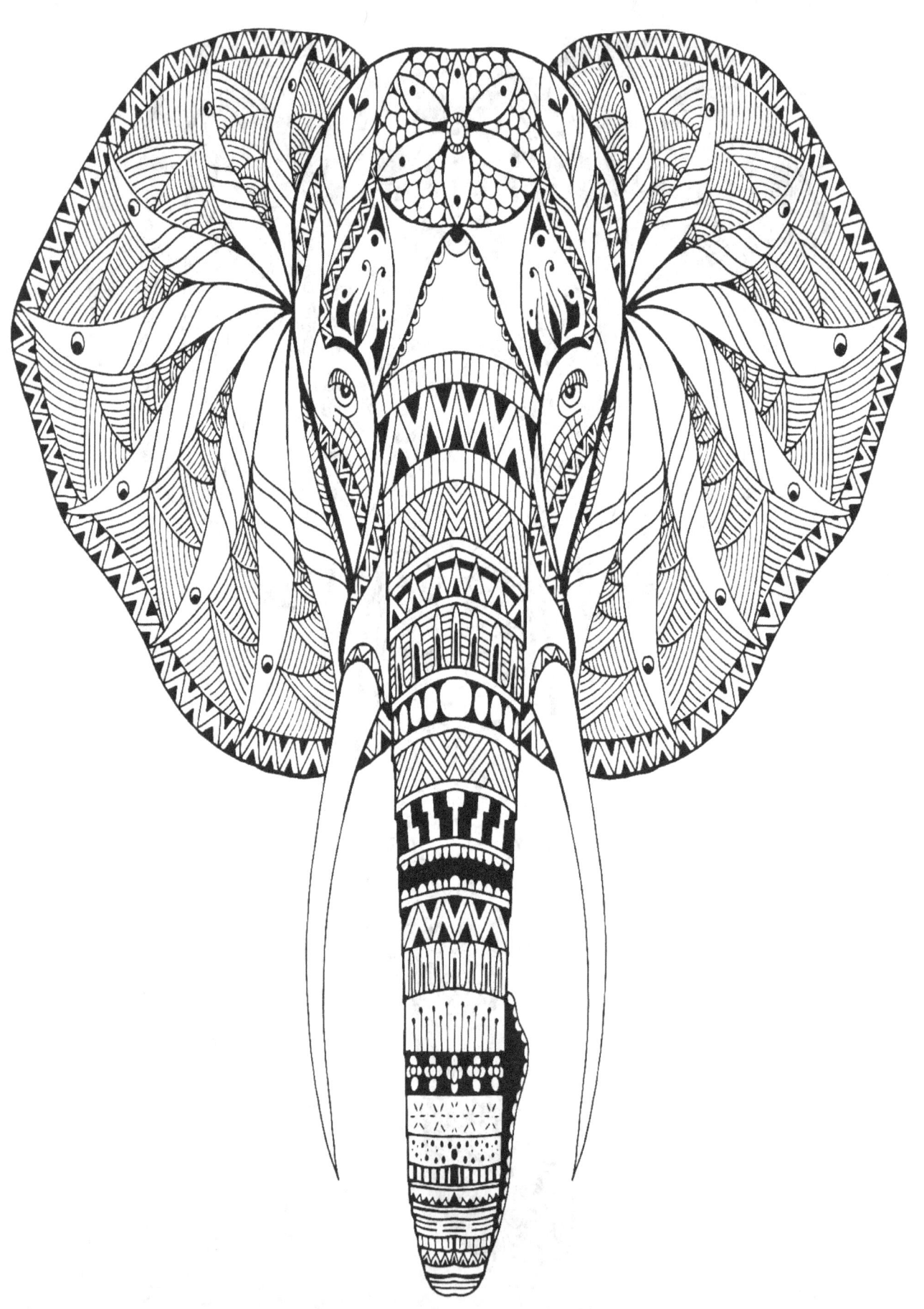

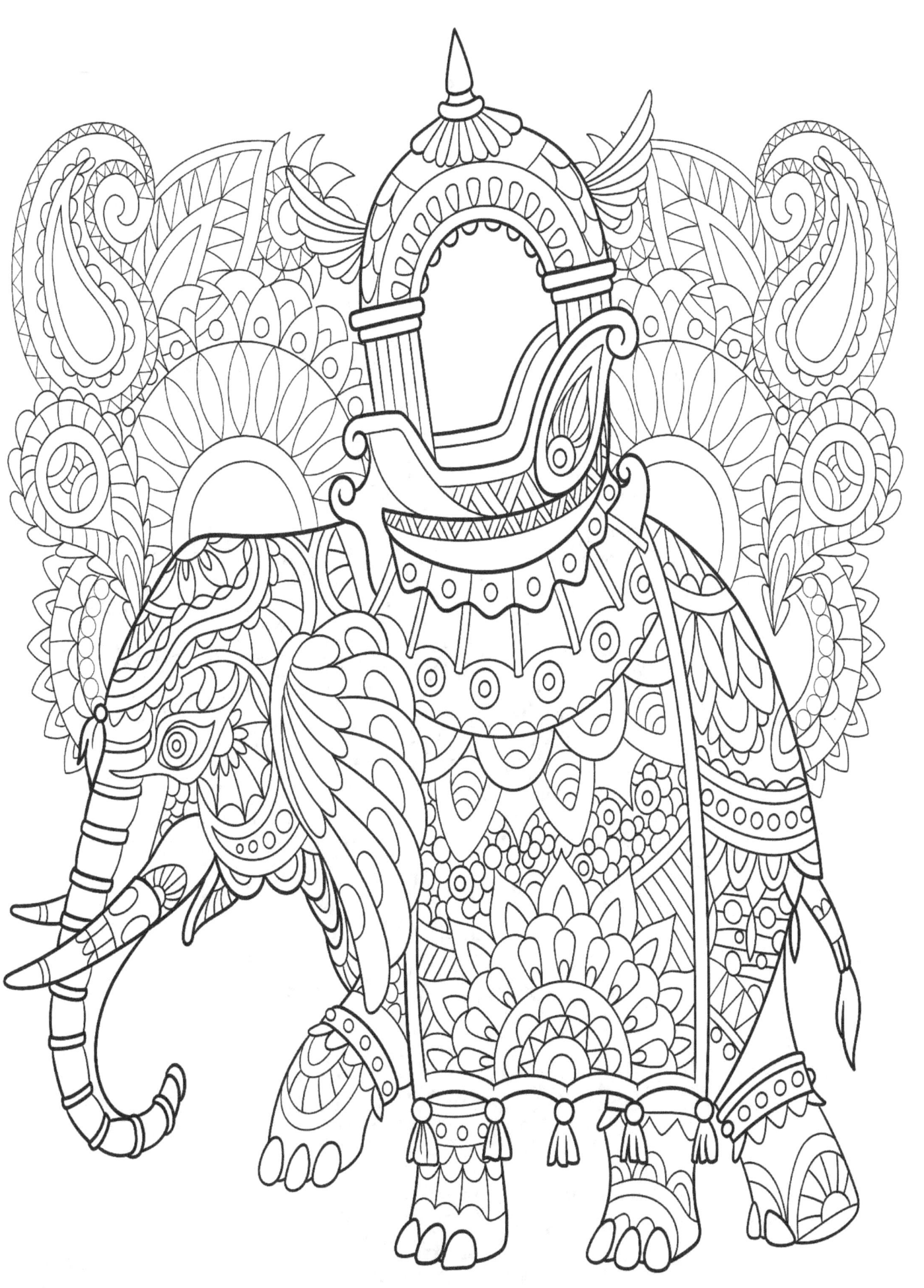

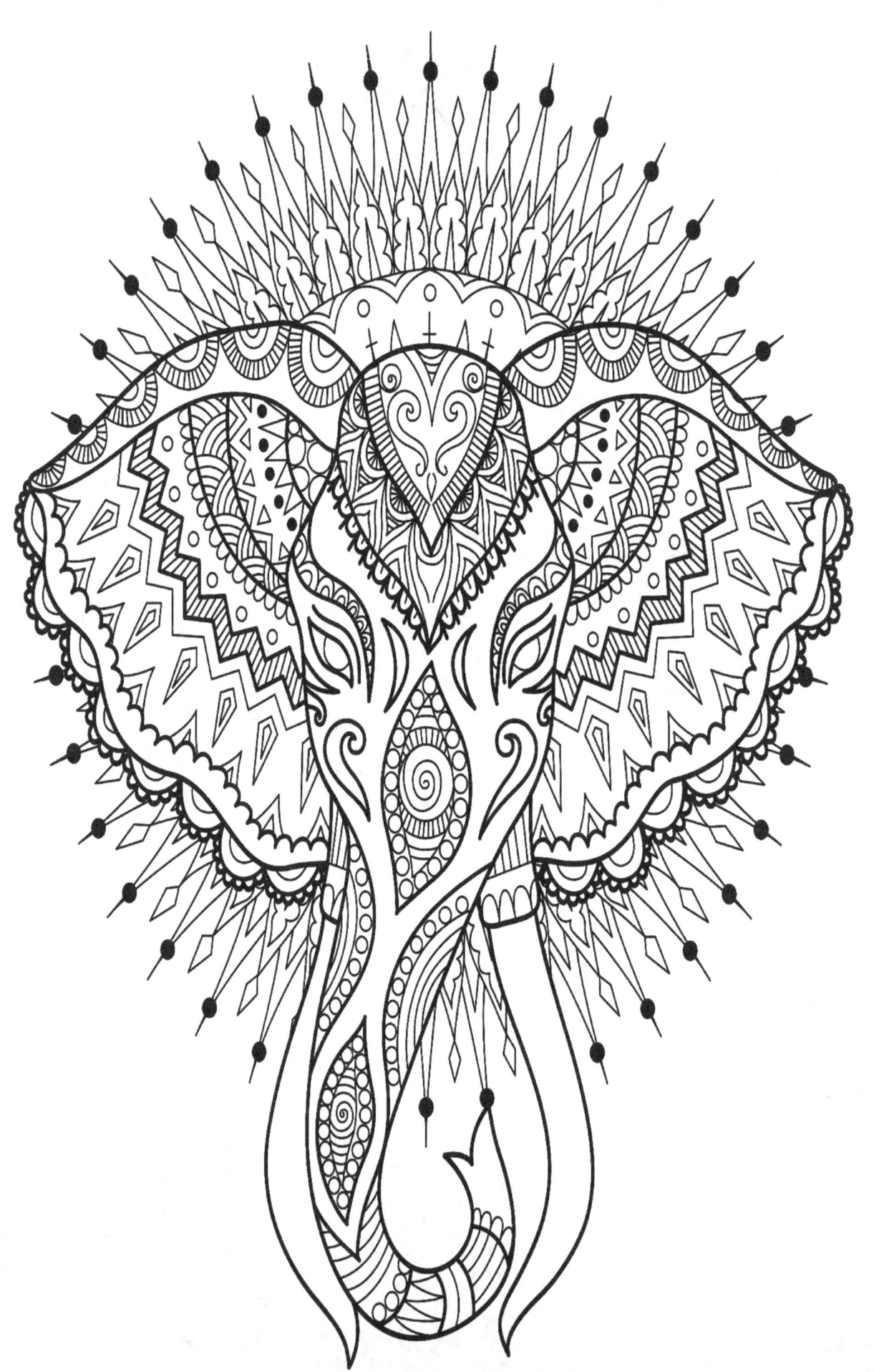

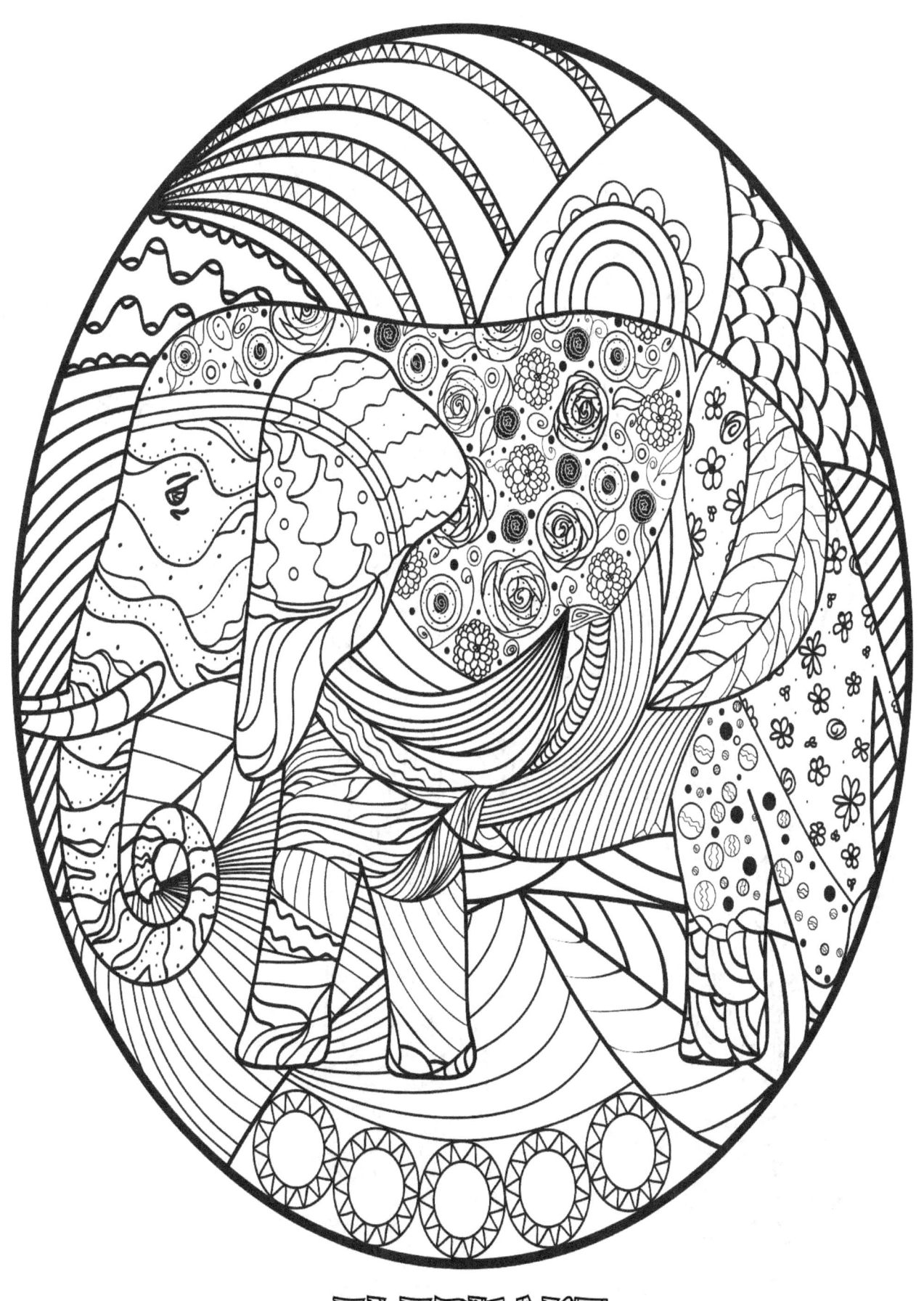

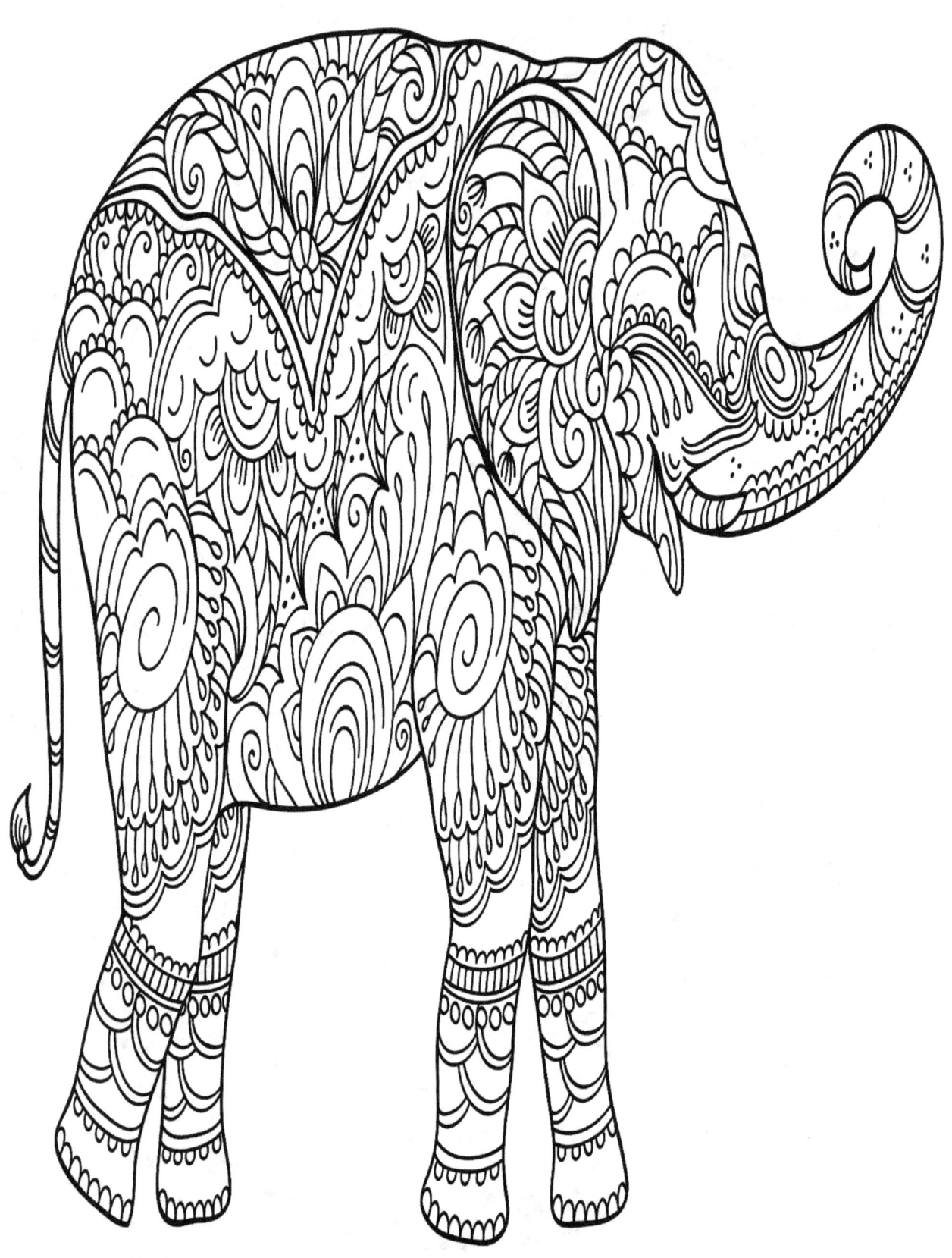

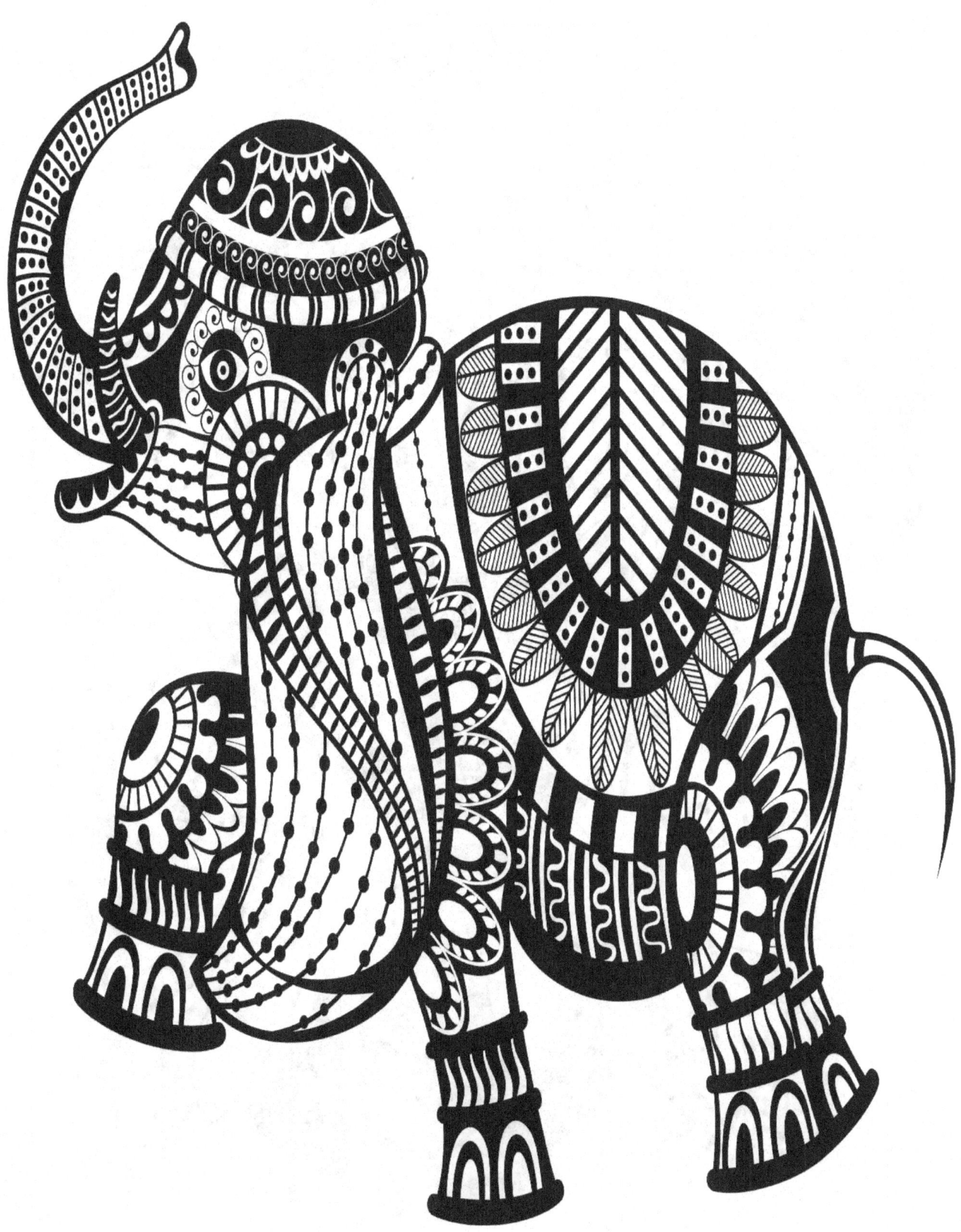

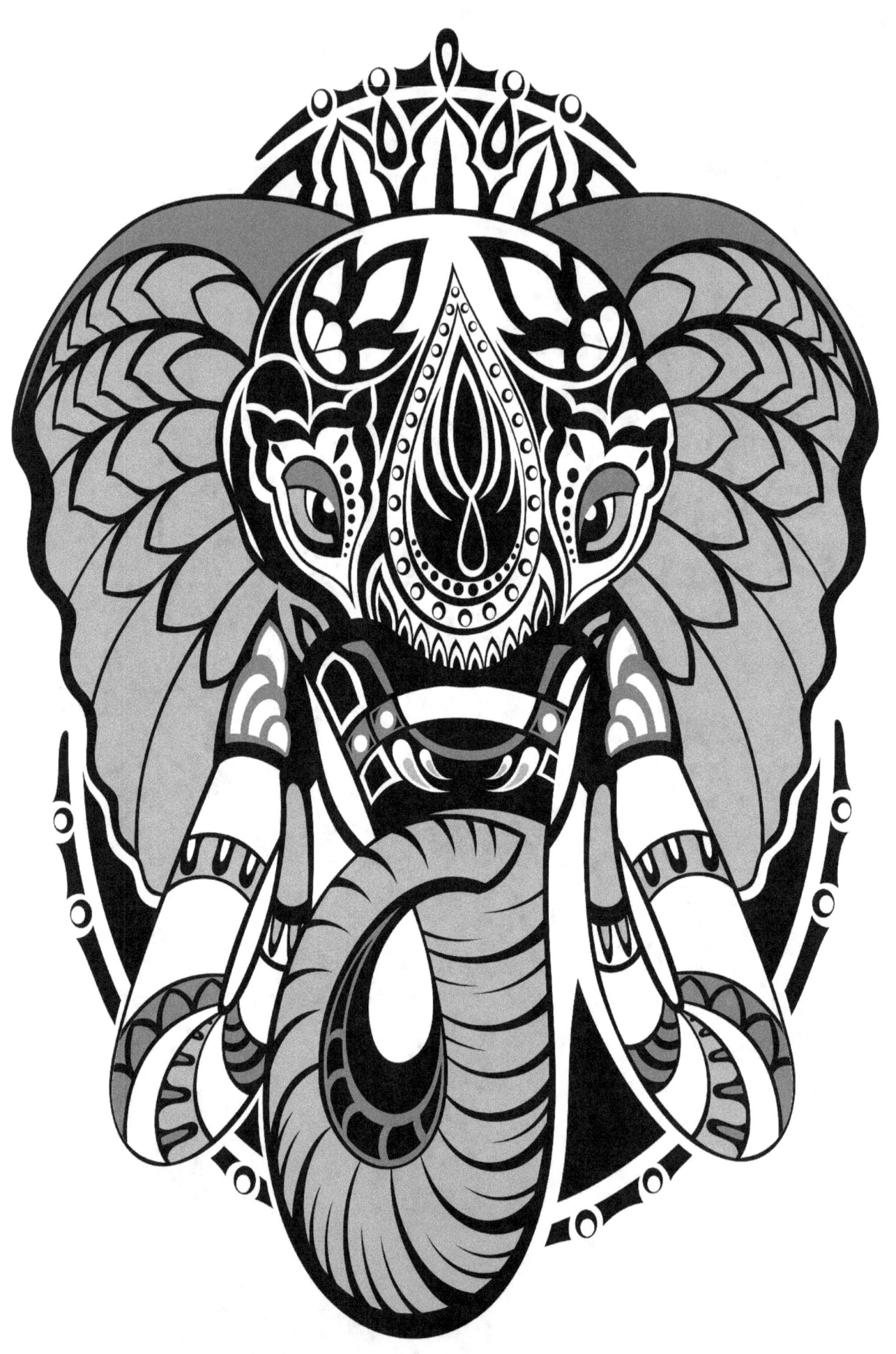

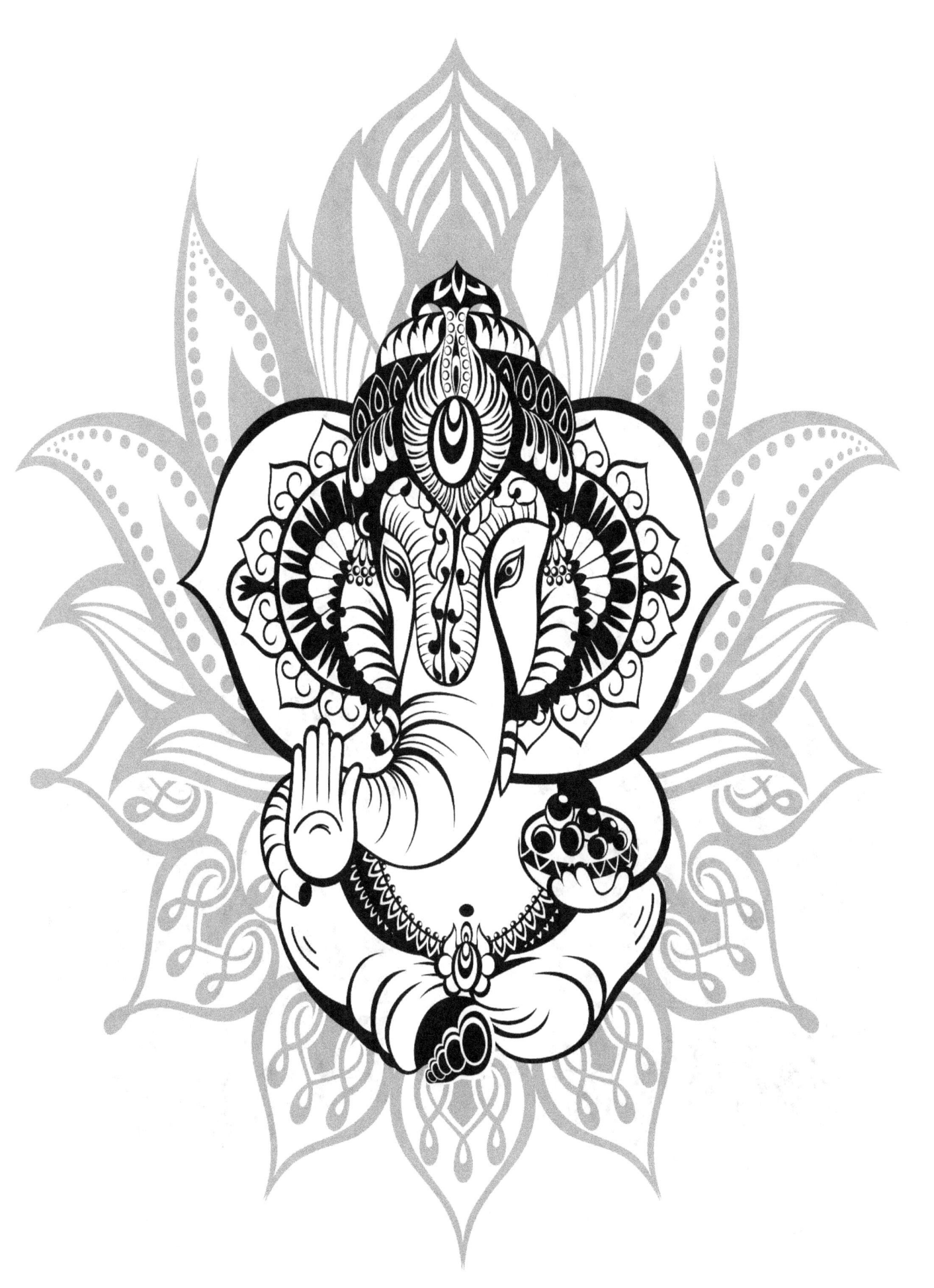

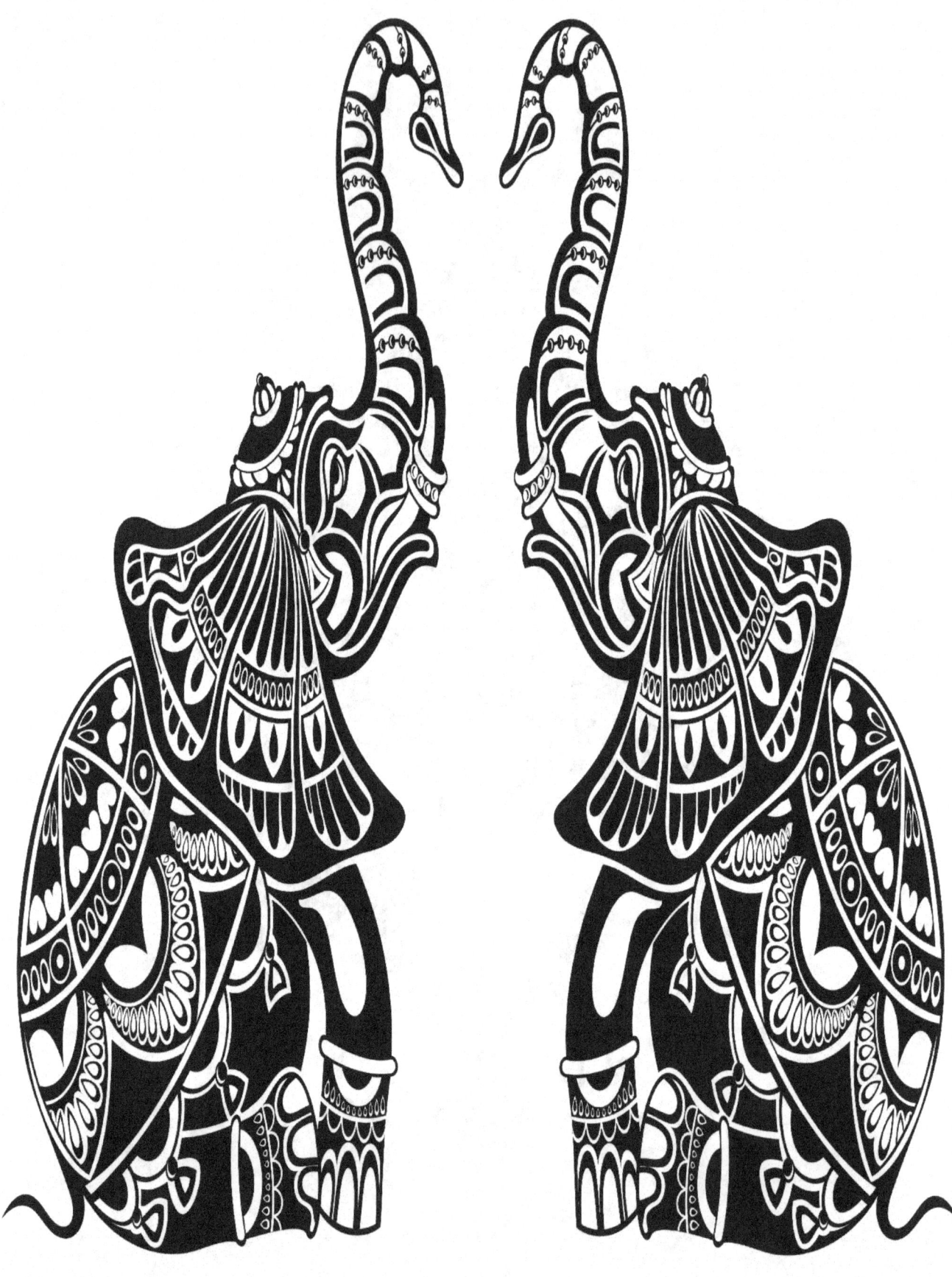

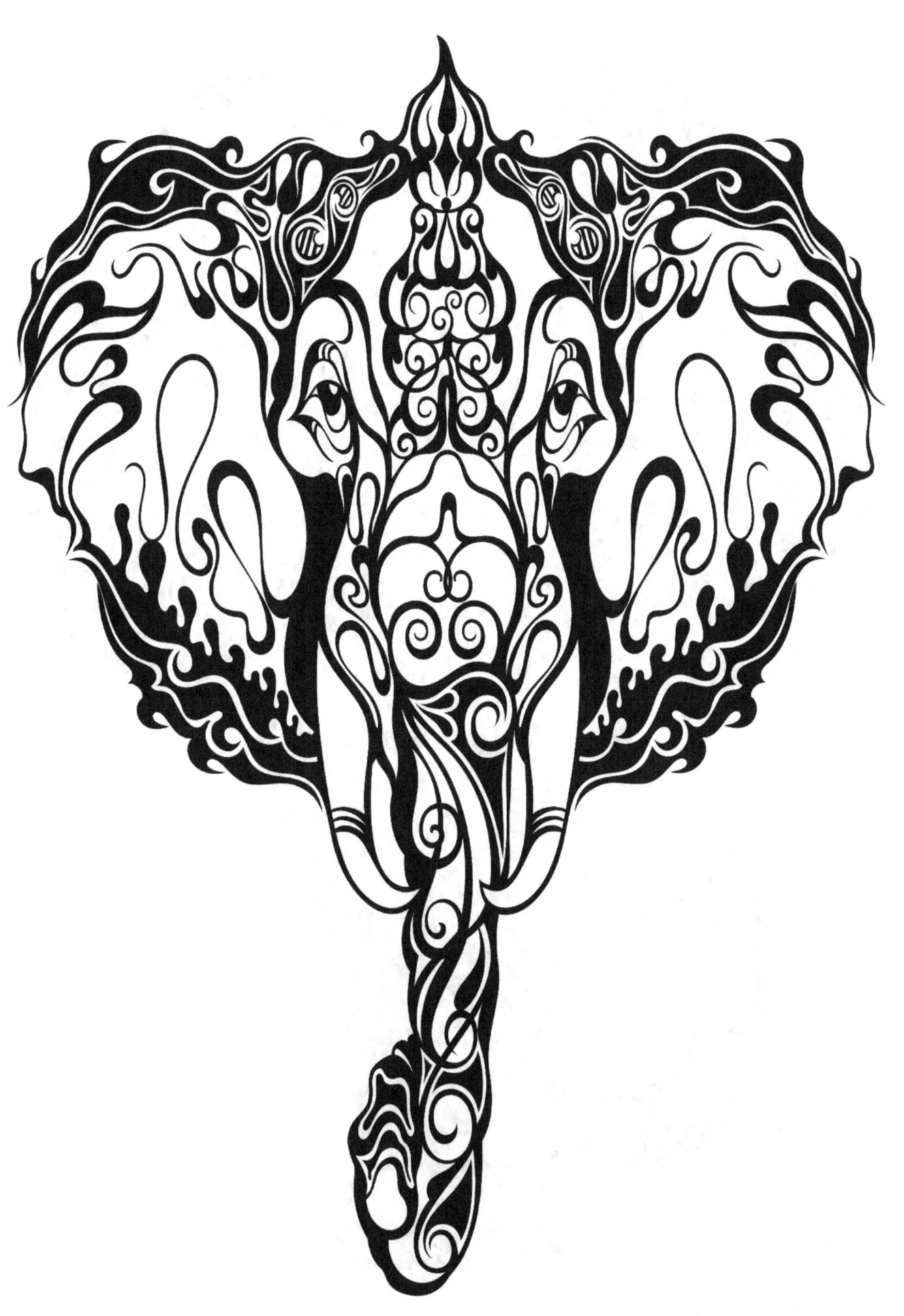

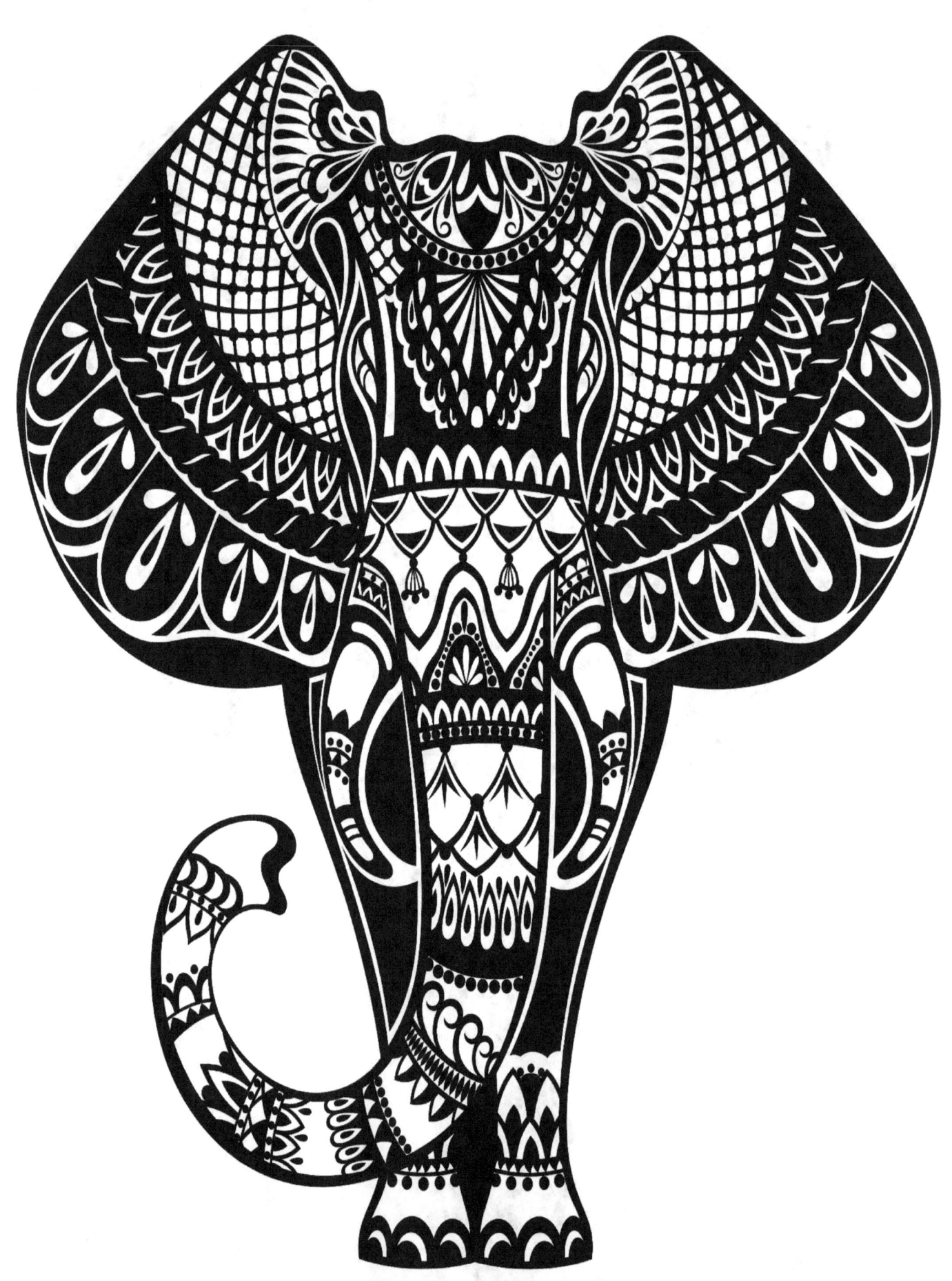

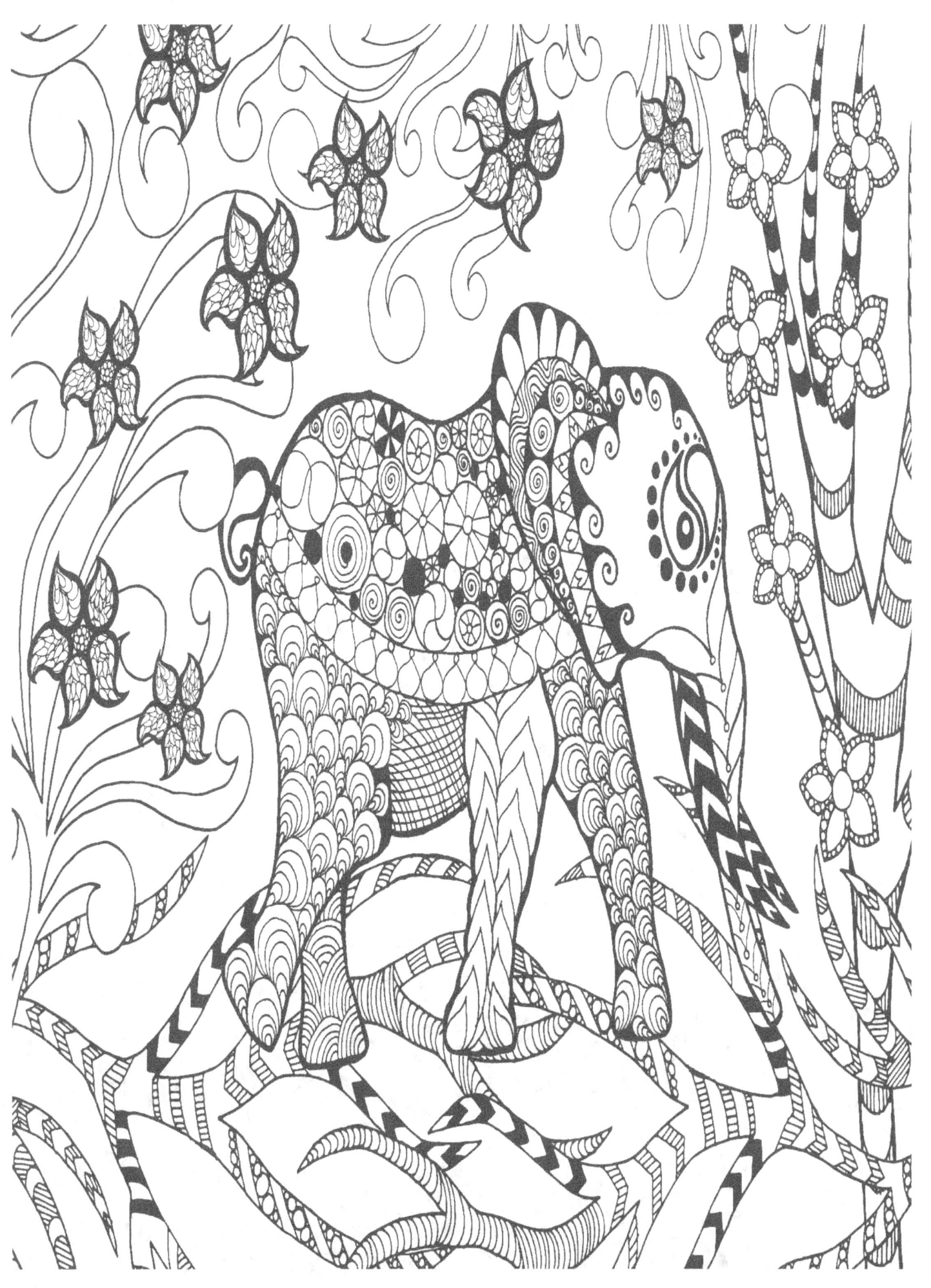

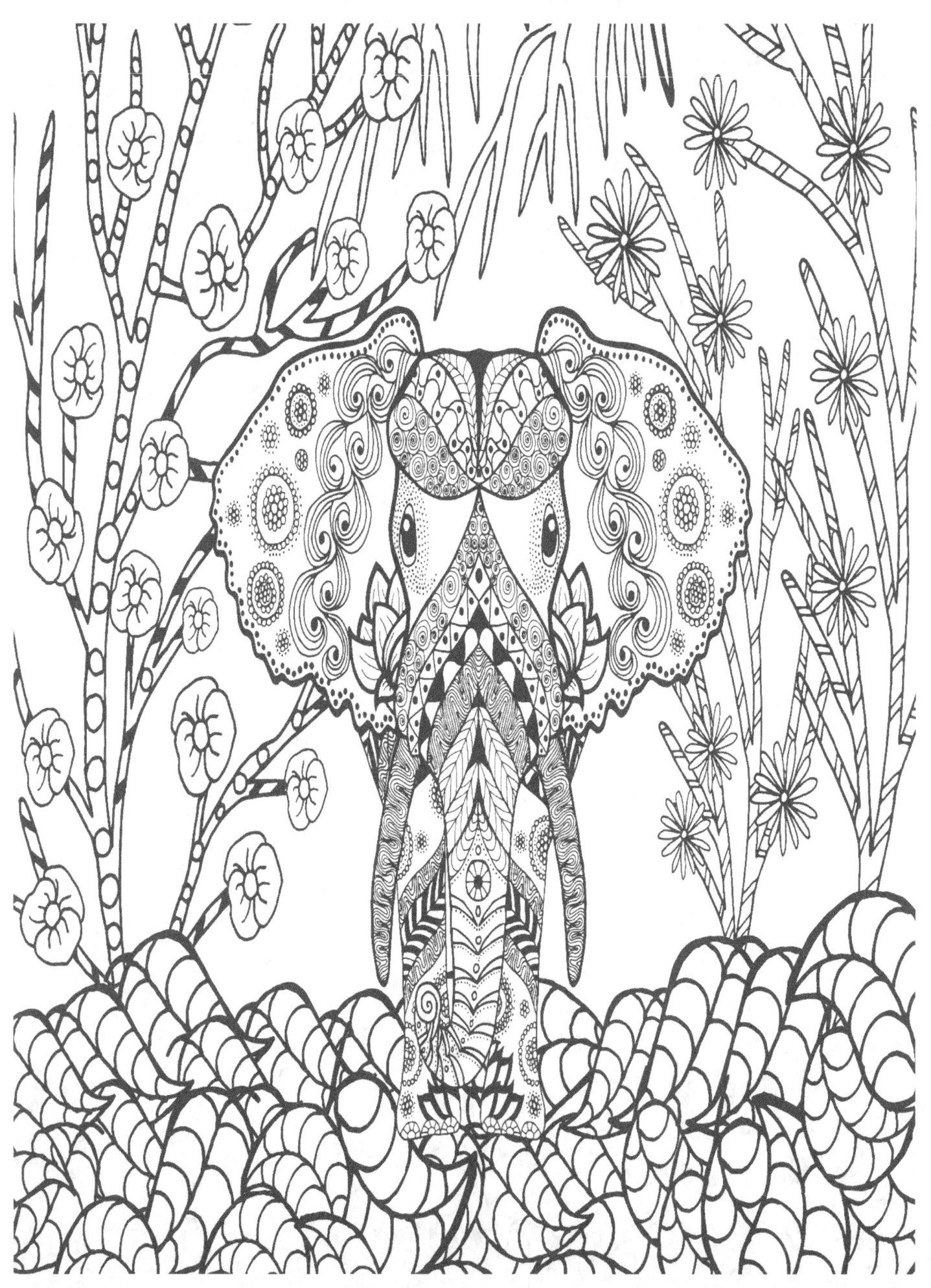

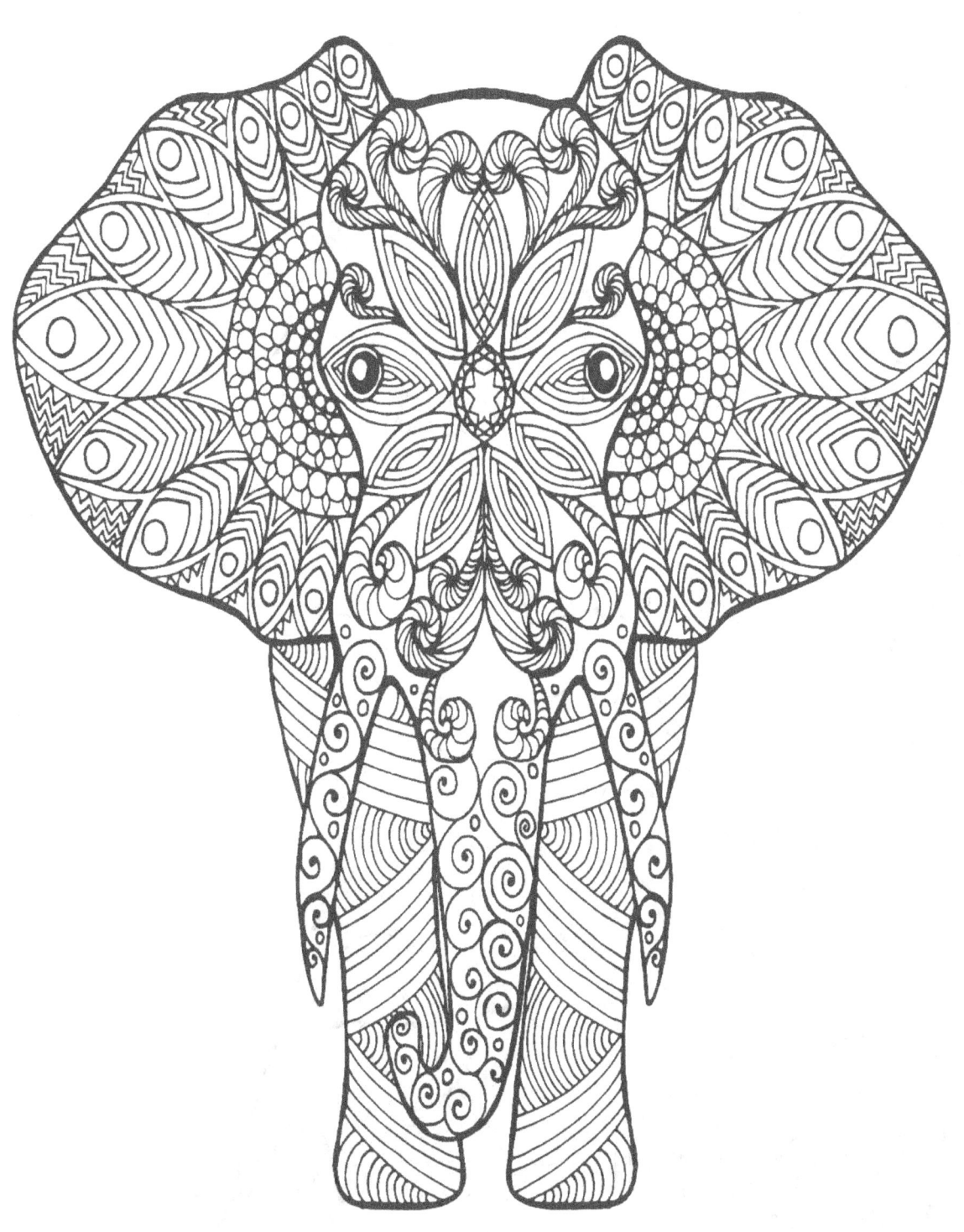

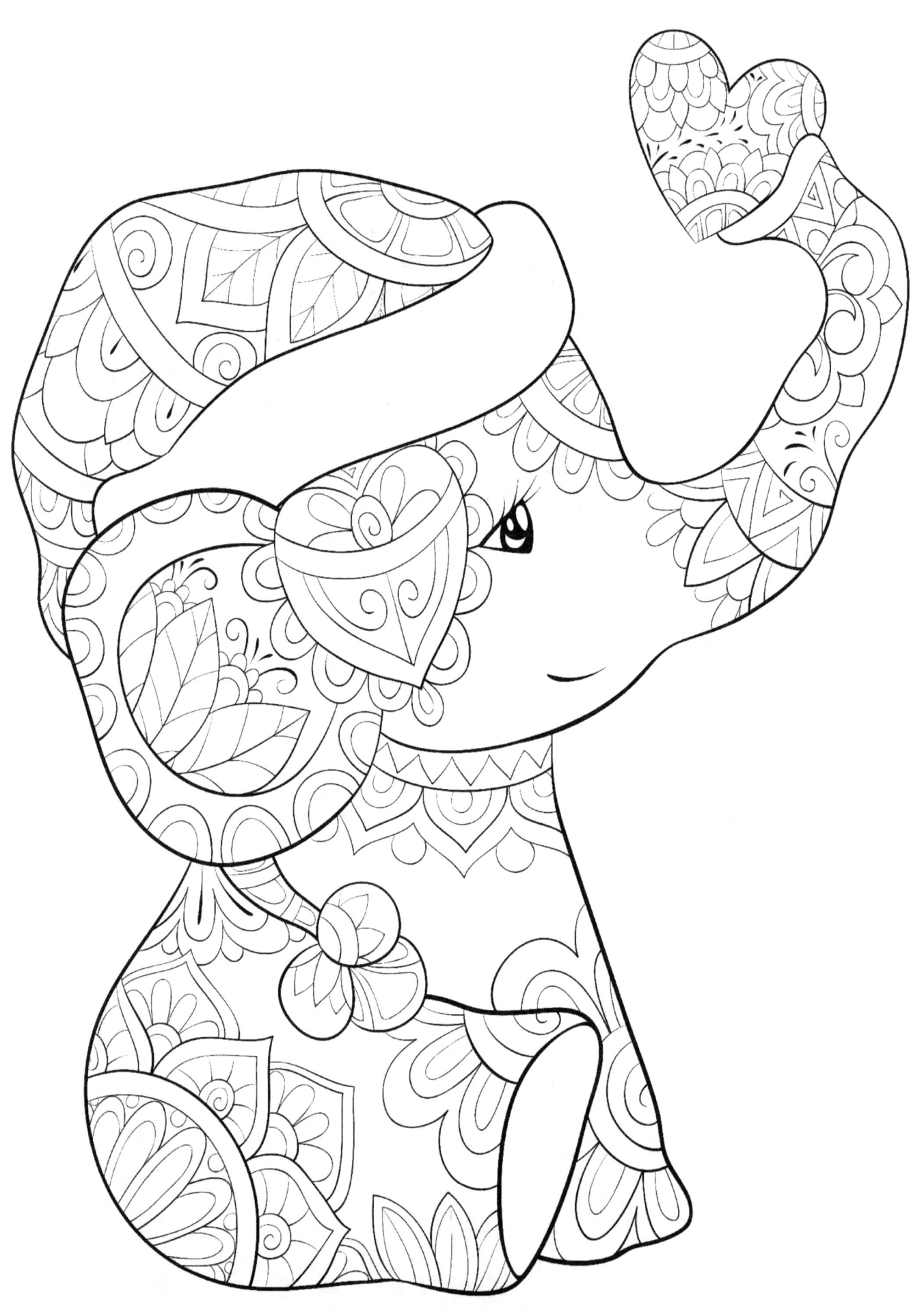

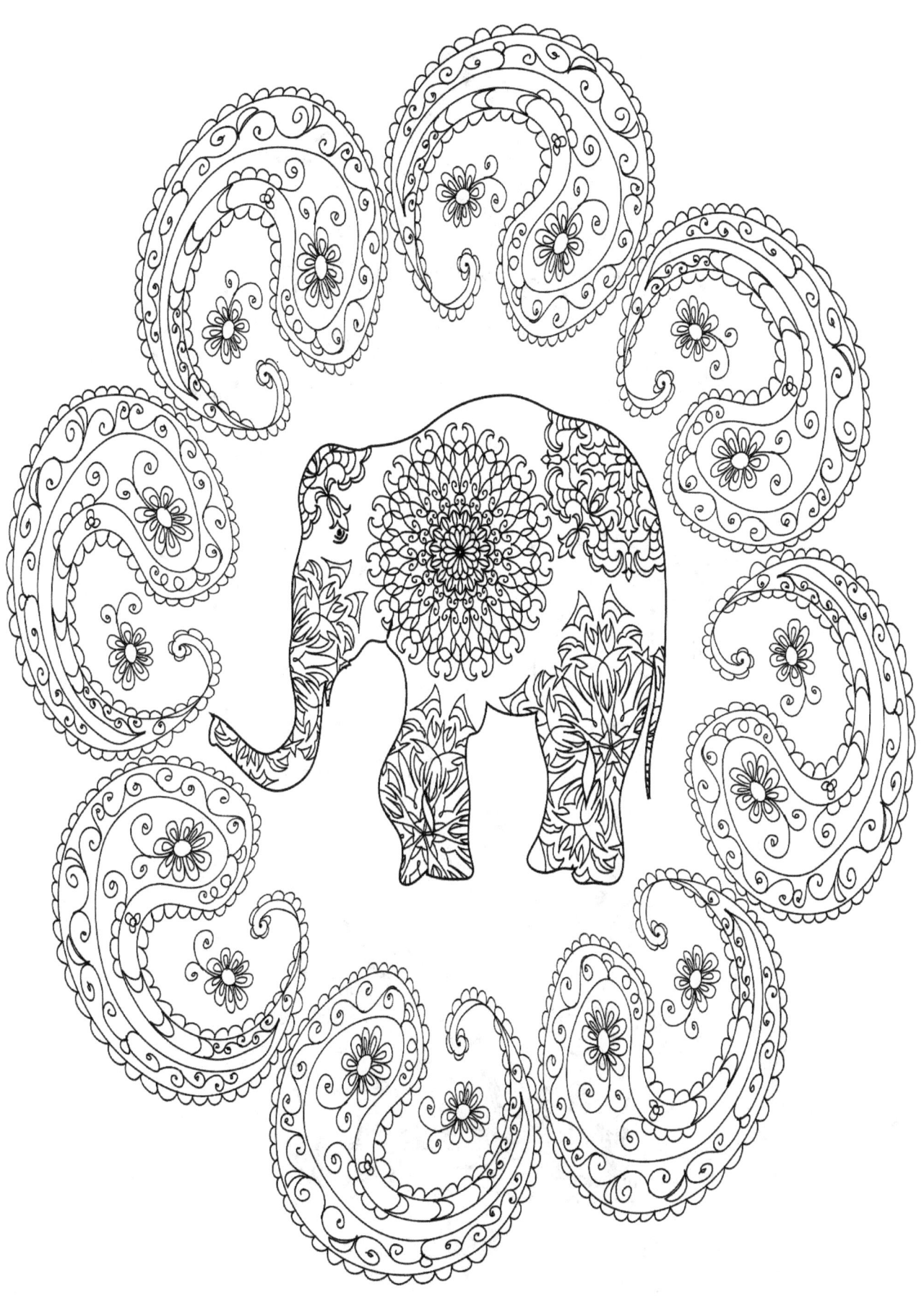

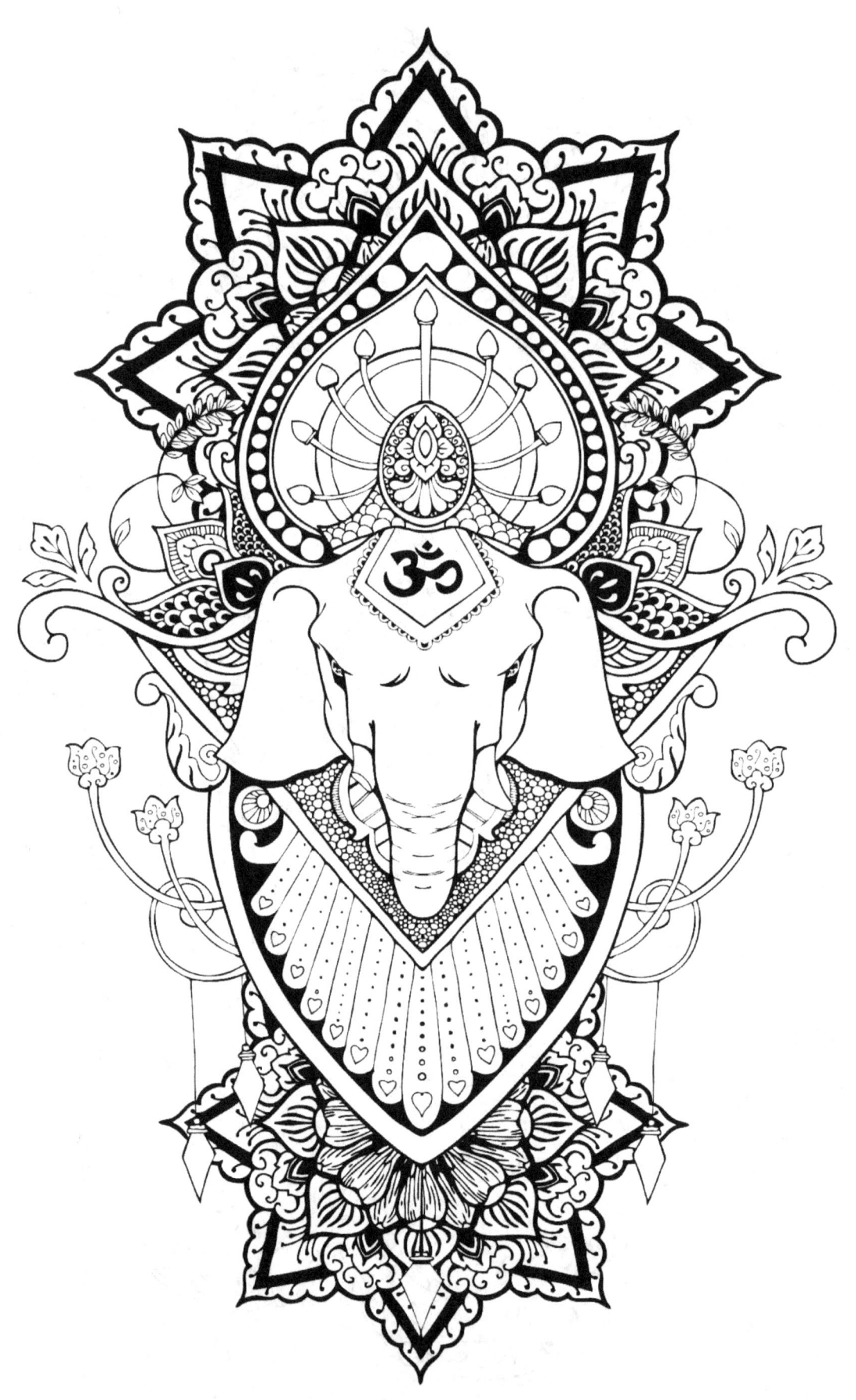

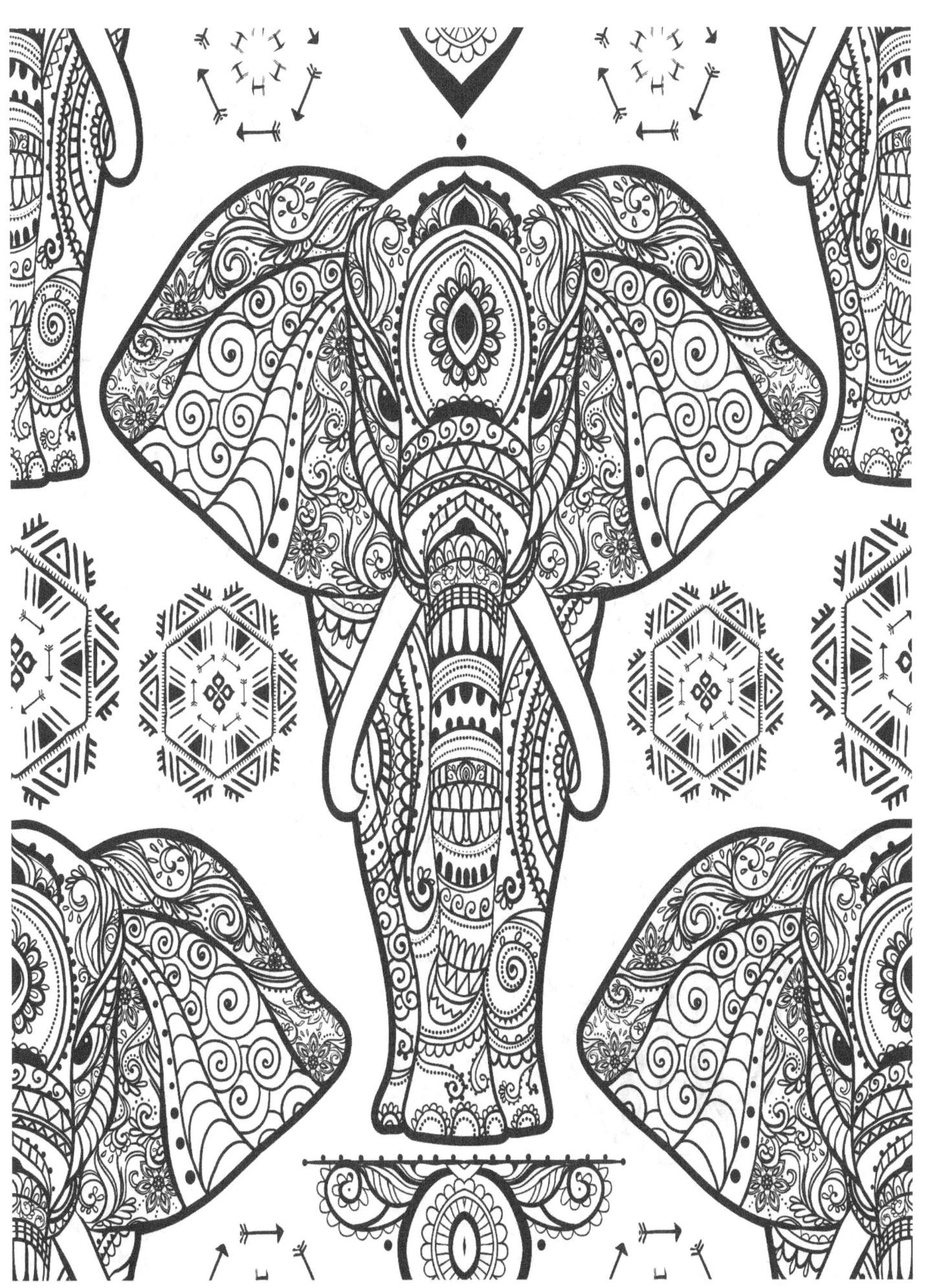

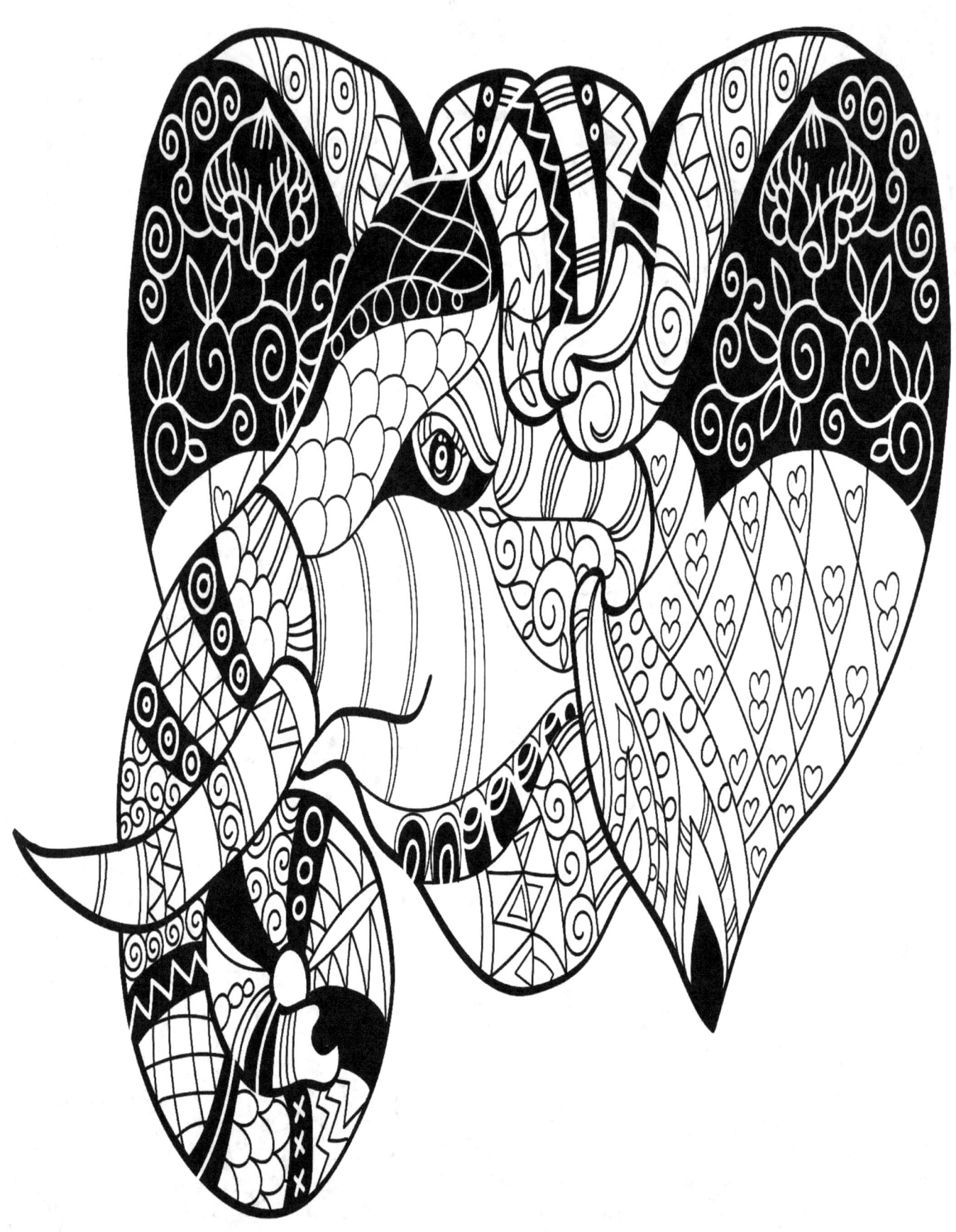

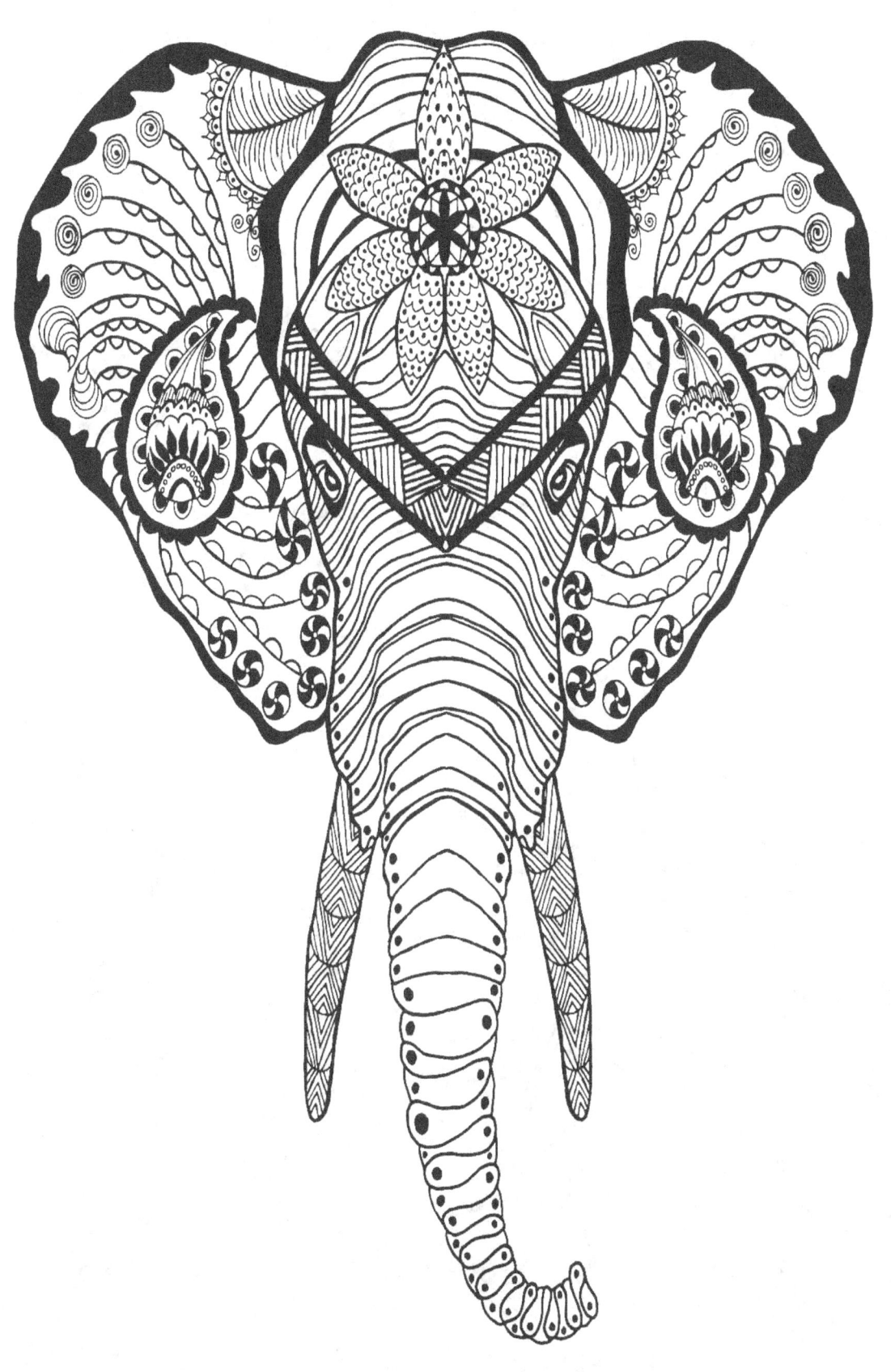

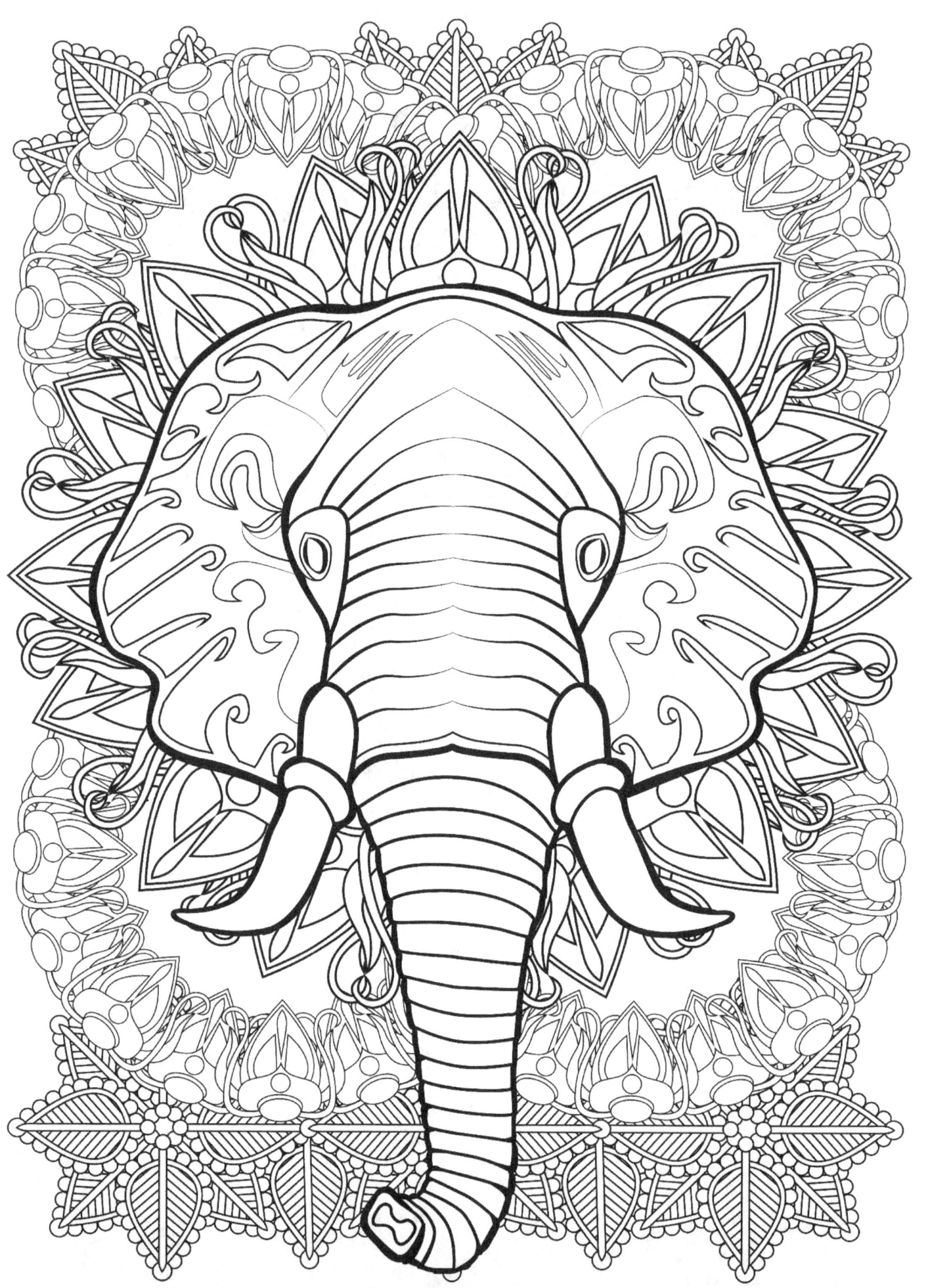

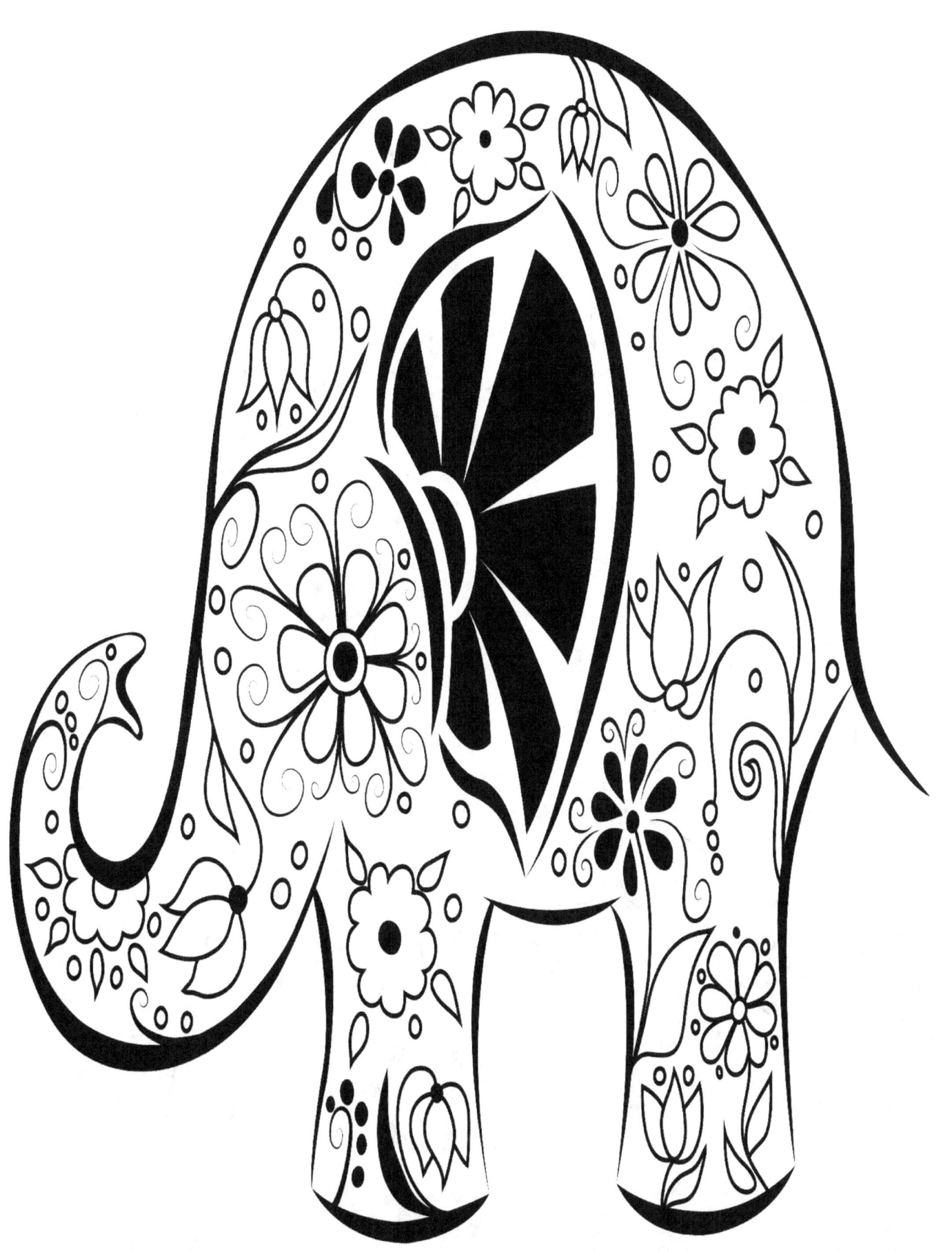

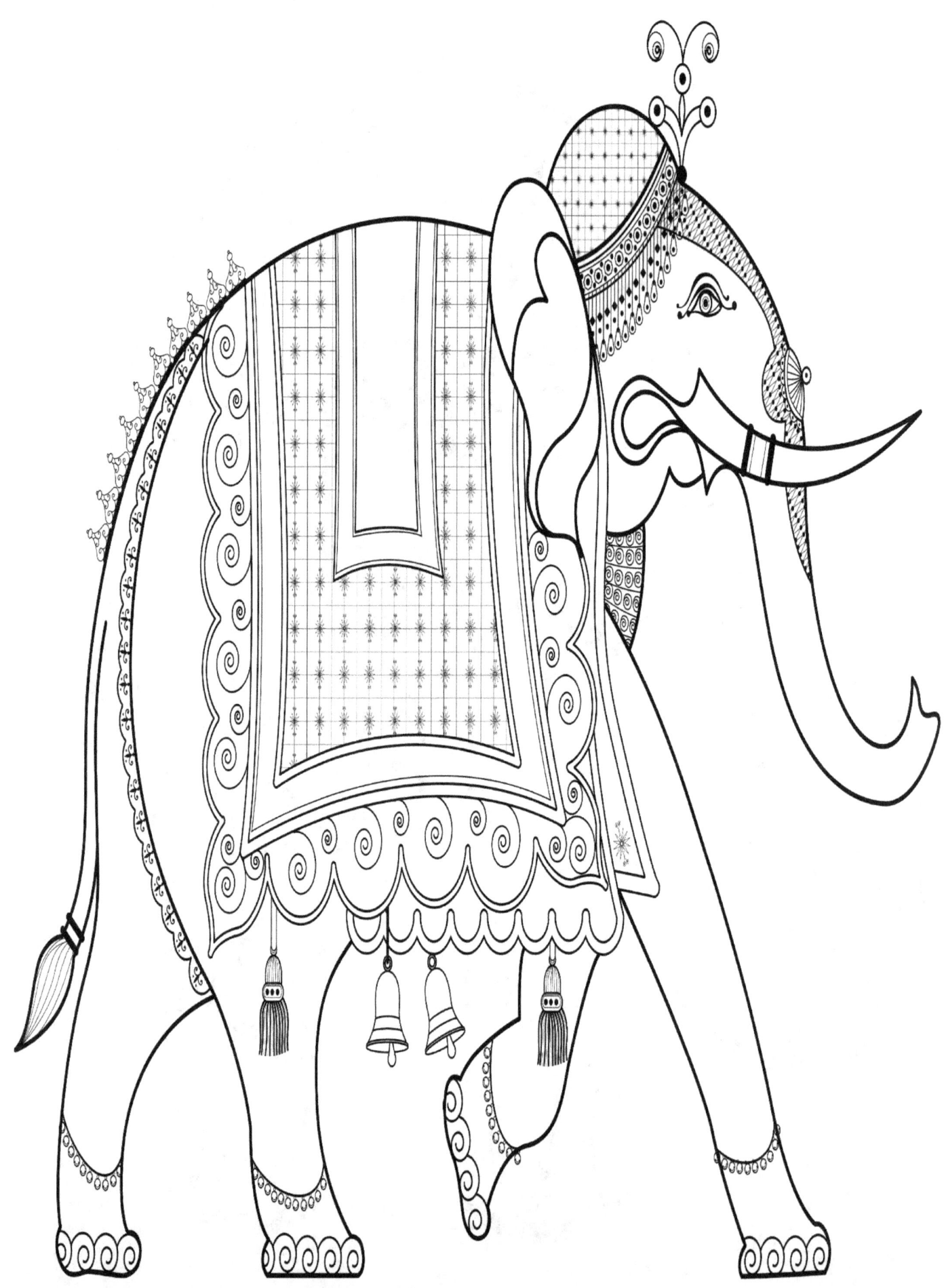

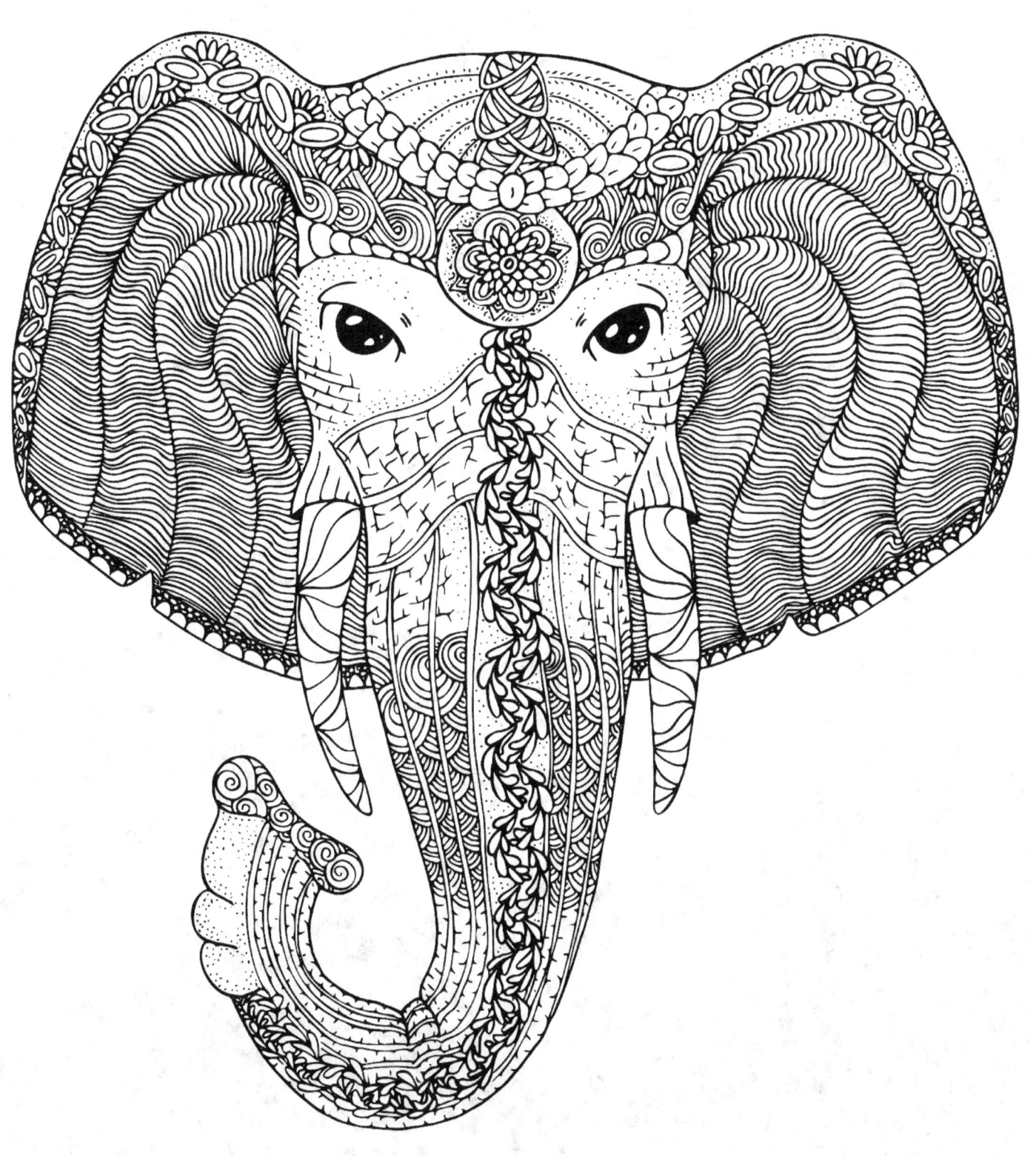

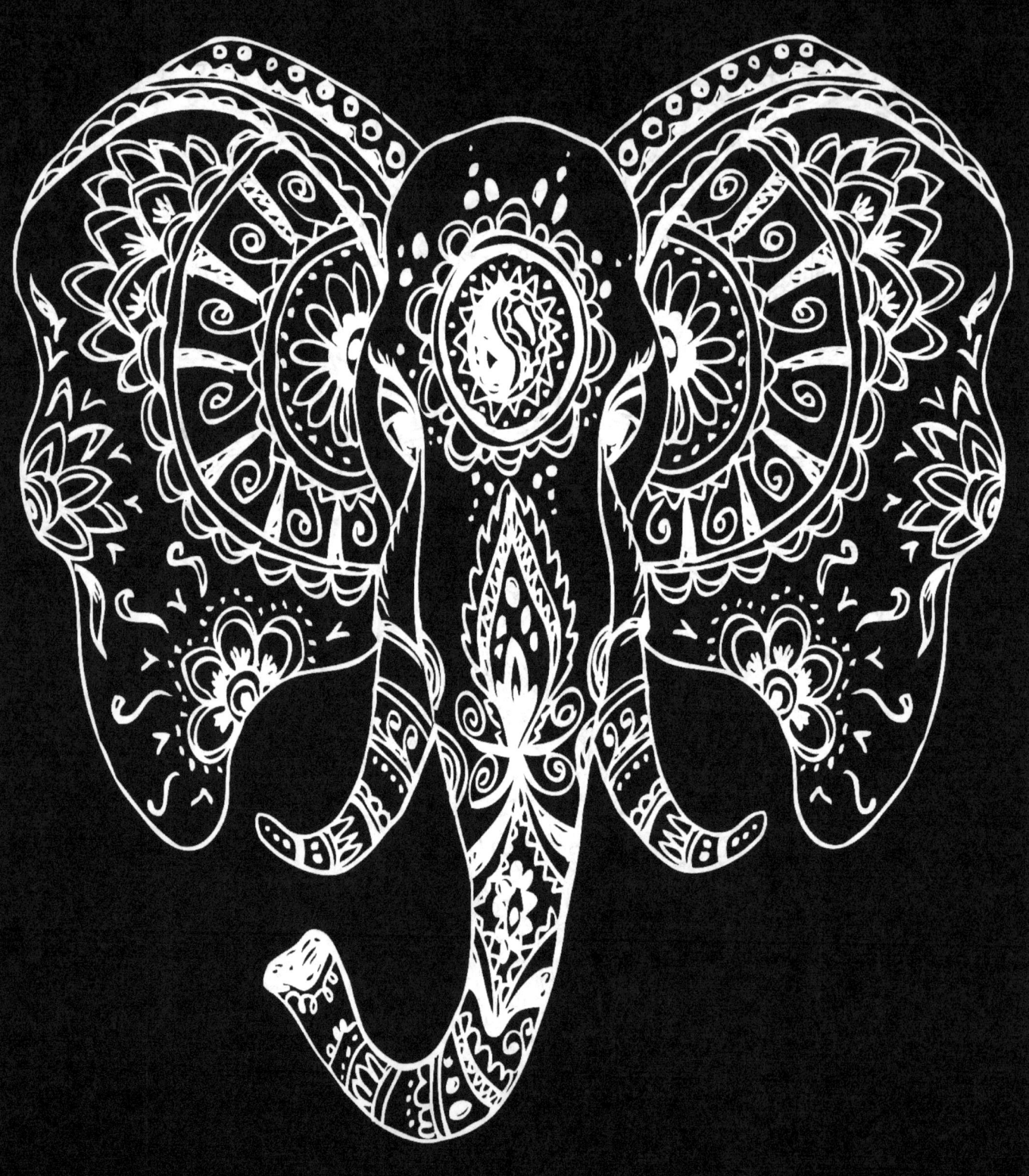

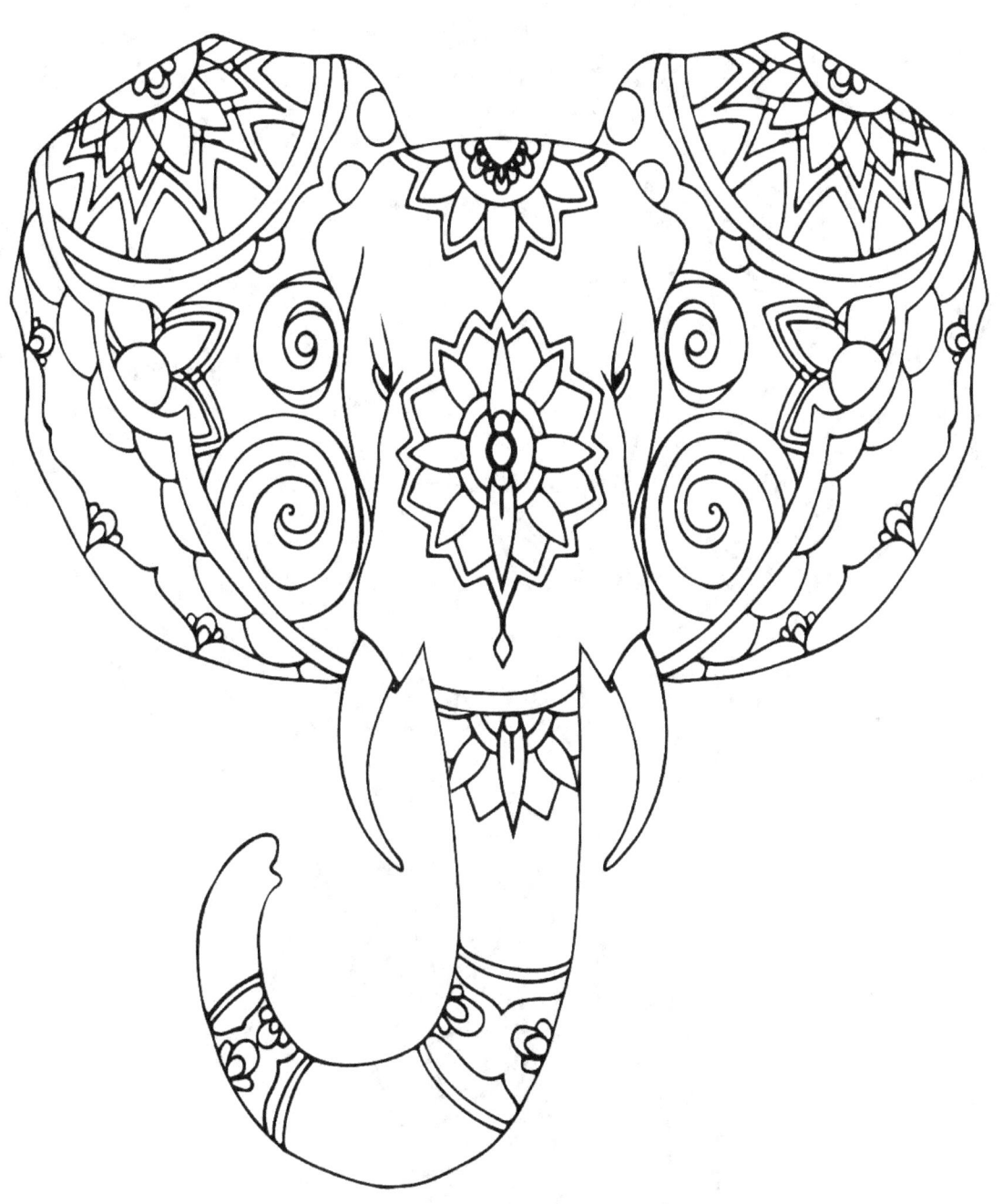

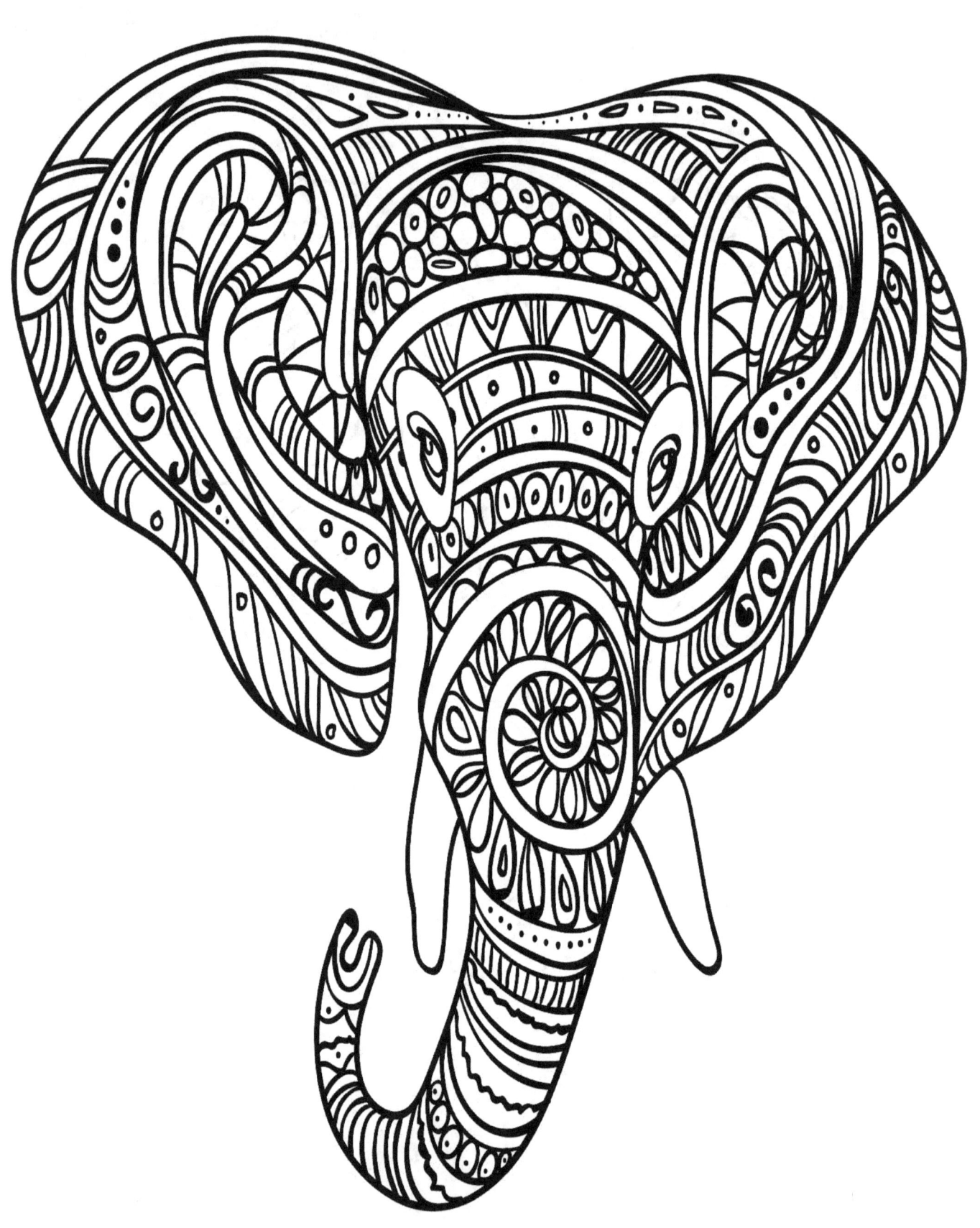

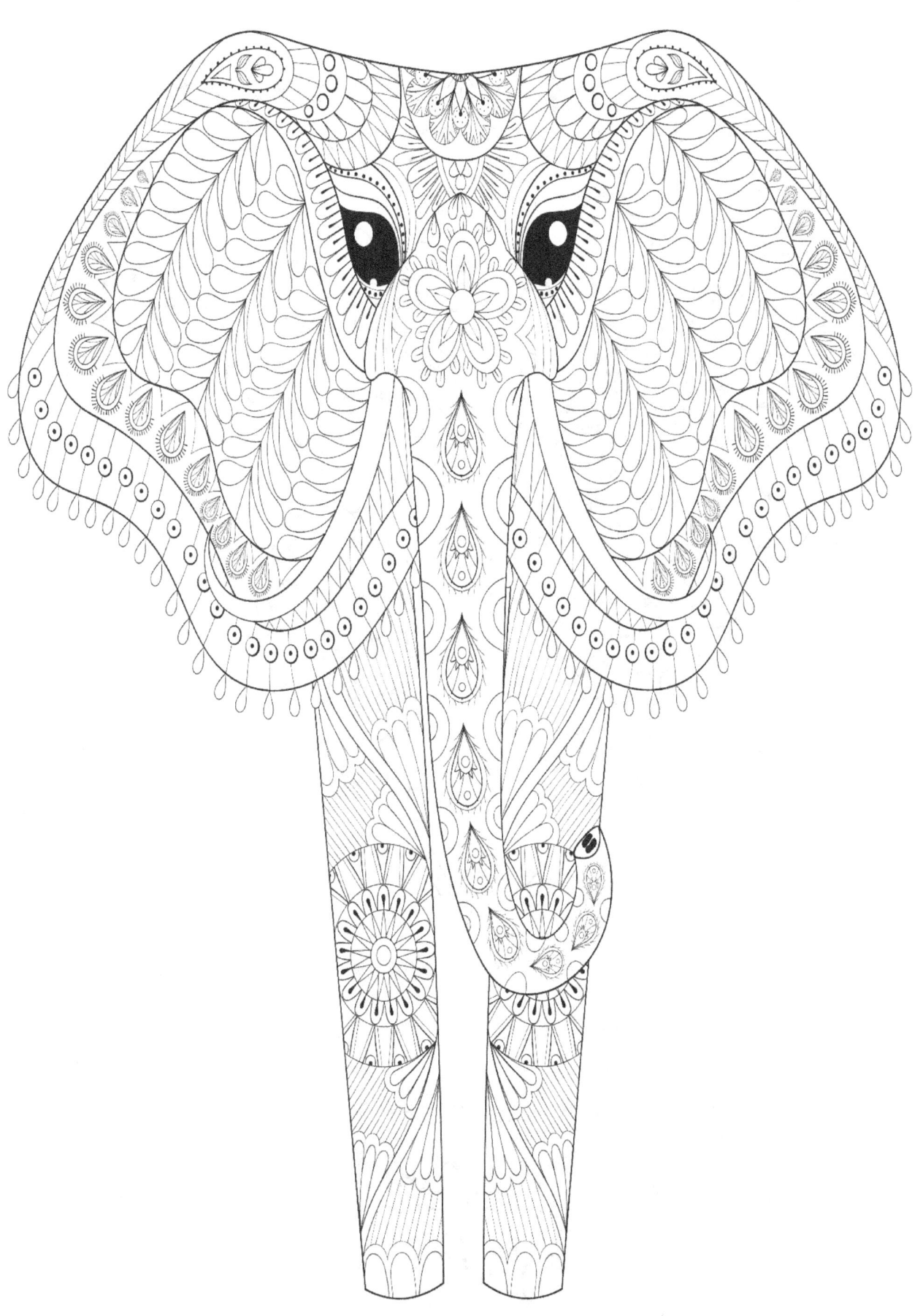

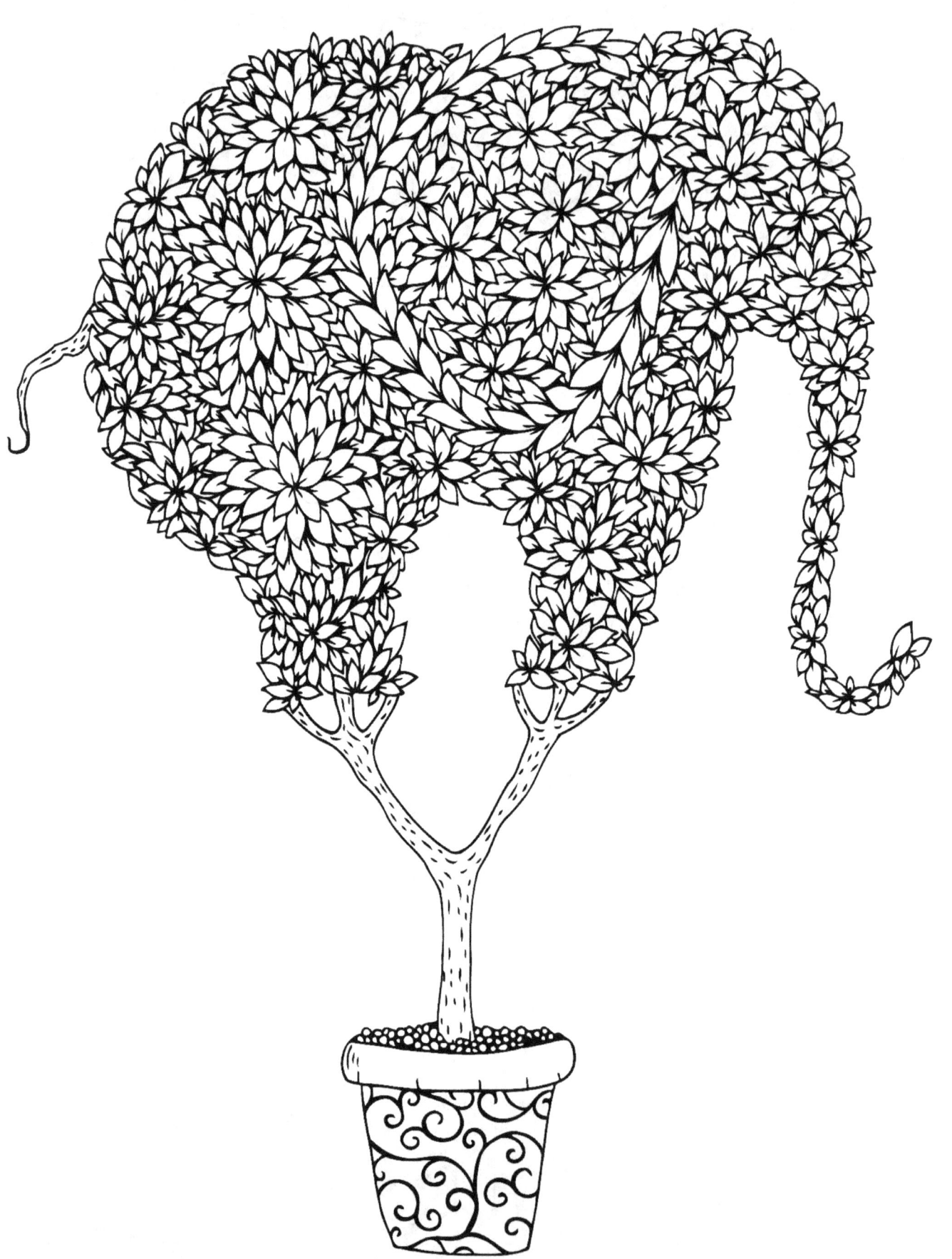

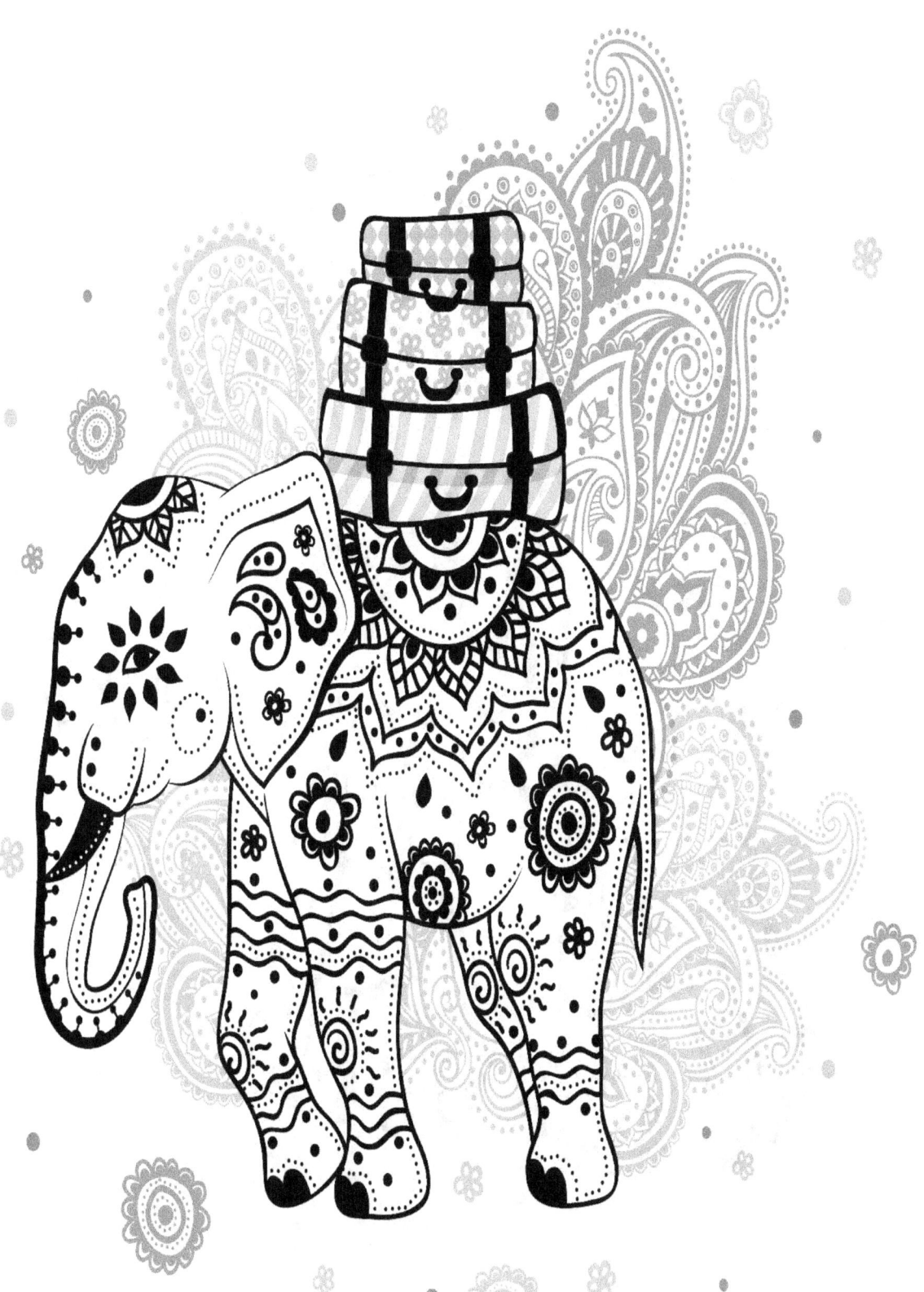

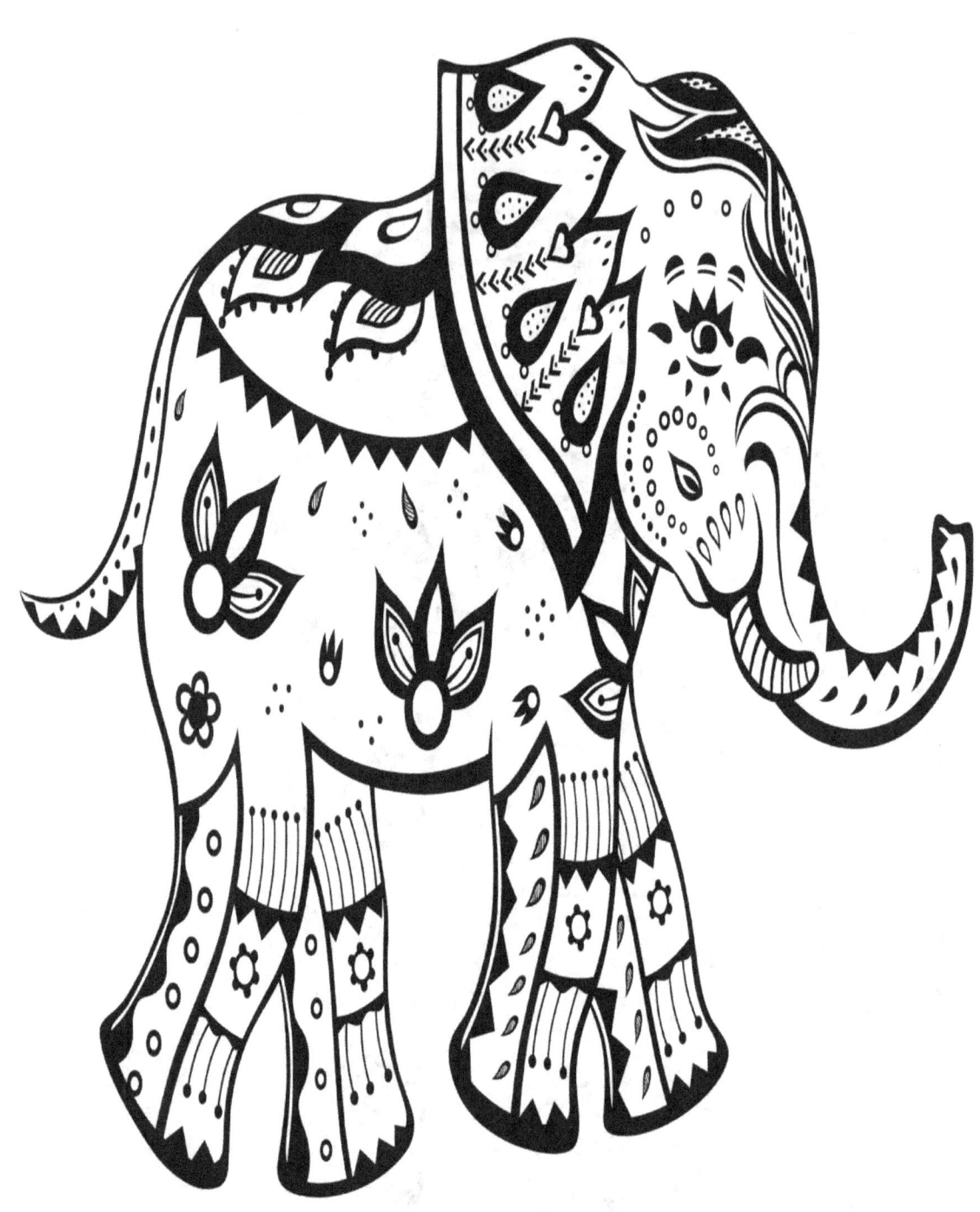

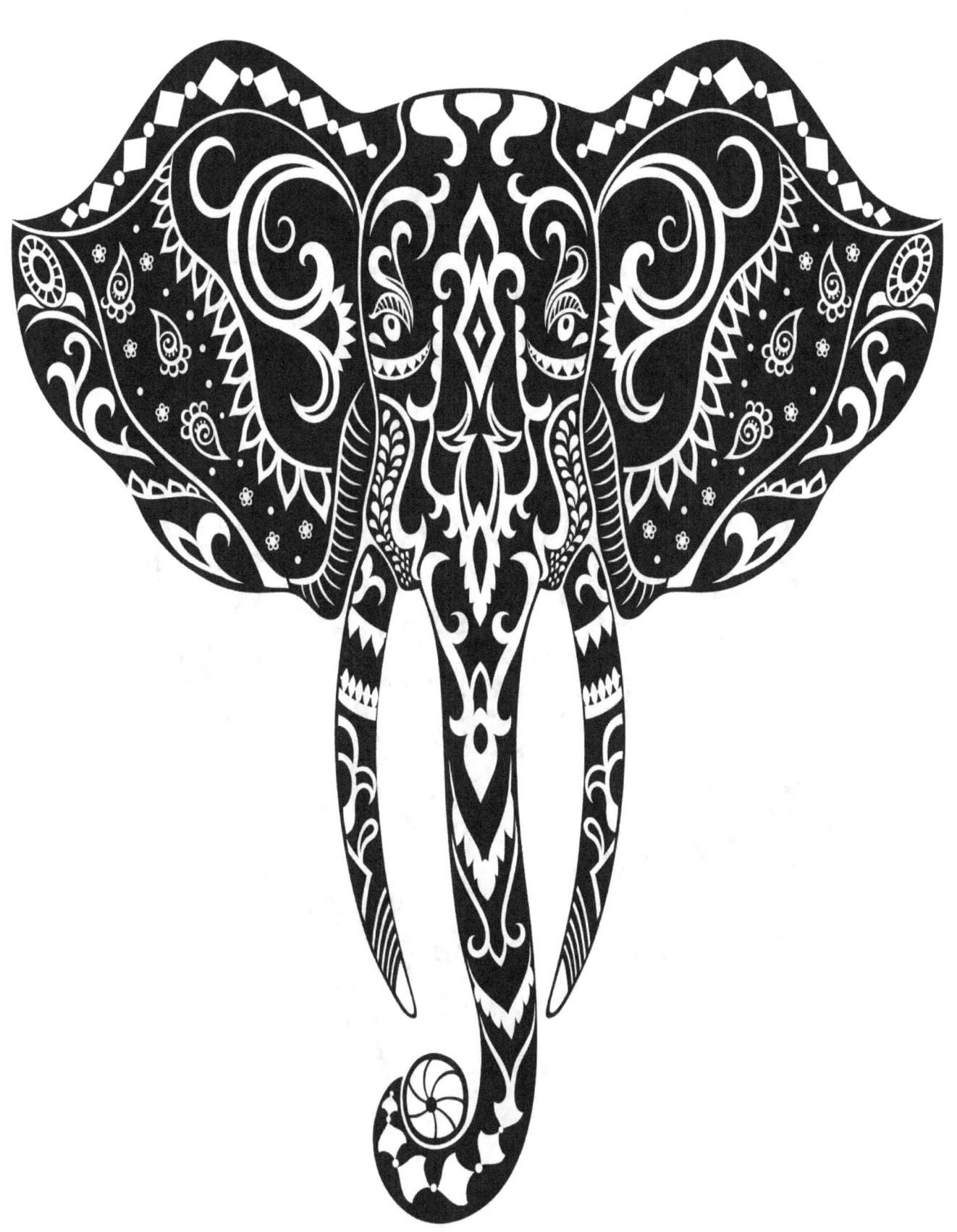

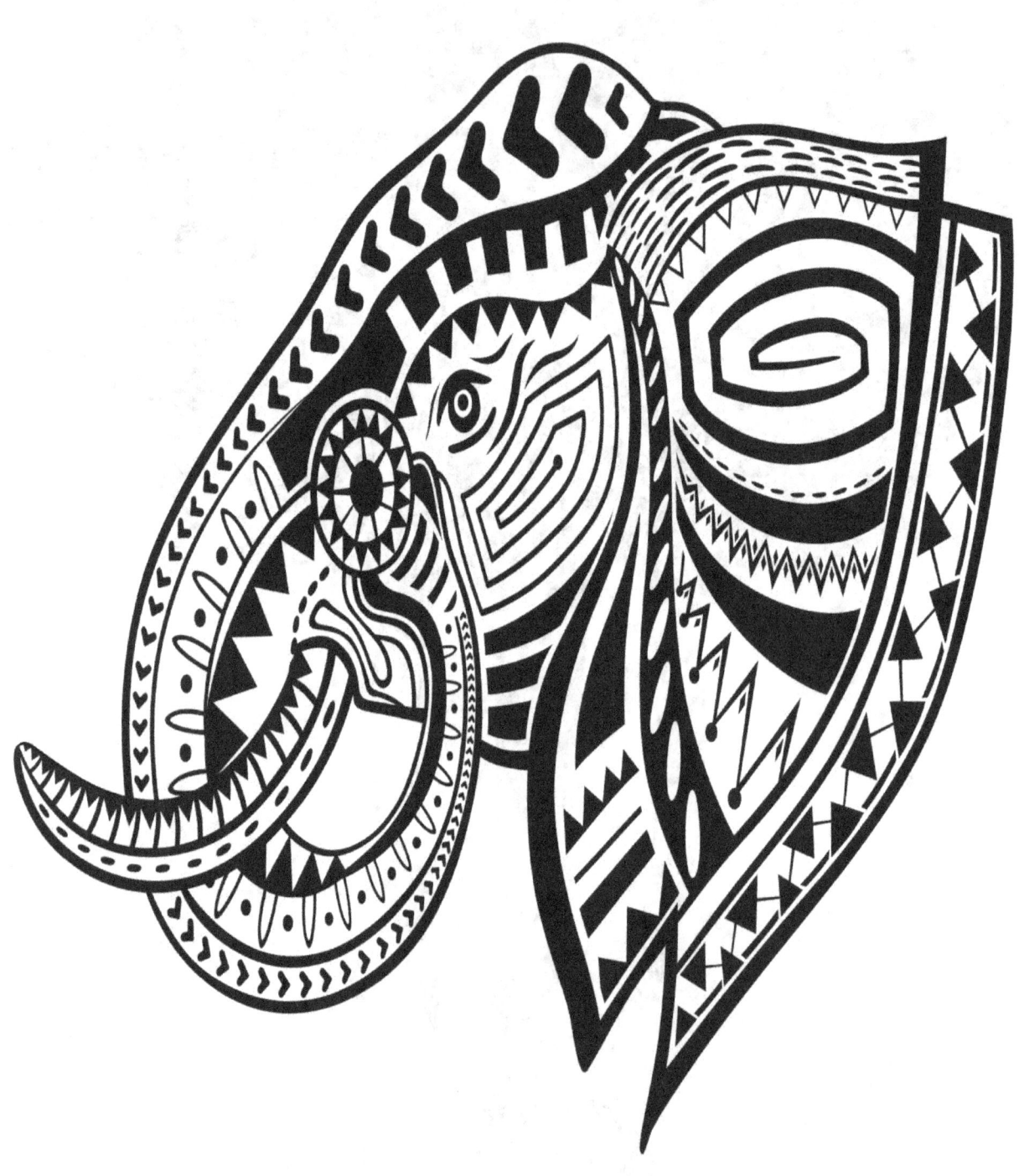

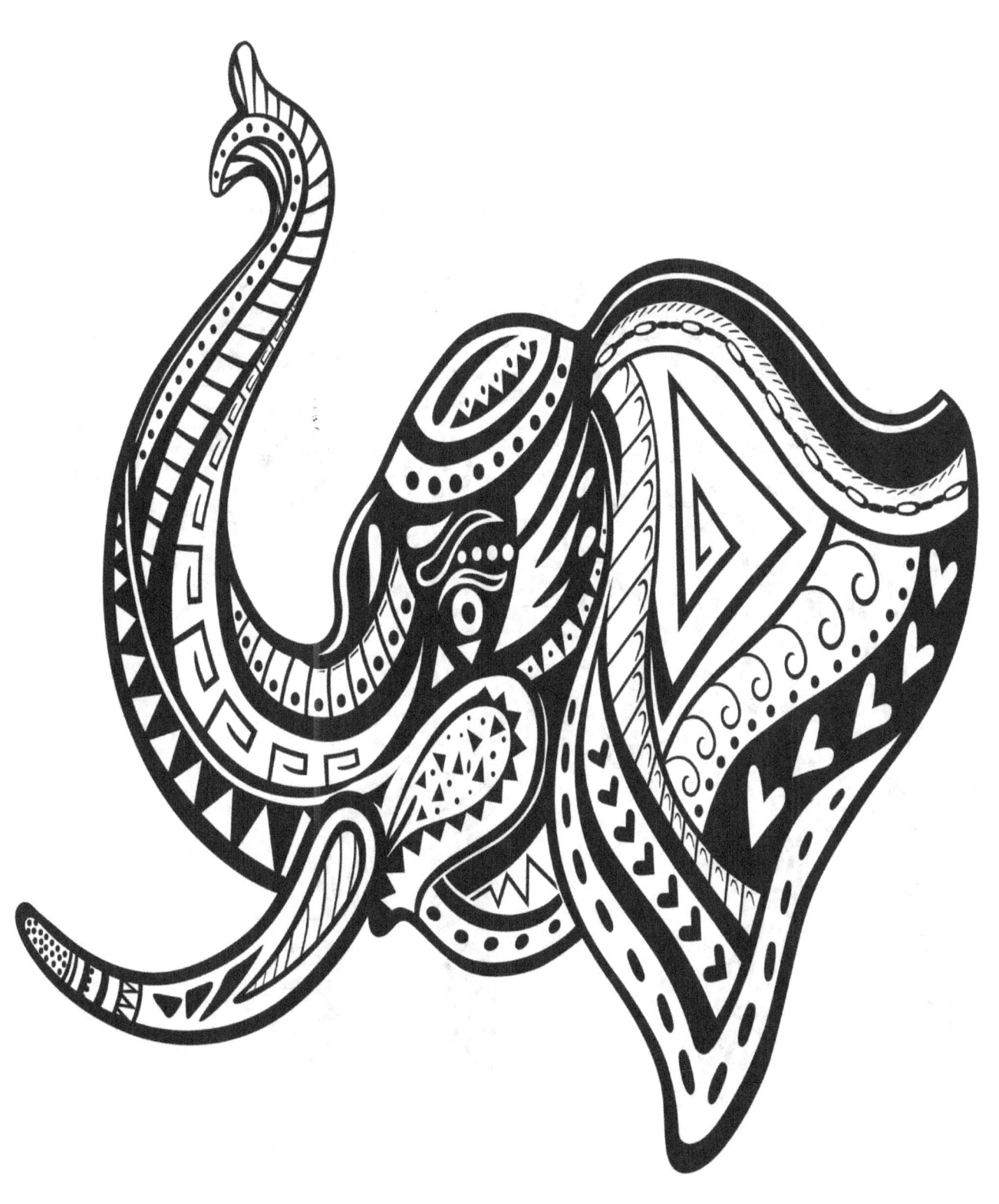

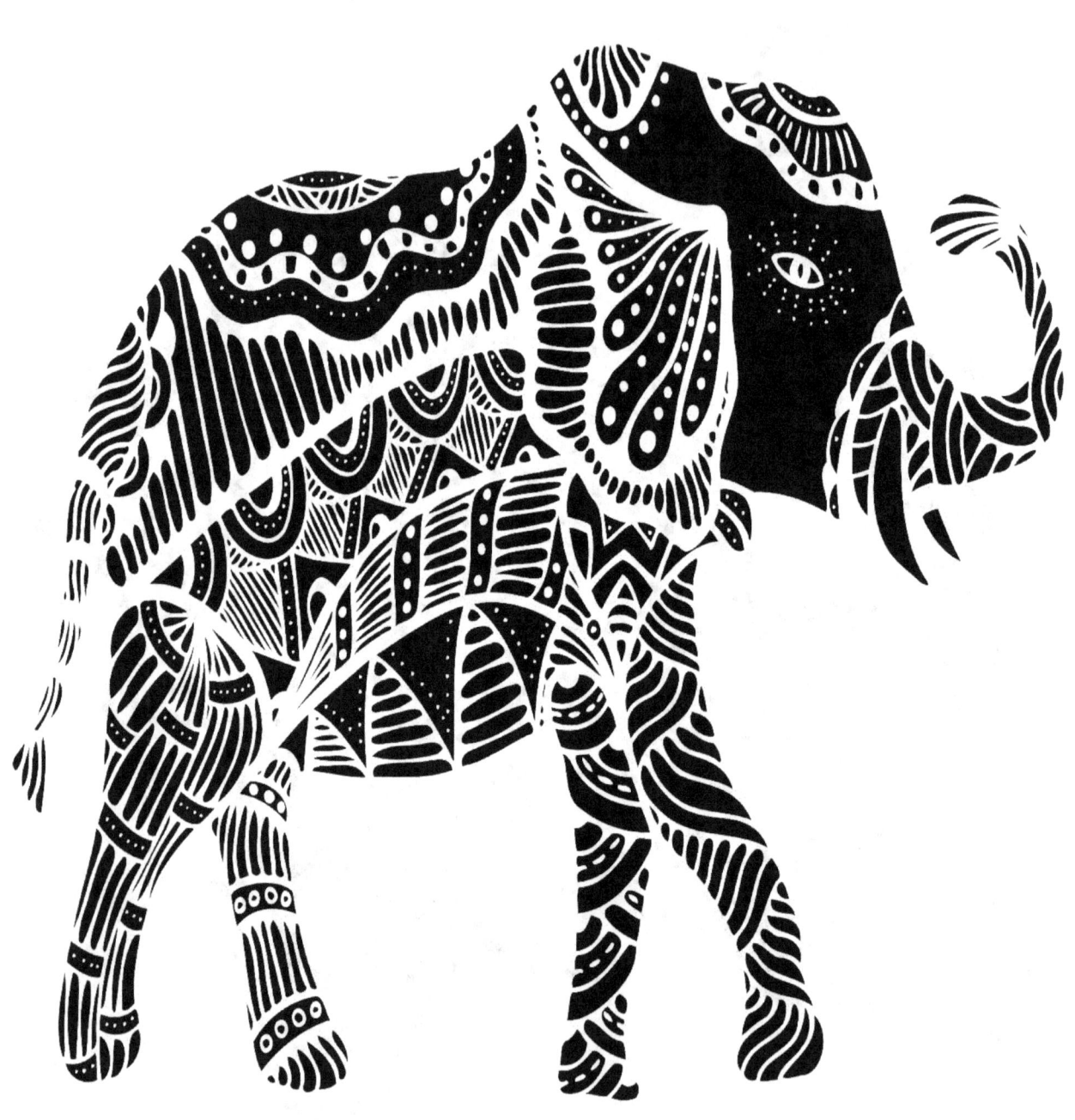

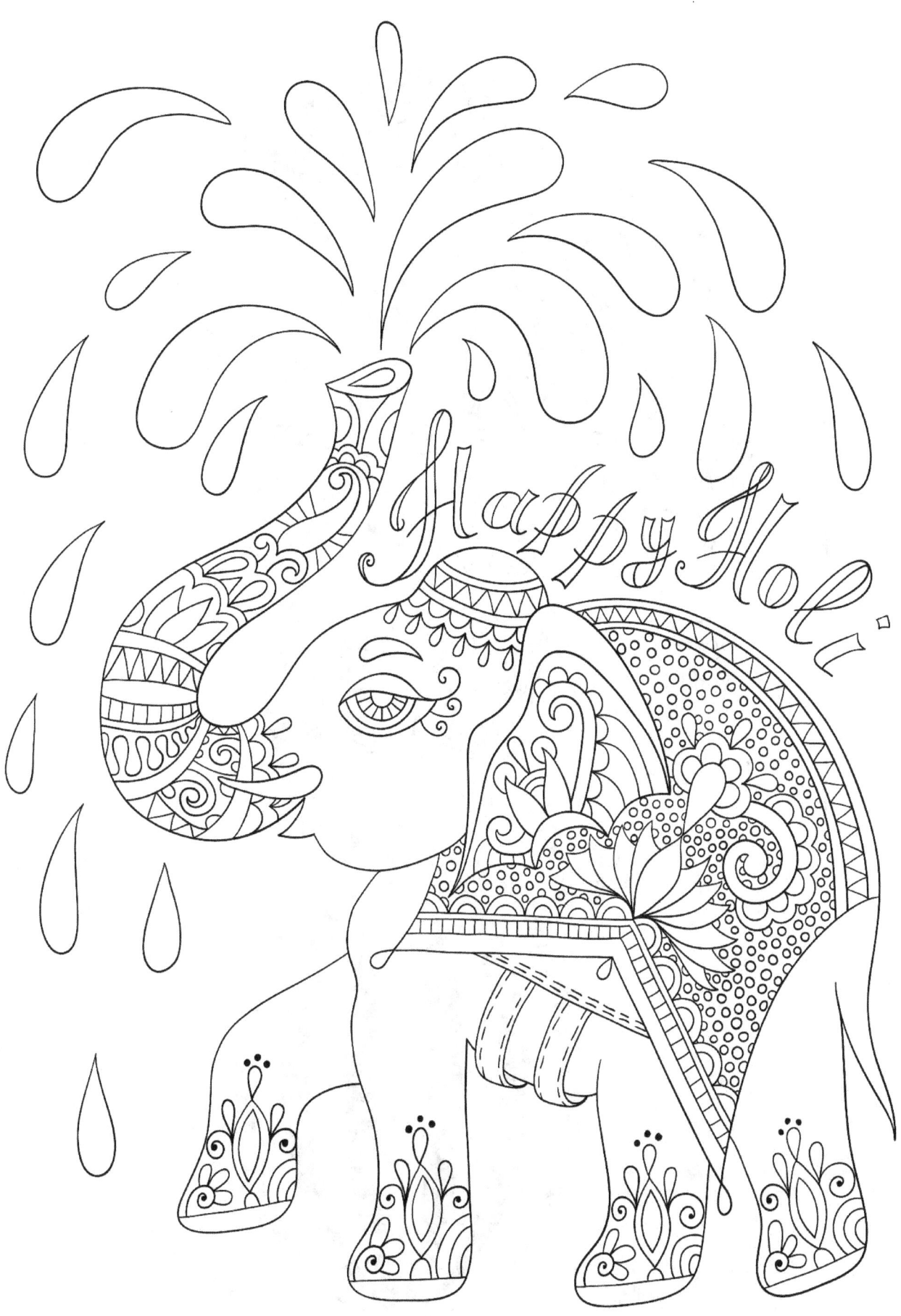

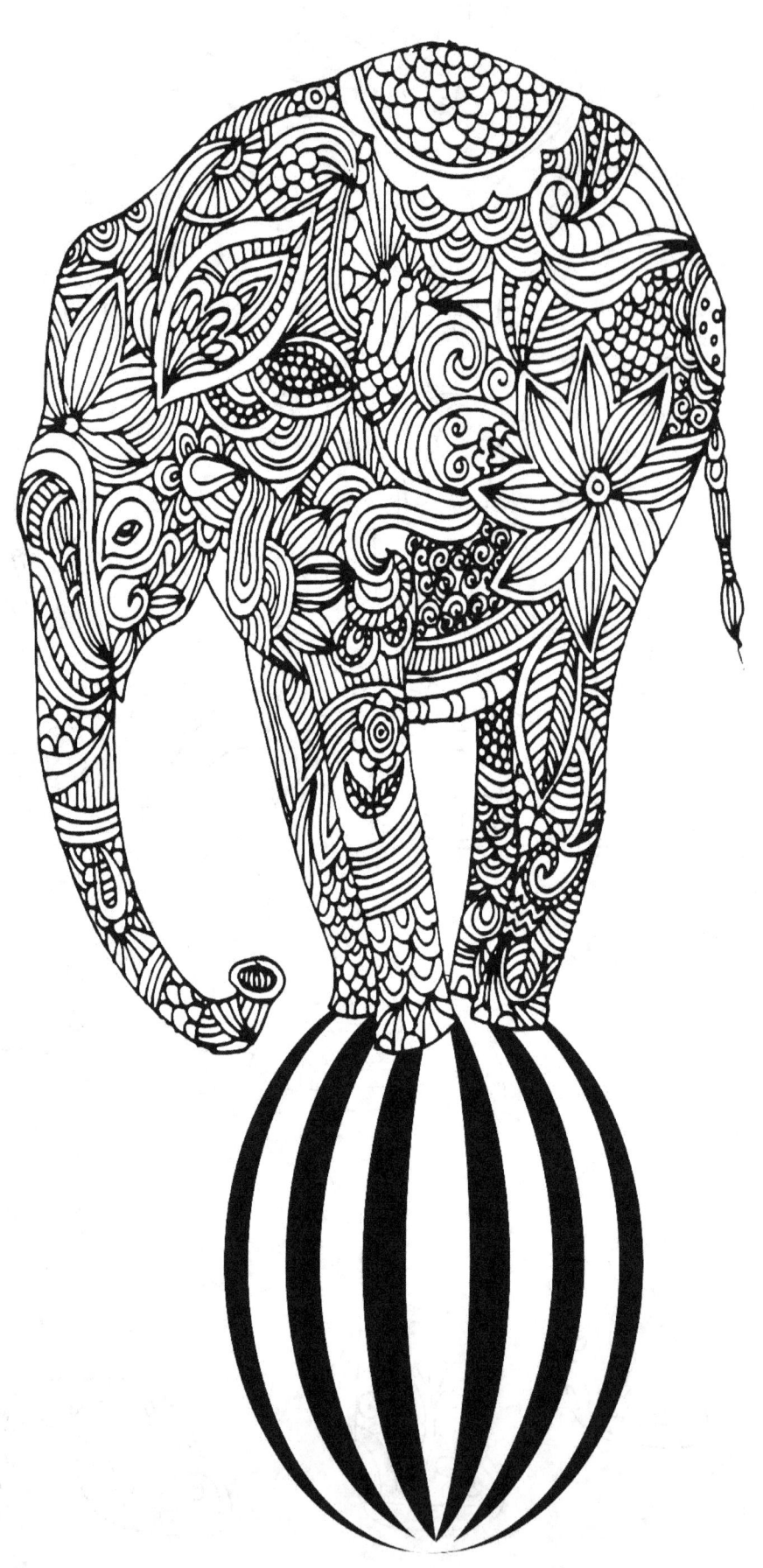

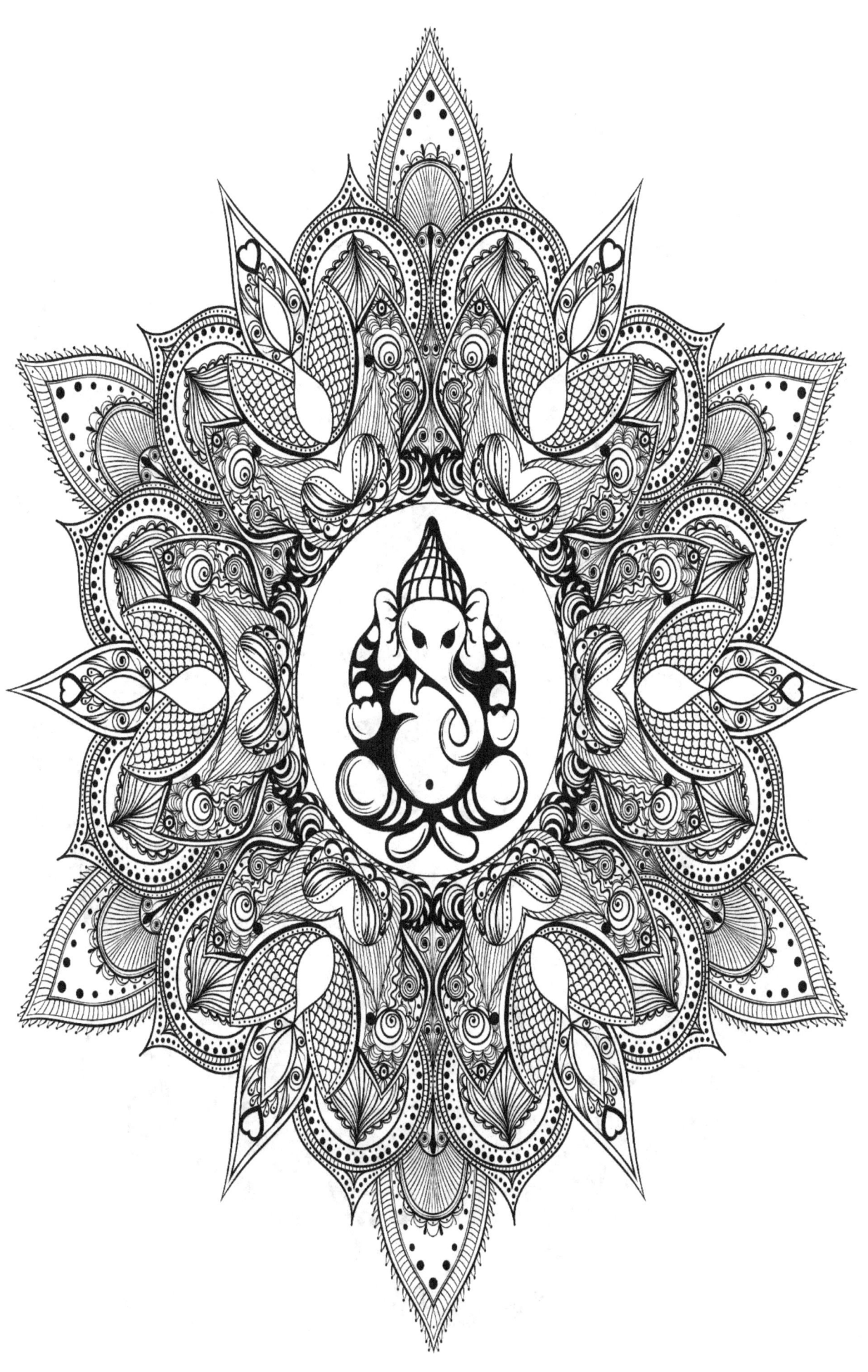

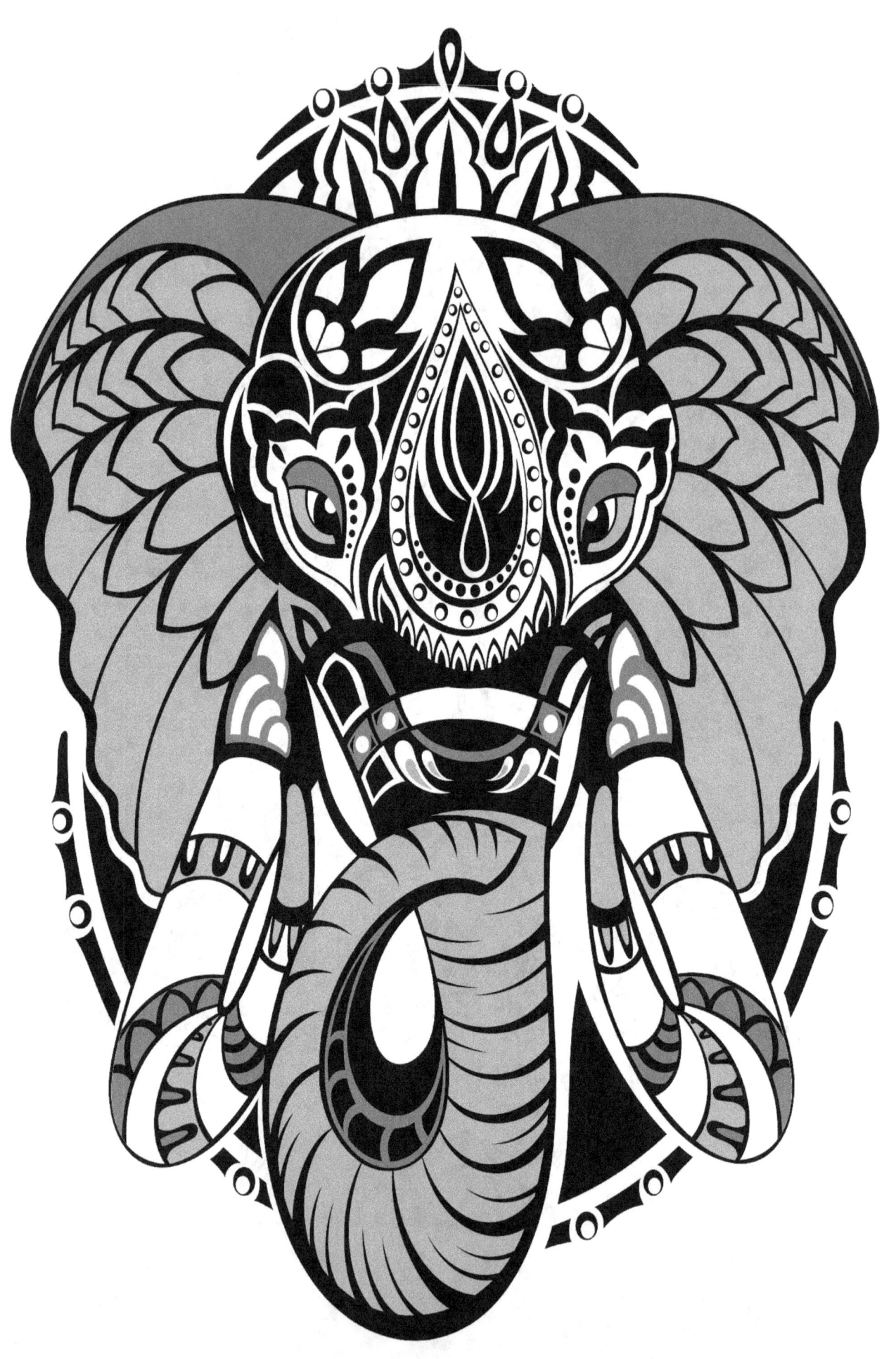

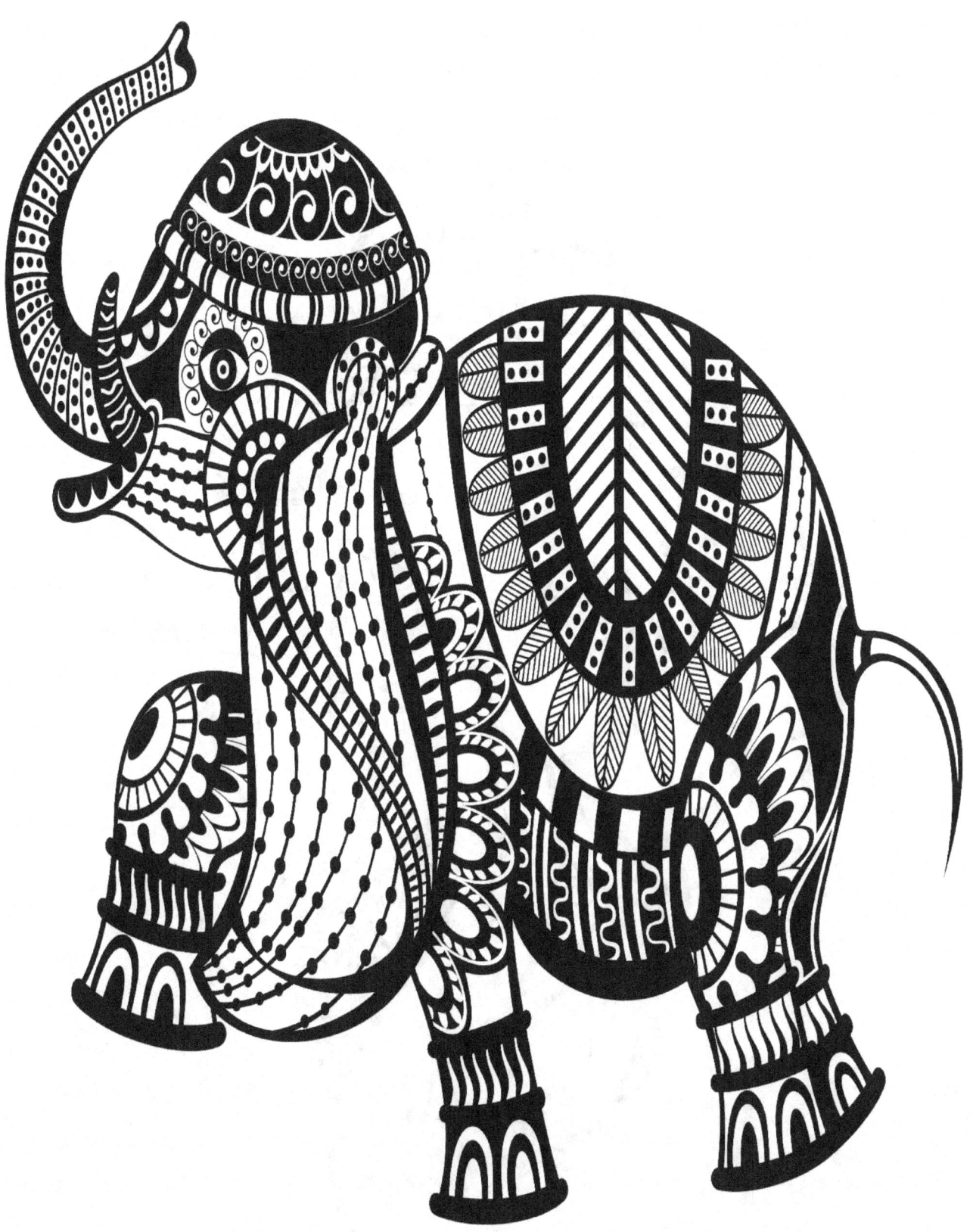

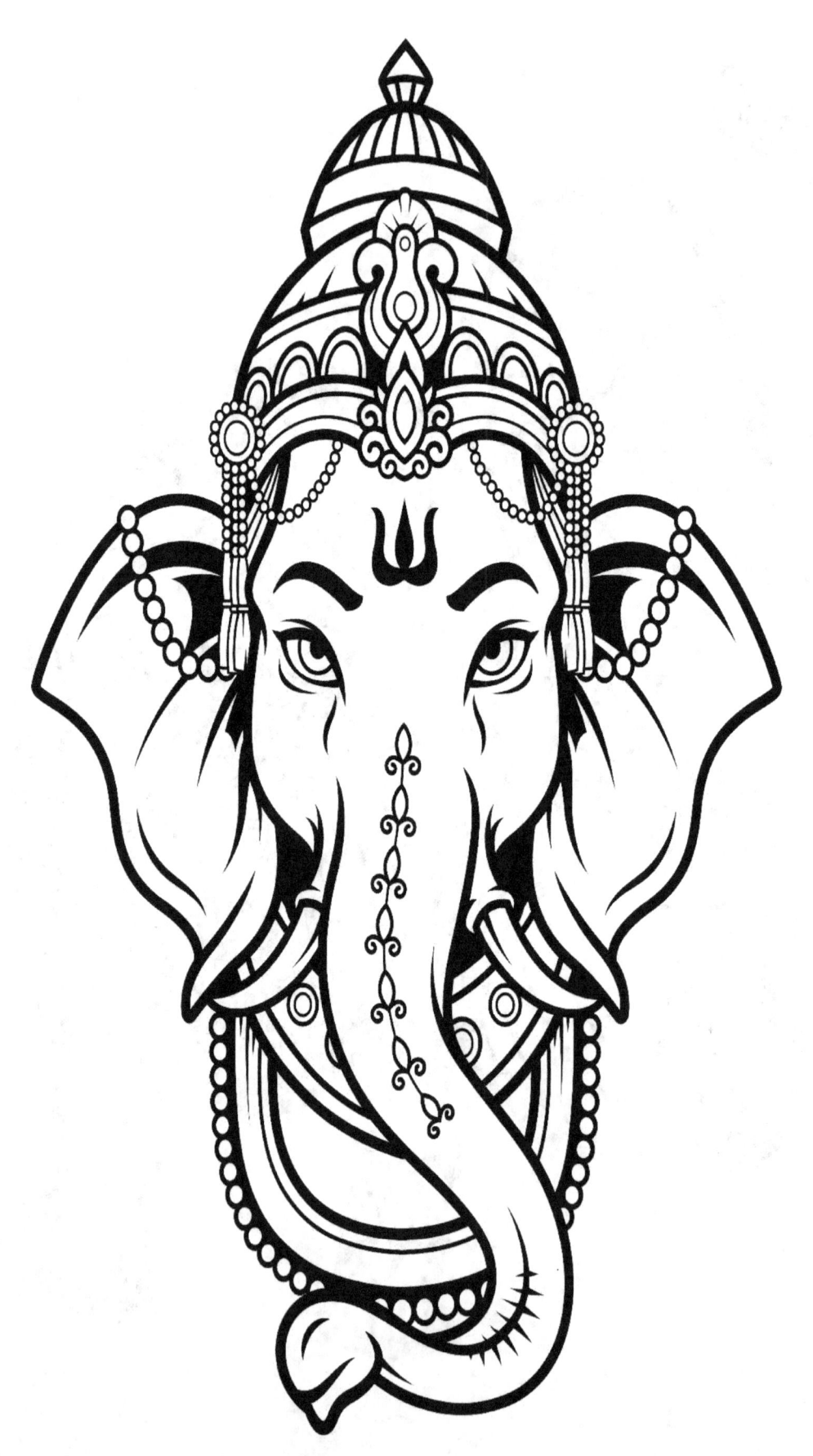

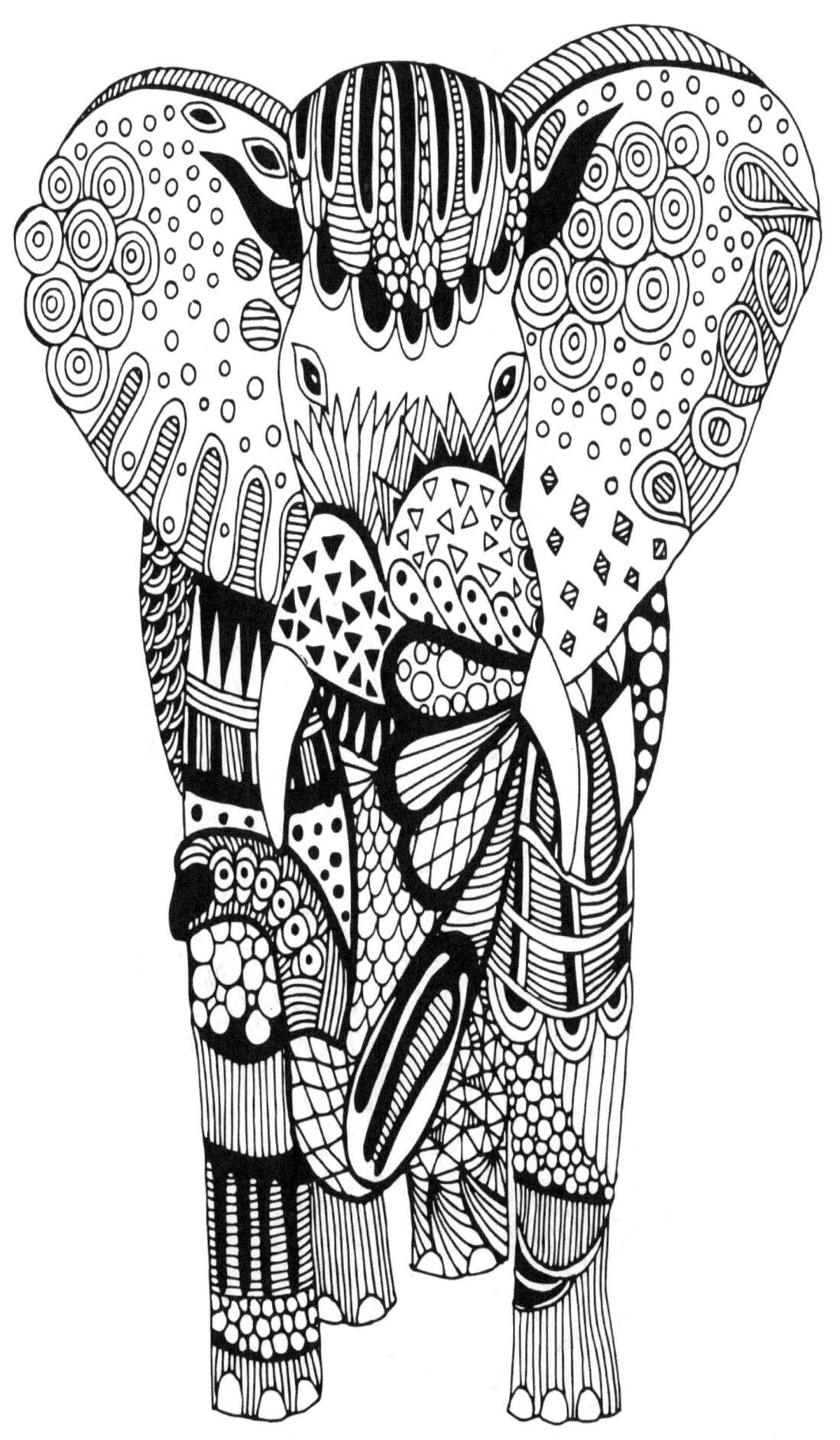

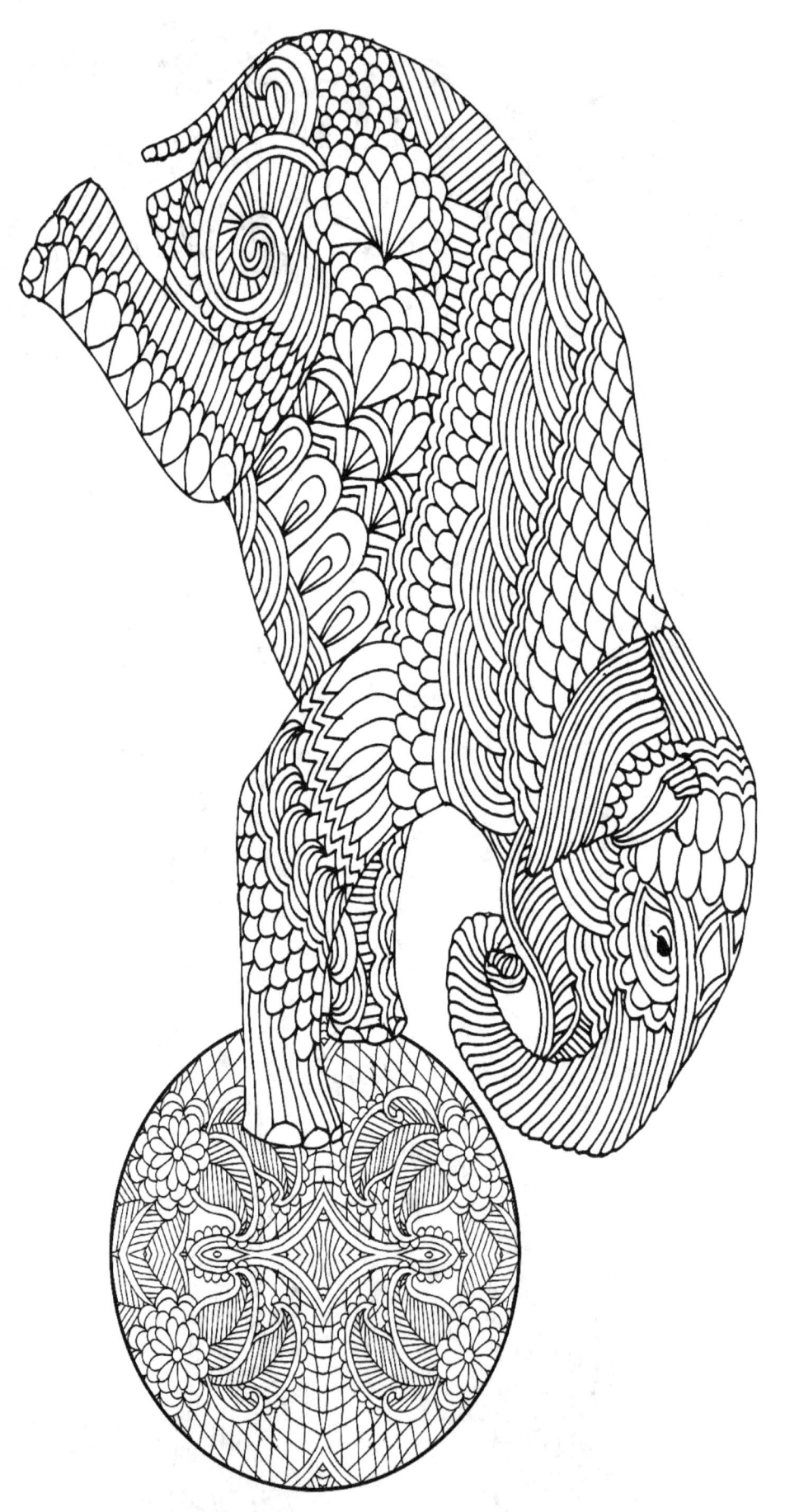

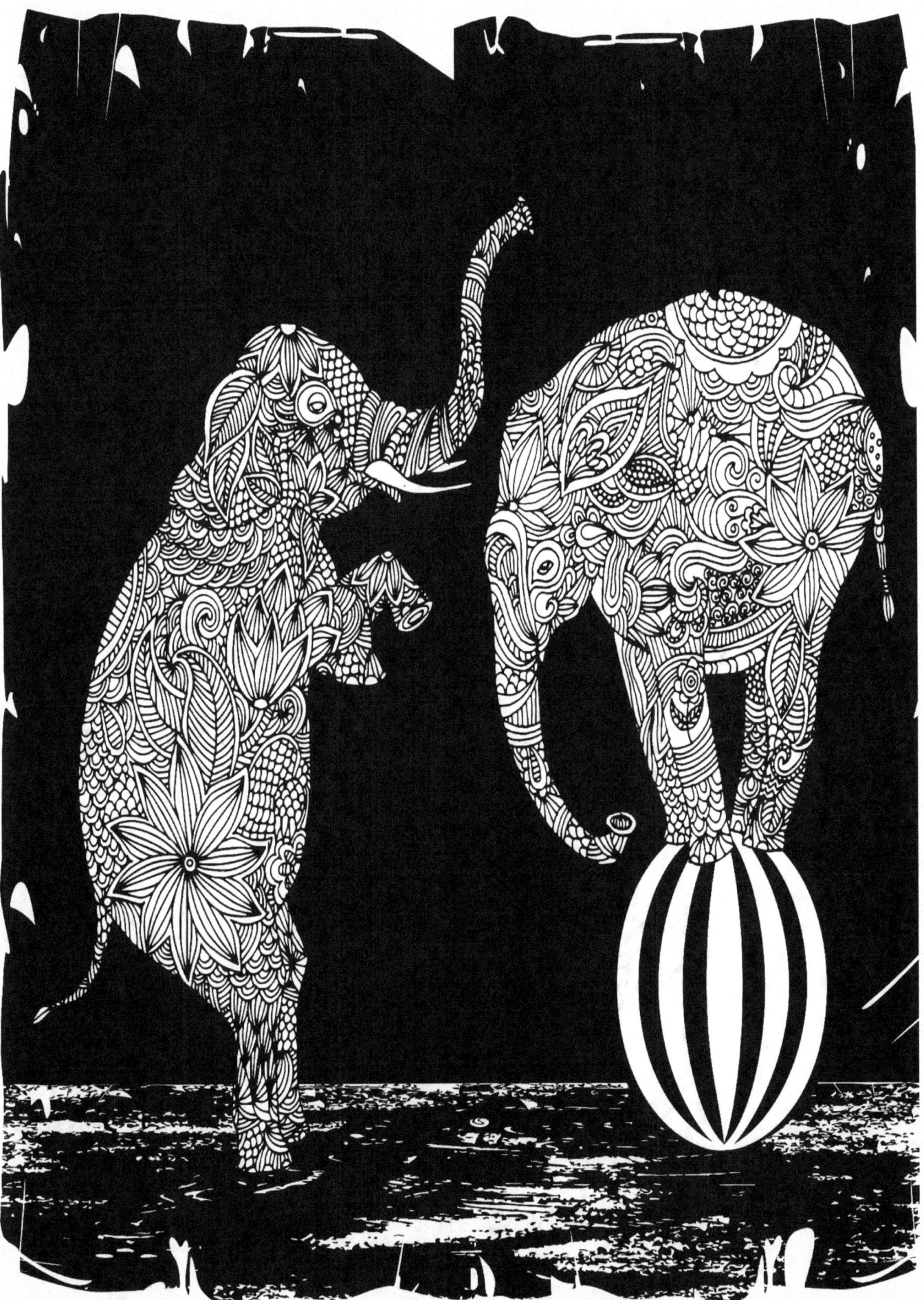

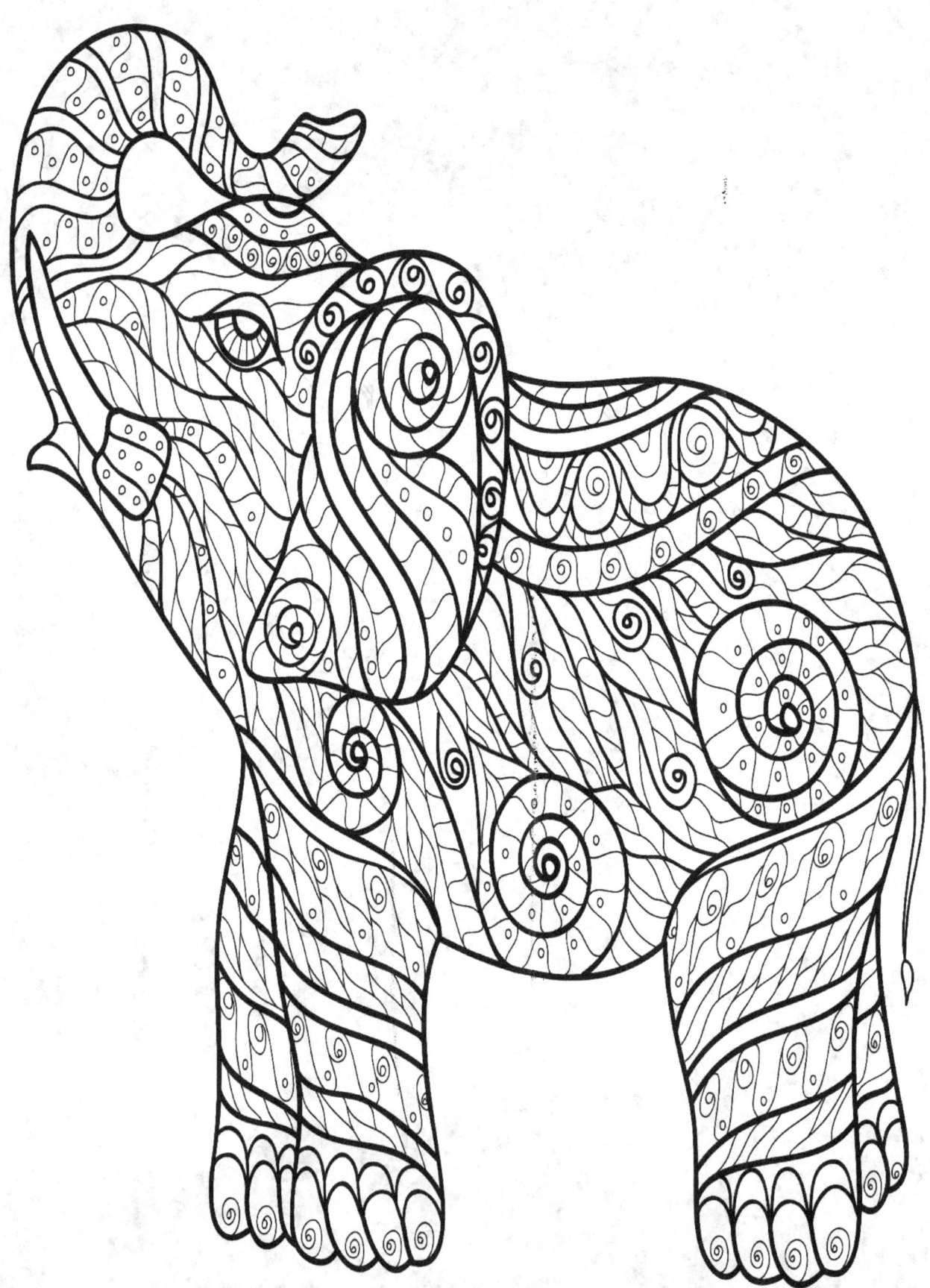

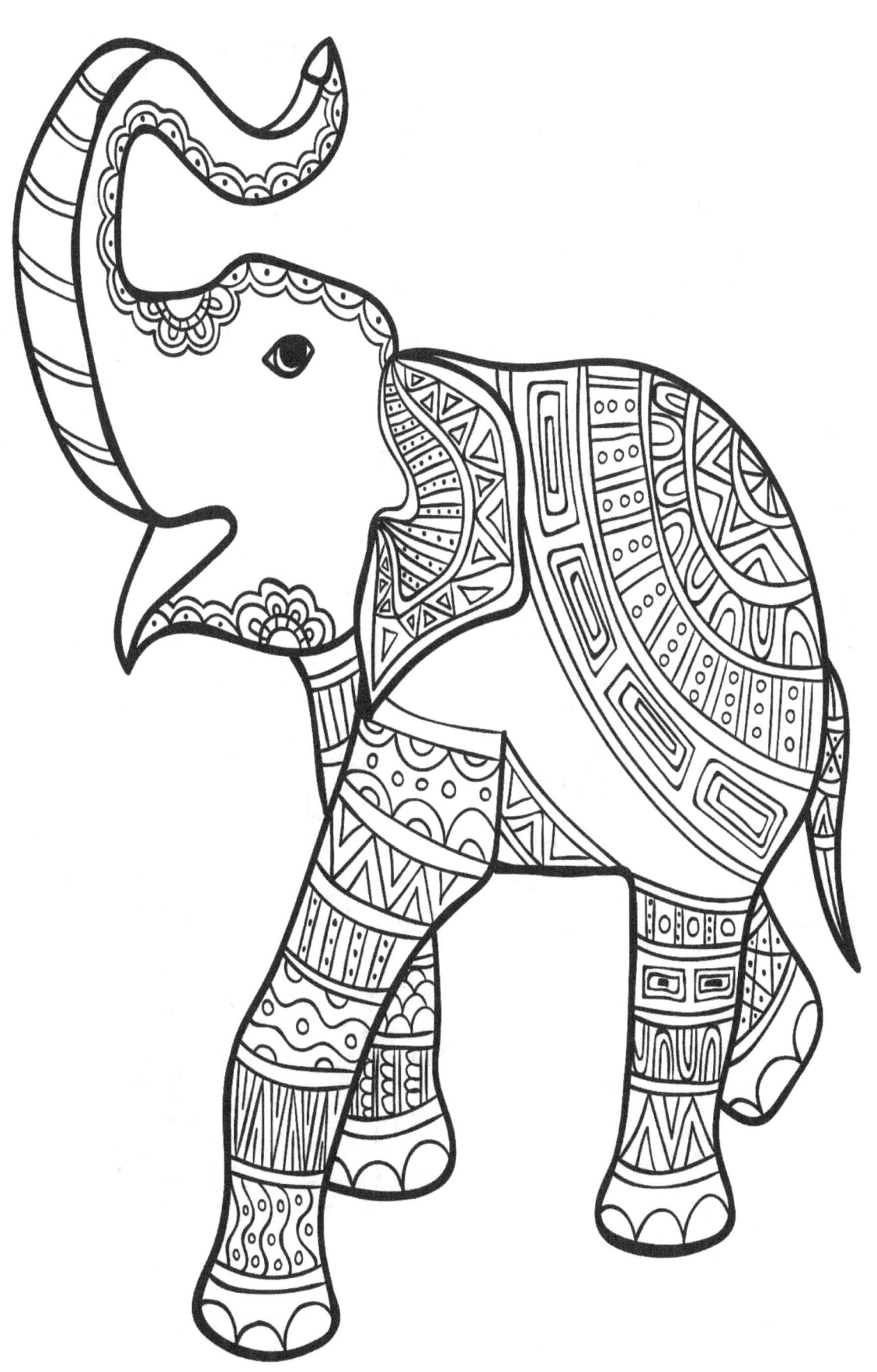

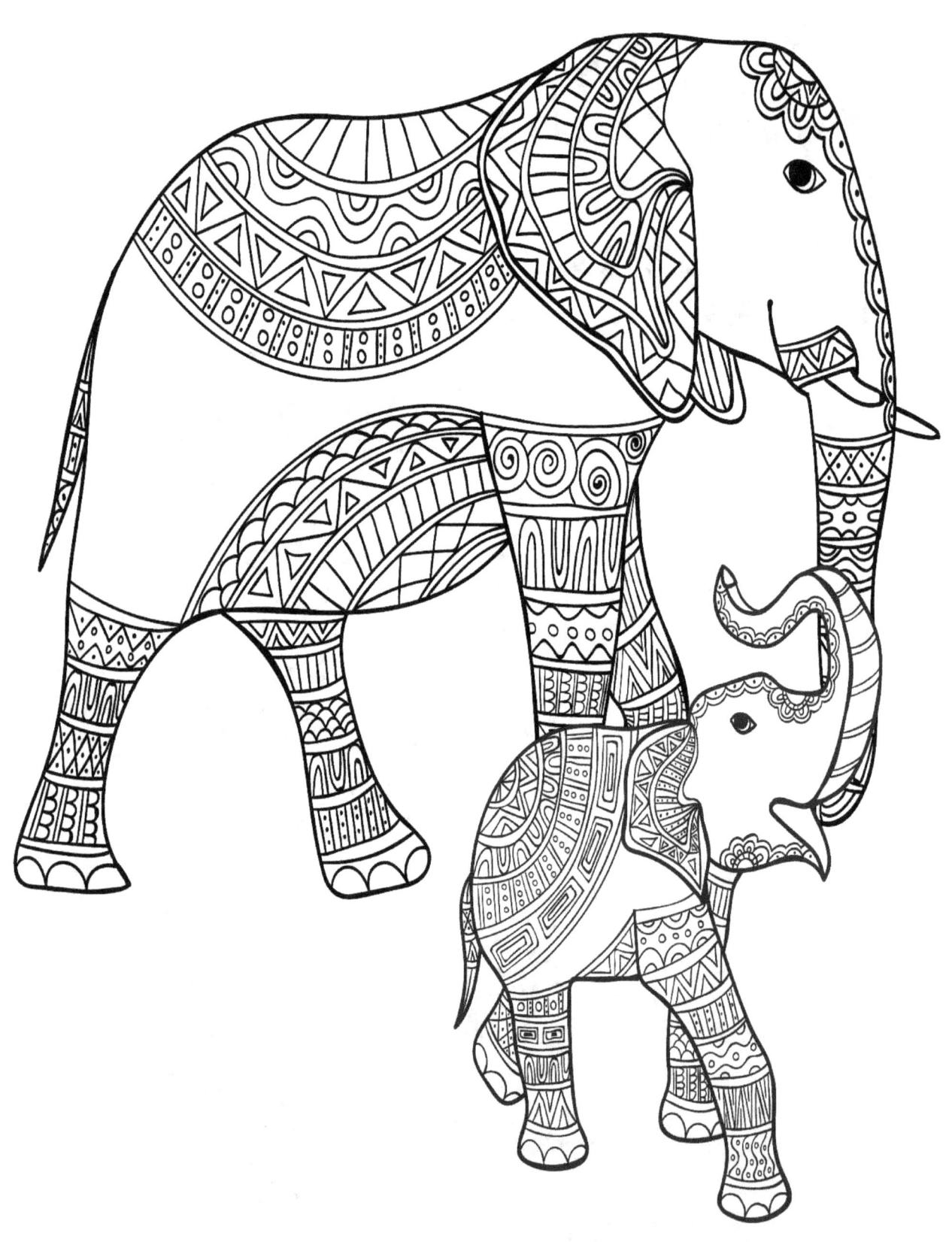

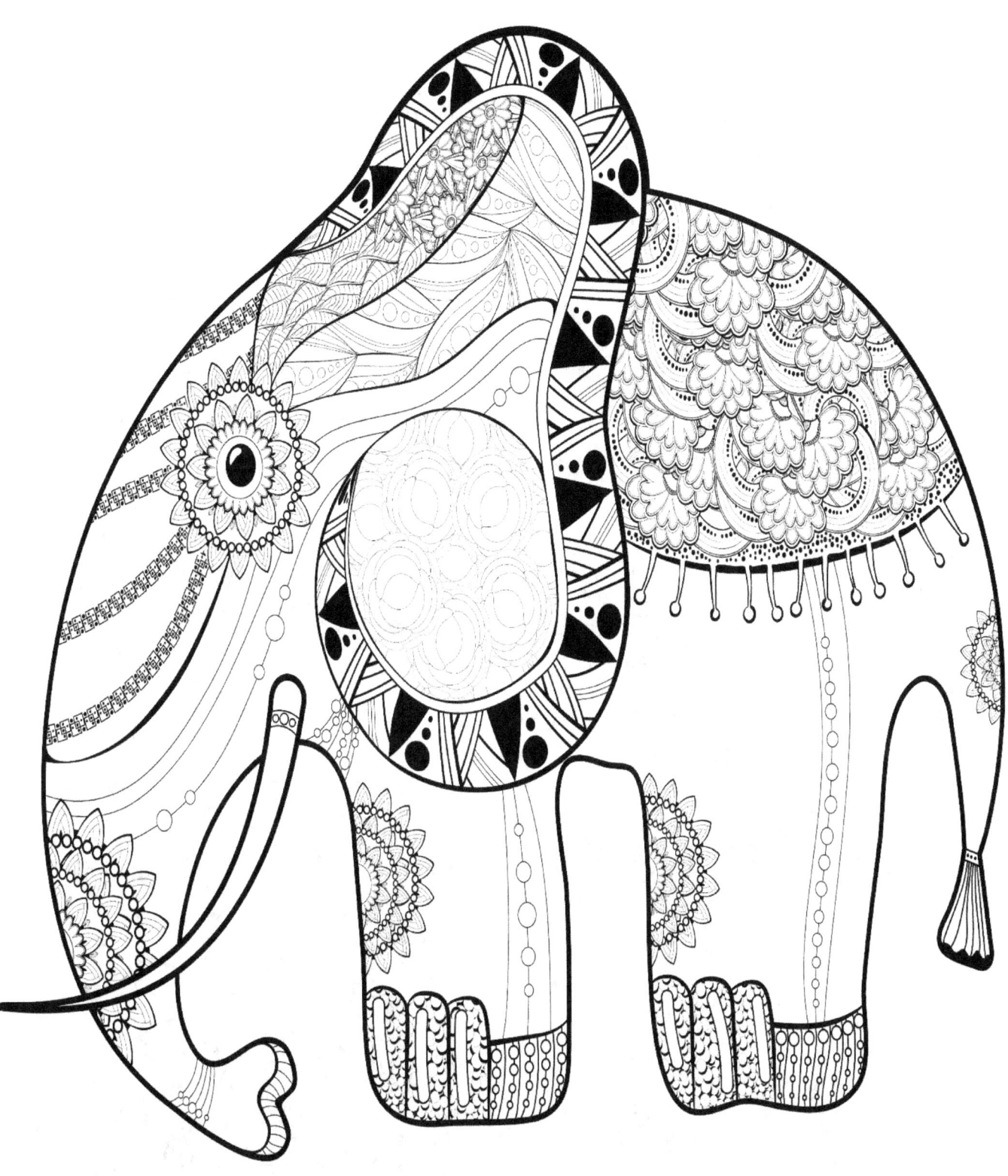

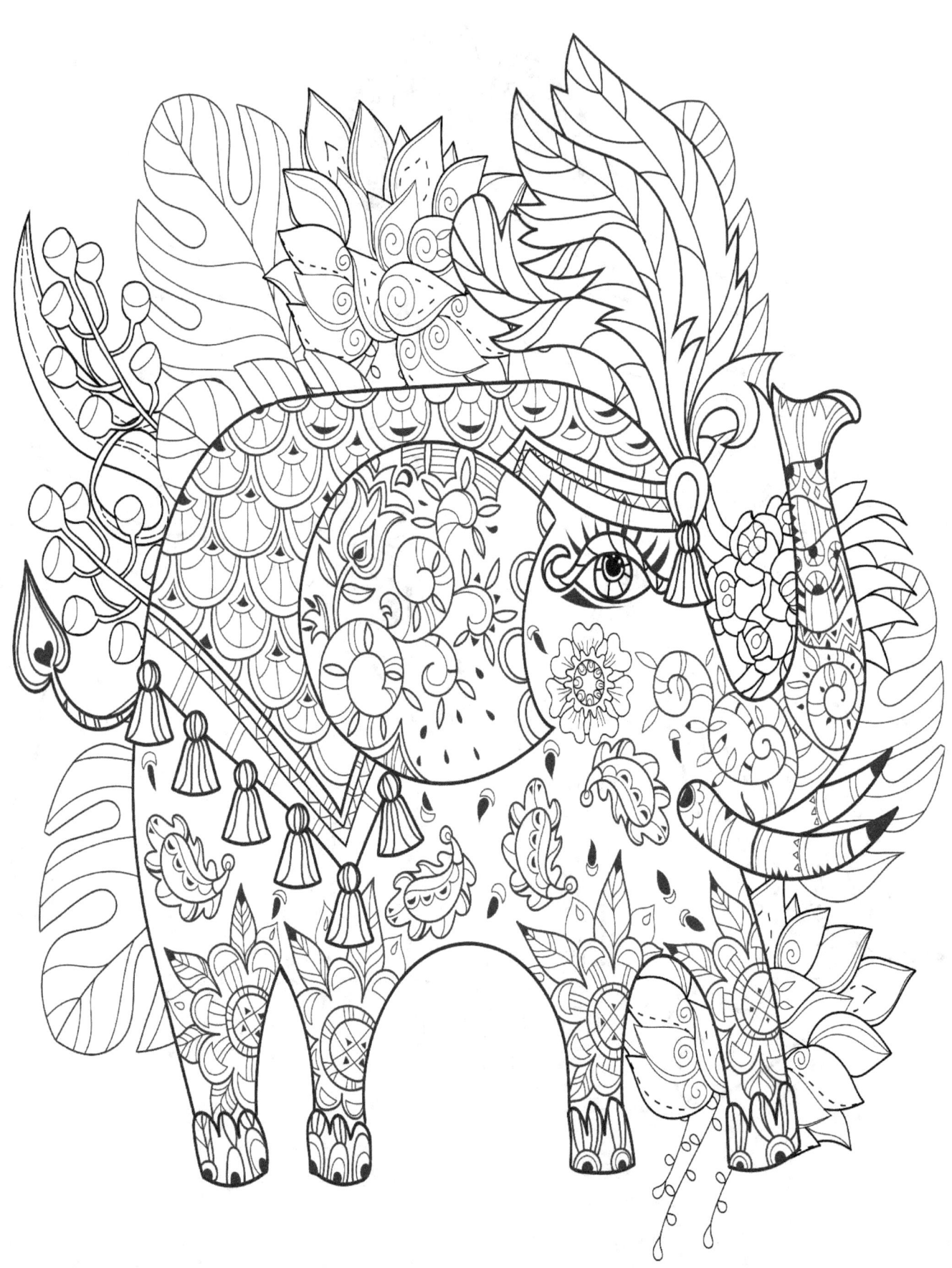

If you enjoyed this book, please leave me a review online.

ABOUT THE AUTHOR

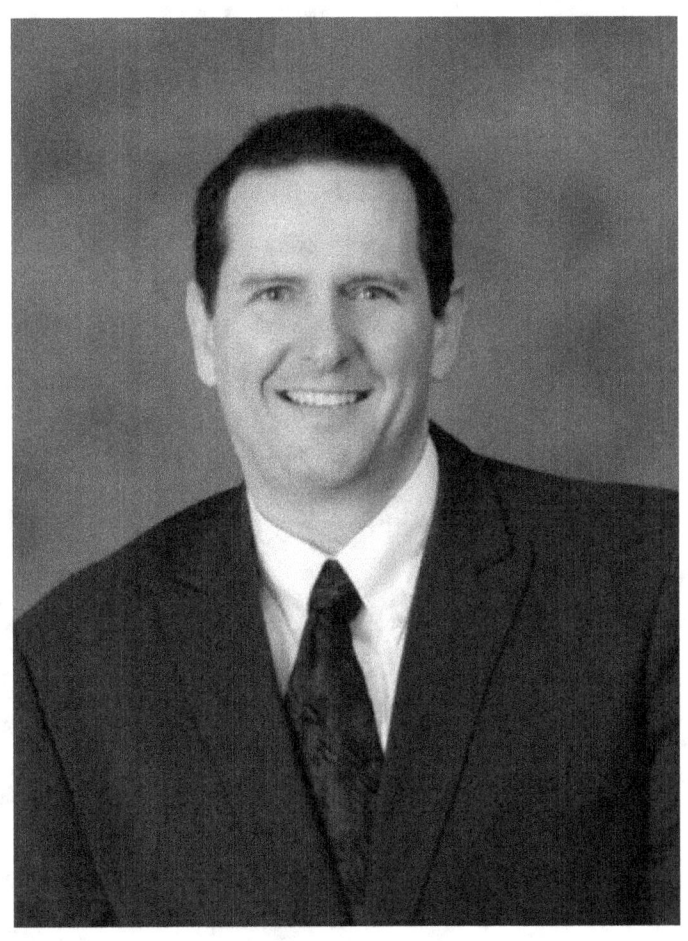

Dr. Wheeler is a physician by day and a writer by night. He enjoys beekeeping, scuba diving, exercise, travel, family time, and of course, writing. He is published through Novel Star for his two fantasy books, Hammer of the Gods: The Nine Realms, Book 1 and The Witch of Endor: Vampires. His poetry book, Mystical Musings: A Collection of Poetry was #1 for a time under audiobooks, poetry anthologies. His other adult coloring books include, Fantastic Designs, Fantastic Animals, Fantastic Dogs, Fantastic Cats, Fantastic Flowers, Fantastic Birds, Fantastic Food, Fantastic Skulls, Fantastic Christmas, Fantastic Dinosaurs, Fantastic Elephants, Fantastic Unicorns, Fantastic Sea Life, Fantastic Owls, Fabulous Designs, Color Me Butterflies and Mandalas and More.

His children's books include, Bumble: The Bee Who Couldn't Fly, Bumble: Beetle Invasion, Bumble: Chicken Tales, each in full color and coloring books. Fairy Tales, a 3 book series about fairies and The Boy Who Thought he was a Horse. Check out Color Me Baby Animals, coloring book.

Dr. Wheeler is currently working on the sequel to his vampire saga, Vampires: Love and Blood.

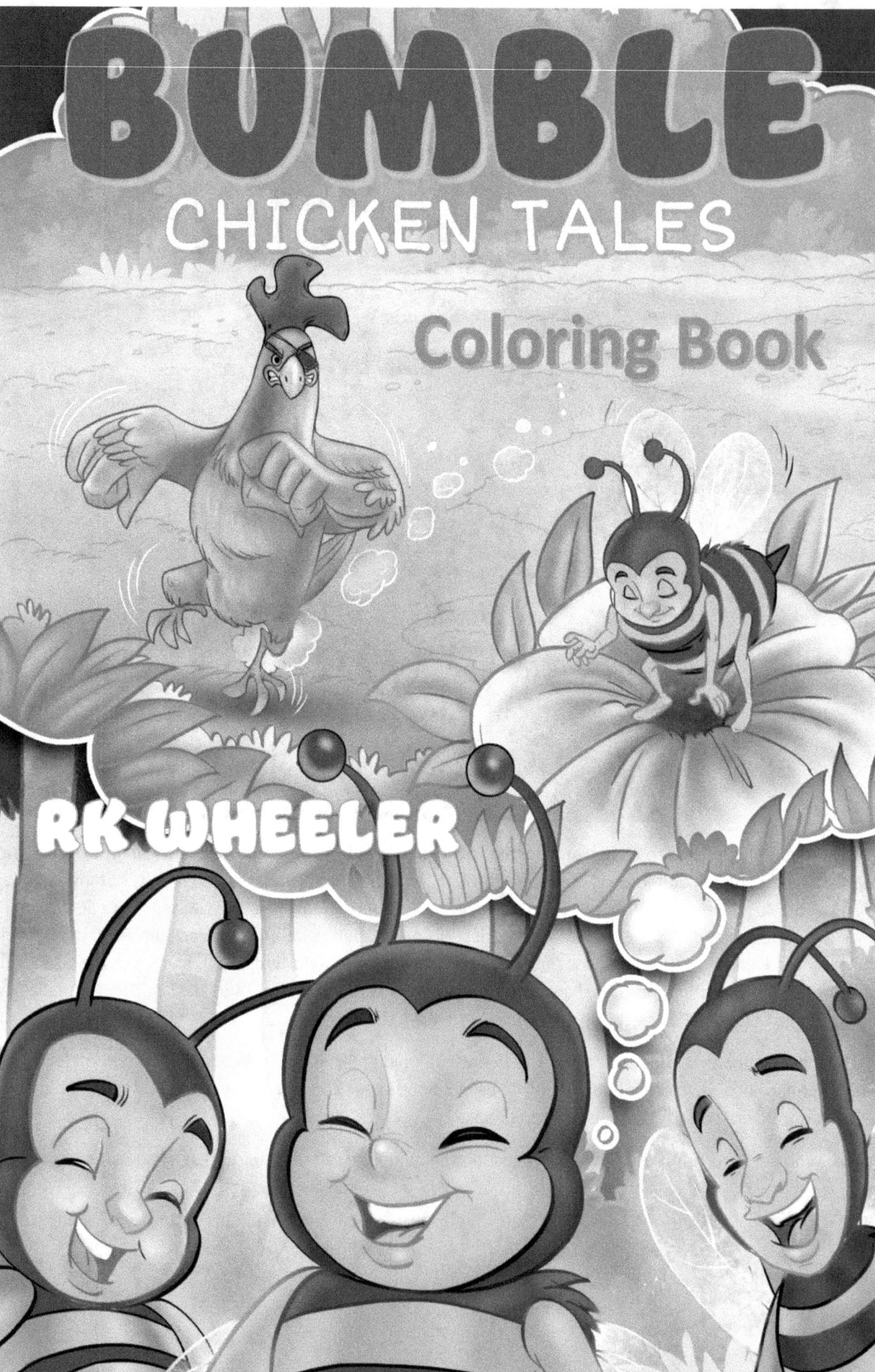

BUMBLE
The Bee Who Couldn't Fly

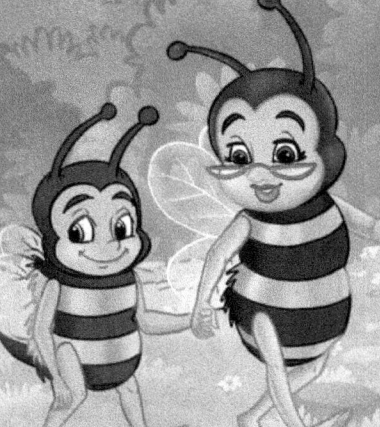

BY

RK WHEELER

The Adventures of Bumble
the Bee: Book I

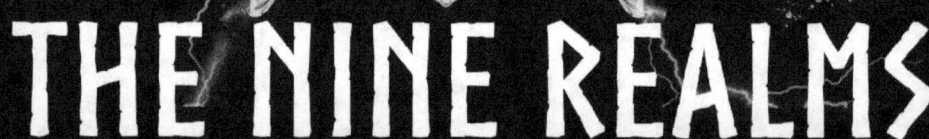

THE WITCH OF ENDOR

VAMPIRES

R.K. Wheeler

RkWheeler.com

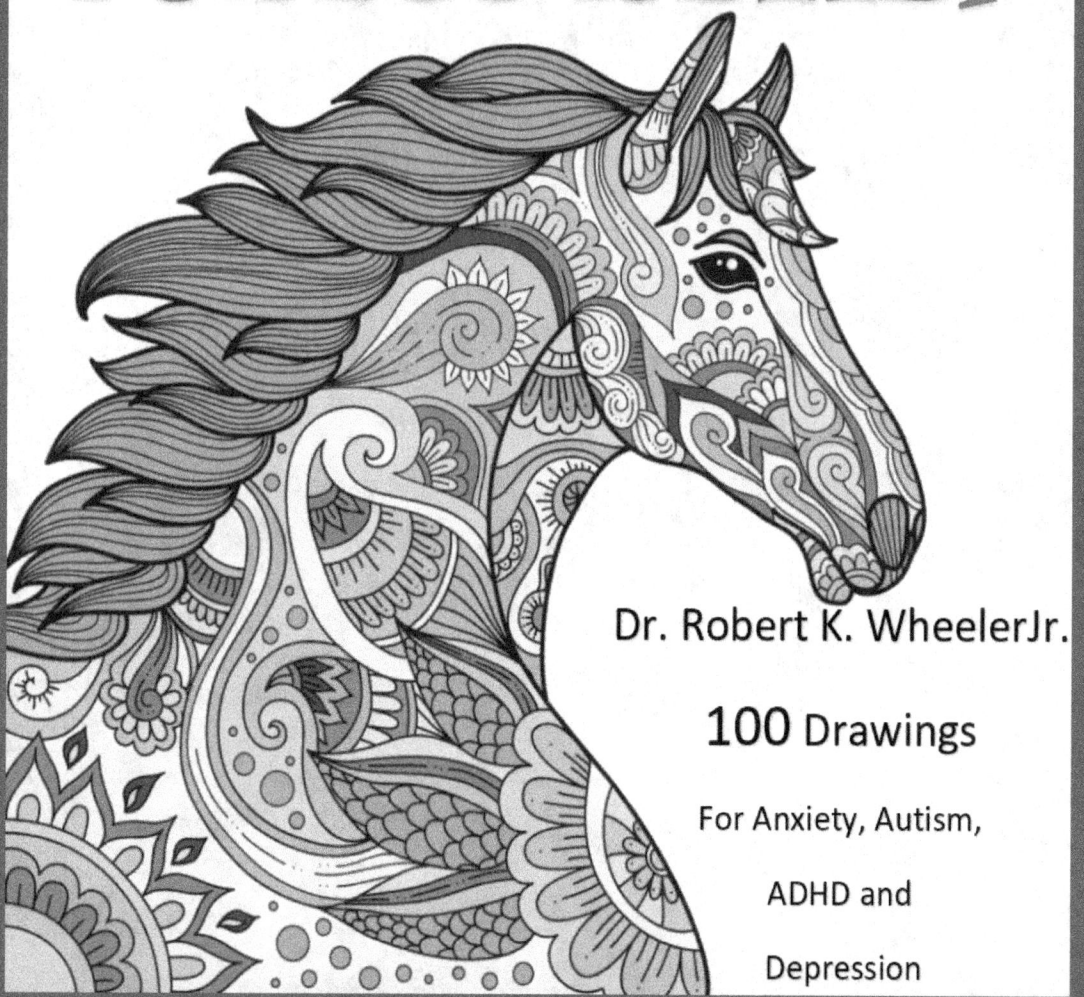

www.ingramcontent.com/pod-product-compliance
Lightning Source LLC
Chambersburg PA
CBHW060422220526
45465CB00008B/2979